Title IV

Interviews
With
Black
Writers

Interviews
With
Black
Writers

Edited by JOHN O'BRIEN

LIVERIGHT : New York

Acknowledgments

A book of this nature could never be completed without the help of many people. I wish to thank especially the authors themselves, who so freely gave of their time and who were so helpful in offering advice; the Michael Brays who gave me lodging in New York; Jerome Klinkowitz who gave an undue amount of time and imagination in helping to edit many of the early interviews; Raman Singh, whose critical work in black literature has been original and daring, for his advice and encouragement; the poet Lucien Stryk for introducing me to the work of Michael Harper and Cyrus Colter; Hiram Haydn for telling me of the work of Alice Walker; Jean Naggar, who was endlessly patient in her work as editor; and most of all, my wife Jeanne, who endured the pains of the book's birth.

The following interviews have appeared in these publications: William Demby in *Studies in Black Literature*, Fall 1972; Ishmael Reed in *Fiction International*, Summer 1973; John A. Williams in *The American Scholar*, Summer 1973; and Al Young in *New Orleans Review*, Summer 1973.

1.98765432

ISBN: 0-87140-561-X (cloth)
ISBN: 0-87140-085-5 (paper)
Library of Congress Catalog Card Number: 72-97488

Manufactured in the United States of America

Contents

William O'Brien
who was there

Robert Vondrasek
who pointed the direction

Jerome Klinkowitz
who taught a method

Introduction

The first problem is describing what is meant by a black literary tradition, where it came from, and what it includes. Most important is that it is a literary rather than racial tradition, defined not by complexion, but by literary styles, themes, myths, heroes, structures, and influences. Not all black writers belong to it. Further, it is not defined by subject-matter. Although race is a thematic concern in almost all black literature, the fact that a writer uses race does not mean that he thereby belongs to a black literary tradition. For instance, Ann Petry, Julian Mayfield, and Cyrus Colter are really outside of this tradition and are better understood if seen in the mainstream of American realistic fiction.

The sources of the black literary tradition are clear enough: folk stories, spirituals, and blues songs that came out of the slavery experience. The tradition is oral rather than written, handed down by word of mouth rather than in books. From the beginning, there seems to be an antagonism toward the written word, partially because it lacks immediacy. Perhaps this is why LeRoi Jones, in his novel *Tales,* rejects "words" as the proper medium of artistic expression, and chooses instead the activity of jazz, making his novel read and sound like a John Coltrane jazz composition. The first attempts at poetry in the eighteenth century, and fiction in the nineteenth, were labored and imitative, and gave little promise of equaling the achievements already made in music.

Both the poetry and fiction appeared to be doomed efforts at entering an American literary tradition that had a headstart. The poets of the Harlem Renaissance—Countee Cullen, Claude McKay, Jean Toomer, Arna Bontemps, and Langston Hughes—began inventing the new forms that would contain the unique experience of black Americans. However, it was primarily in fiction that black writers created their own tradition and developed original styles, themes, and forms. W. E. B. DuBois' *The Souls of Black Folk,* although not usually considered a work of fiction, is the archtype of the black novel. Overtly a series of political, social, and economic essays on the history and future of black America, it is a tightly conceived book, held together by images, recurring motifs, strains of music, characterizations, and a concluding short story which suggests the fictional nature of the entire book. Its impulse is mythic, its form epic, and it is shaped less by the rigid forms of logic than by artistic necessity. After DuBois, we find the novels of Claude McKay (*Home to Harlem* and *Banjo*) and Jean Toomer (*Cane*) which continue both in form and theme what DuBois initiated in *The Souls of Black Folk.* All three writers took the hard realities of sociology—formerly the exclusive domain of the naturalistic writer—and transformed them into imaginative and innovative works. Where readers expected straight naturalistic fiction appropriate to the subject-matter, they found highly lyrical and experimental fiction. And this inclination toward experimentation has remained constant in the development of the black literary tradition, baffling readers as much today as it did back in the 1920s. From his beginnings, the black fiction-writer labored under the tension of what he was expected to do and what, in fact, he was doing.

Richard Wright, by following in the tradition of DuBois, wrote one of the most misunderstood novels in American literature—*Native Son.* Rather than conforming to the naturalistic tradition of showing a character victimized by his environment, the novel traces Bigger Thomas's transcendence of that environment. The hero Wright creates follows a path similar to that traced by the heroes in DuBois, McKay, and Toomer, and can only be understood when related to the tradition expressed in those other heroes. Rather than deterministic (the only way the white American writer has been able to treat urban life), *Native Son* is an existential novel in which freedom from the limitations of personality, environment, and history is possible.

Then came Ralph Ellison's *Invisible Man*. Like its predecessors, it contained all the forms, themes, and musical devices that characterized the black novels before it. Because it also dealt with the whole spectrum of American experience, it reached a very wide audience. The 1960s witnessed the greatest flowering of fiction by black writers since the Harlem Renaissance. Ishmael Reed, LeRoi Jones, Ernest J. Gaines, William Melvin Kelley, Charles Wright, John A. Williams, and John Wideman appeared not as products of American literature, but as the children of the black literary tradition which had already established its own forms, styles, myths, heroes, and themes.

The black writer has not so much created new themes in literature as he has retold old ones, giving a new perspective to and interpretation of the human situation. Identity is the central concern of almost every black writer who belongs to this literary tradition. The problem for the hero in black fiction, as DuBois argued at the beginning of this century, is one of synthesizing his African heritage with his life in America. He must somehow combine two cultures, seemingly forever at odds with one another. This conflict is most often explored in a character who has been raised and educated in a Western tradition, but who cannot achieve his true identity until he acquaints himself with his racial and cultural origins. Symbolically, this tension is frequently represented in terms of the North (white) and the South (black). Identity can be found only by discovering a way of fusing these antagonistic forces. Until the 1960s, this tension could be only potentially resolved. The typical ending of the black novel is open-ended and suggests a resolution in the future. Thus we have Du-Bois girding his traveler for a journey, McKay preparing his characters for future voyages, Toomer having his hero ready to ascend the stairs, and Ellison making ready for the day when his Invisible Man can emerge from the basement he has been hiding in.

Unlike the attitude in American literature in general, this attempt at wholeness, this effort to reconcile the divisions within man is at least always potentially realized. The black novel knows no defeat. This literature implies faith in man's ability to triumph over his experience, to learn by it, and to return to life sustained by his new knowledge. Whereas American literature is generally a record of man's inability to transcend the past (either historical or personal), black literature consistently reflects an individual's and a society's ability to escape the past and prepare for a future. In other words, this literary tradition has no sense of or belief in determinism. This antideterminism may in part be attributed to the absence of theological concerns in black literature. Without this sense of God, the black writer avoids the dilemmas that face so many other American writers. Problems of good and evil are never raised to an abstract plane, where man is helpless in trying to discover their obscure meanings. This whole philosophy suggests that the black American writer does not belong to the Calvinistic tradition of thought that has so strongly influenced the American consciousness. No characters in black literature are driven by the mad need to subdue the force of evil, as is Melville's Ahab, nor are they wracked by the doubts of Hawthorne's heroes, nor by the disbelief that Hemingway's characters wish they could escape. The black writer conceives of good and evil in terms of man-made creations which—since man has made them —he can change.

The recognition that man is the maker of his own myths is present throughout black literature. It is this recognition that permits black writers so easily to recast old myths to serve man rather than control him. We can see someone like Clarence Major breaking free from sexual myths which, according to Leslie Fiedler, haunt American fiction. In Major's fiction the body is not in conflict with the soul; the body is not the source of temptation. The only characters in black literature to experience sexual inhibitions are those who have been overly affected by white culture and morality.

But if sexual myths are man-created, so are racial ones. Rather than overtly attacking racism, black writers are more concerned with establishing a black mythology which grapples with the imagination (where myths originate), rather than with politics. There we find Ishmael Reed's novels retelling the story of the old West, or John Wideman, going back in time to discover the roots of the African culture, or the Invisible Man experiencing the black version of the Horatio Alger story. The black writer is trying to establish alternate myths to those which have fashioned the Western and American mind so far, myths that will not depict the black man as the symbol of evil and the black race as the threat to civilization.

The styles used by black writers to convey their own particular literary tradition vary from the naturalistic style of a Richard Wright to the surrealism of Ishmael Reed or the lyricism of Jean Toomer. But there are almost always innovations, attempts to produce in fiction or poetry what the jazz greats did in music. The influence of music has been substantial: there are evidences of it either in the rhythms of a particular passage or in the larger structure. Just as the terminology of Western music, with its accent upon regularity and formal structure (Bach and Mozart) has little relevance to jazz, the terminology we have for Western literature has little relevance to black literature. The form, as Michael Harper argues about his poetry, is modal rather than rationalistic, dictated by instinct rather than intellect. At the same time, it is an oral tradition, begun with the slave narratives and folk tales. But writers are not limited in styles. Ernest J. Gaines returns to the Southern plantations for his sources and depends upon oral narrative, more, perhaps, than any other black writer. An Ishmael Reed or a LeRoi Jones uses language less as a medium for rational communication than as a way of mesmerizing readers by sounds and rhythms. The meanings are there, but we are led into them not by the traditional devices of plot and character, but through episodes that are held together by recurring images.

Again, however, there are several black writers whose styles are best understood by relating them to more conventional movements in American literature. For instance, the stark naturalism of Cyrus Colter or the realism of Ann Petry belong, it seems to me, to the mainstream of American literature. Although he uses blacks as the central figures in his stories and novels, Colter is not concerned with exploring the myths of black experience nor is he interested in employing those distinct literary forms developed by black American writers. In the person of John A. Williams, we have a hybrid writer whose style is realistic but whose themes come out of the tradition of DuBois, Toomer, and McKay. All of these comments suggest that black writers work as individual talents, unrestricted by either white or black traditions.

There exist a number of critical fallacies about black literature which continue to impede the black writer in America. The first, is that the greatest service the black writer renders is not artistic, but political and sociological; that he reflects the mood of black Americans and affords insights to a white audience concerning the elusive thing called the "black experience." Even the *Literary History of the United States,* the Bible of literary scholars, cites the tradition of Negro writing as having begun with Claude McKay and Countee Cullen and as being presently continued by "publicists" like Adam Clayton Powell! Not only does this critical approach to black literature limit the writer to certain themes and styles, but it also demands that he concern himself with only that element of the "black experience" which is political and social.

An extension of this first fallacy is the idea that there is a bond of some kind between all black writers, and that it is legitimate and nececessary to speak of them as an homogenous group. The deluge of black literature anthologies issued in the 1960s perhaps best demonstrates this critical attitude. Rarely was there any rationale for including writers other than the fact that they were black. No literary distinctions were made. Writers were not there because they belonged to a unique tradition in American literature, but because they were black. Experimentalists are side by side with naturalistic writers; those who write about racial matters are next to those who did not; those concerned with the "black experience" appear with those not the least interested in it. In other words, the black writer does not exist as an individual, but as a type.

Although such groupings may please both white racists and black nationalists, it is strange that professional critics, trained to distinguish between rhetoric and art, should be guilty of such an error. Yet, as John A. Williams points out in his interview, book reviewers consistently, when discussing books by black writers, compare the book before them only to books by other black writers. The danger of such criticism is that in effect it either dismisses every black writer who does not seem to conform to the formula of what the black author should be, or it forces him into a mold, whether or not his work belongs there.

Finally, the black writer is rarely talked about as an artist. Such matters as style, form, structure, symbols, and characterization are usually ignored by critics. Most criticism of black literature is devoted to a discussion of the "message." This indifference to form has led to the great misunderstanding about themes. Meaning and form are inseparable, and it is only by ignoring form that one can think of black writing as "protest" literature. Nevertheless, the majority of critics, white and black, liberal and conservative, have yet to begin talking about black literature as literature. Lacking the support of critics, several black writers themselves have spoken out to urge critics to apply the same critical standards and perceptions that are given to their white contemporaries.

There are built-in limitations in the interview format. Oftentimes they seem to be without direction in the sense that they lack a central idea or thesis that is stated and developed. Likewise, the interview depends upon spontaneous conversation in which the quality and clarity of expression sometimes suffer. The objections are admittedly valid; but the interview format, because of its flexibility, allows for a breadth that an essay cannot encompass. The subject of each interview is the author himself. There need not be the orderly and logical development of the essay. In this way, many things can be touched upon without the necessity of demonstrating an intimate connection to a central idea. Although it does not have the depth an essay might possess, the interview is free to wander over a landscape composed of whatever seems interesting. There is also something wholly fascinating about what an author has to say about himself and his work. The spontaneity of the form is compensated by careful editing by both the editor and the author. In each case we tried to shape the raw materials in the best way possible without destroying the sense that these are conversations between a critic and writers.

Interviews

With

Black

Writers

Arna Bontemps

No other man in America today can speak with as much authority as Arna Bontemps about the great literary phenomenon
known as the Harlem Renaissance. It brought together the most
gifted black writers of the 1920s and issued in a literary revolution whose effects are felt as strongly today as they were then.
For the first time, blacks were published in unprecedented numbers and the works they produced decisively shaped the form and
tenor of what is called black literature. Arna Bontemps is perhaps the Renaissance's foremost scholar and has written some of
the most significant fiction and poetry to come out of that movement. His work includes three novels, *God Sends Sunday* (1931),
Black Thunder (1936), and *Drums at Dusk* (1939), the collection
of poems *Personals* (1964), several children's books, biographies,
and anthologies of black literature. He soon will publish a collection of essays on the Harlem Renaissance gathered from students
in a seminar which he conducted at Yale.

A concern with the past informs all of Bontemps' fiction and
poetry. On the one hand he attempts, in a poem like "The Return," to restore the broken link with an African heritage so that
he can "keep the dance of rain our fathers kept/and tread our
dreams beneath the jungle sky." On the other hand he also uses
the past in his two historical novels to focus on the determining
force of history and the causes and nature of revolution. An

aborted slave revolt near Richmond in 1800 is the subject of his most accomplished novel, *Black Thunder*. *Drums at Dusk* uses the Haitian slave-revolt led by Toussaint L' Ouverture to explore revolution from the point of view of the power being overthrown. In both novels history itself emerges as the protagonist who either permits or disallows man's attempt to change existing social and political structures. As with his poetry, Bontemps' success lies in his ability to draw upon folklore and folk idiom. Motivated by many of the same concerns as the realistic writers of the 1930s, Bontemps avoids their limitations by turning to myth and history as the true subjects of his novels. He returns to the slave narratives and their oral tradition for his inspiration and style.

The interview was conducted in the spring of 1972 in Mr. Bontemps' office at the Fisk University library. He endured the four-hour session with patience and wit, a few times asking me to aid him in recalling parts of his novels which were written almost forty years ago. He now lives in Nashville, teaches at Fisk, and is currently at work on his autobiography.

INTERVIEWER: Mr. Bontemps, you mention in your preface to your collection of poems *Personals* that many young blacks were arriving in Harlem at the same time as you did and that many had the same hope of becoming writers. Did you know at the time which ones were going to be important? Were there any surprises?

BONTEMPS: I recognized Langston Hughes, Countee Cullen, Jean Toomer, and Claude McKay immediately. All of these hit me within the first year or two in Harlem. Claude McKay's *Harlem Shadows* was the only one I had read before coming to Harlem. In 1923 I missed Toomer's *Cane*. When I went to New York in 1923 a friend of mine from Los Angeles wrote me that she had heard about *Cane* and that I should read it, so I did, and I was very shook-up by it. Cullen and Hughes—I had read both of them before their books were published and I knew that they were on their way. Wallace Thurman I knew from Los Angeles. He didn't come to New York until a year after I arrived. Actually he floundered around for about three or four years. It was not until about 1929 that his first novel and play were published. He was the man of the moment in 1929. That sort of surprised me. I found that he was so cynical about himself and others that he might not make it. Many of the things he tried between 1925 and 1929 had failed. I had known him longer than I had known any of the others and I had not felt too sure that he would make it because he distrusted himself as much as he distrusted others. Some that I had expected more of did not produce. Eric Walrond, who wrote *Tropic Death*, I thought was very promising. I had thought that Rudolph Fisher would become a giant, but the first thing he did was the best. In fact, his very first story, "The City of Refuge," which appeared in *Atlantic Monthly* he was never able to reach again. He wrote a couple of novels after that, both of which seem almost negligible now. Zora Hurston looked promising and I anticipated that she would develop, but I did not think that she would turn out to be identified with reaction.

INTERVIEWER: Are there writers who you feel still have not gained proper recognition?

BONTEMPS: There are those who feel that Zora Hurston doesn't begin to have the rank among American writers that she deserves. Others feel that Nella Larson is more important than she has gotten credit for being. There were others—as I said—who didn't develop as much as I expected. Wallace Thurman went astray, but his was a failure of health as much as it was of talent. Nothing after 1929 was up to what he had done by then, and he knew it. To some extent Rudolph Fisher was like that. Like Thurman, he died almost right during the Harlem Renaissance.

INTERVIEWER: You said in that same preface that the Harlem Renaissance came close to giving America a "new aesthetic." Could you elaborate on what that aesthetic involves and how it differs from that which existed then?

BONTEMPS: Perhaps not in detail, but I can suggest what I was thinking about. First of all, the white aesthetic eliminates folk sources and sociological topics; it says that these are not legitimate material for art. If you accept that, you really eliminate the black writer's whole range of experience from serious literature, because about a third of all he knows is folk and about another third is classified—rather arbitrarily—as "sociological," and only one third comes out of the traditions of the English language which he is using. He is so inhibited that he's left out. So, if you could create another literature which employs folk motifs and which doesn't shy away from the problems of urban living and race relations, you have a new aesthetic.

INTERVIEWER: Do you find a division in black literature between those writers who use folk sources and those who use sociological materials? Perhaps Toomer exemplifies the former and Ann Petry the latter?

BONTEMPS: Yes, if you work with generalities. Jean Toomer is consciously preoccupied with folk living. But when you read all of *Cane* you find that he is also involved with the sociology of inner-city living in Washington, D.C. and Chicago. You have in Toomer this poetic eye trying to resolve this mix, in his story "Kabnis." The more innovative writer would not make a clean distinction between the two. He would not accept the urban problem as being sociological alone.

INTERVIEWER: Perhaps that's the artistic triumph of people like Toomer, McKay, and contemporary writers like LeRoi Jones, Clarence Major, and Ishmael Reed, because they are able to transform traditionally realistic material into another literary form.

BONTEMPS: Yes, that's it exactly.

INTERVIEWER: Why do you think that writers like Toomer and McKay were so ignored in their time? Was it largely because of the innovations they were making in the novel?

BONTEMPS: The time wasn't right. Even if they had written different things, the American culture was such that it would not have accepted them. They couldn't have written anything that

would have been wholly acceptable as long as they were identified as blacks. Our first attacks had to be directed against the
closed doors; just as the generation of the sixties had to be preoccupied with getting into restaurants, theaters, and trains, so the
writers of the Renaissance had to be concerned with trying to get
published by standard publishers. Prior to that there had been a
period of twenty years in which no publisher issued a serious
piece of literature by a Negro. There were a few quite under-
standable exceptions, such as Booker T. Washington. He was
unique and he really wasn't a literary man. But James Weldon
Johnson wrote a novel in 1912—now treated as a classic in its
field—which he couldn't get published by a major publisher. He
was in New York and had plenty of entree, but it wasn't until
after the Renaissance people broke through the door that a publisher brought back that old novel and it has never been out of
print since. So, the Renaissance writers were trying to open
doors, to get into magazines. That was the challenge for these
writers. When someone would get published there was a lot of
noise and this accounted for the attention drawn to them. After
that they were confronted with another problem that does not
face the writer today—the books didn't sell. There was the resistance of the booksellers, the resistance of white readers, and then
the fact that black people didn't read novels at all. And they had
good reason for not reading because all they had read in the past
had been so damaging to their own feelings. The next challenge
to the Harlem writers was to change the minds of blacks, to
break down the resistance of booksellers, and to make some in-
roads into the white audience as well. None of these are confronted by the writers today. They were pretty successfully conquered during the Harlem period. After the Depression was over
with, the gates were wide open. So, it was easy for Richard
Wright to come in.

INTERVIEWER: Do you think that McKay and Toomer realized how innovative they were being in their fiction?

BONTEMPS: I think Toomer did. Toomer was consciously
trying to find new ways to write through the use of symbols. He
was preoccupied with them and talked about them. But I don't

think that it's possible for a writer—even a black writer—to do something that doesn't have its roots in the tradition of the language. None of these writers wanted to divorce themselves from the tradition of the language.

INTERVIEWER: Did you know McKay and Toomer very well?

BONTEMPS: I didn't know them in the way I knew Cullen and Hughes. For one thing they were both about ten years older than I was and they were not around Harlem at the same time. Toomer popped in and out. McKay was abroad for the whole of the Renaissance. I didn't see him until after he came back when the Depression was over.

INTERVIEWER: Why do you think that Toomer only published the one novel? Owen Dodson suggested that Toomer just seemed to fade into oblivion.

BONTEMPS: Again, the audience and the receptivity of the publishers and booksellers were all against Toomer. Add to that his innovation. I regard that as the explanation. His time has only now come. He was so far ahead of his time. I only wish that he had lived three or four more years to see it.

INTERVIEWER: Did he reach a time when he did not like to be considered as a writer?

BONTEMPS: I wouldn't say that he didn't like to be considered as a writer. He wrote all his life. He was discouraged about his writing I believe. I think more than anything else he wanted to be a writer, and he was disappointed that he never had an audience. But the influence of Gurdjieff made him settle for another kind of recognition.

INTERVIEWER: What was the influence of Carl Van Vechten on the writers of the Renaissance? Was he a center around whom many of the writers revolved?

BONTEMPS: He was a figure there but I don't think it was based upon his own writing. I don't think a single writer tried to imitate him. If any did, it was Thurman who disapproved of him most. Van Vechten was sort of a middle man. He was responsible for getting some of the younger writers published. He was excited by the upsurge in self-expression in Harlem and he promoted a lot of it. But I was not in his circle for a number of reasons. I suppose one reason was that I got married soon after arriving in New York and I was preoccupied with making a living. So, I couldn't run around as much as some of those who were unattached.

INTERVIEWER: What caused the Harlem Renaissance to break up?

BONTEMPS: It was the crash of the stock market on Wall Street in 1929. It took it from 1929 to 1931 to reach uptown to Harlem. You heard a lot of things but it was not until 1931 that you could tell that anything had happened on Wall Street. That is what ended it; it was a blow to publishing. Recovery didn't come until the New Deal. By then the black writers of Harlem were all scattered.

INTERVIEWER: Why did so many black writers expatriate?

BONTEMPS: So many? I'm amazed that so few did. Nothing like the number of white writers that went abroad in the twenties. Very few blacks went and very few stayed very long. More went after World War II. William Gardner Smith, Richard Wright, Chester Himes. Wright went because he could better support himself there. Chester went a little later because he was actually doing better in France than he was in America.

INTERVIEWER: Could you compare what went on among the writers of the Harlem Renaissance to what is happening among the young black writers of today? Although they do not live within a few city blocks of one another, is there a closeness and vitality among them that reminds you of the writers in the twenties?

BONTEMPS: I see more contrasts than I do similarities. There is a comparable impulse motivating this generation, but the circumstances have changed, so that the differences are conspicuous. For one thing, Harlem was Harlem because it had a locus in New York which was the cultural center of the nation. Now this impulse is dissipated throughout the whole country. I don't think that this is bad; as a matter of fact, I think that it may be very good. But it makes it *seem* different. There are many young black writers who are anxious to conceive of something similar to the Harlem Renaissance, but now everyone has his own local loyalty. I think that we are really far away from unification. And I don't think that now we have anyone writing verse that compares with Hughes or Cullen. There are more dramatists now and I attribute this to the different characteristics of our time. This is the time of the demonstration, this is the era of the visual demonstration. History is coming into it. And that is closer to drama than it is to poetry. I encourage young writers to imitate the Harlem group. If history will let them, perhaps they will make the same sort of impact.

INTERVIEWER: A number of contemporary black writers still insist that publishers continue to discriminate and that there are really only superficial changes since the Renaissance.

BONTEMPS: I would say that if it's difficult to get published today, it isn't for racial reasons. They don't have that obstacle.

INTERVIEWER: You have described the kinds of racism that the Harlem writers had to overcome in the publishing world and several contemporary black writers have pointed to continued racism on the part of the critics which they are having to combat. Do you think that the black writer finds it difficult to avoid becoming politically involved because he is made all the more conscious of racism when he attempts to publish? Does that political involvement help or hinder his art?

BONTEMPS: My own feeling is that modern man, the artist included, is directly affected by politics in our age. When it comes to being a doctrinaire participant in the political structure, I think that a writer can be hurt more than he can be helped by too strong an identification and too strong an allegiance. When I first knew Richard Wright and Ralph Ellison both of them were deeply involved in party-line communism and both felt that they were hurt more than they were helped by it. I always avoided it because, having grown up in an environment where my father had been a preacher, I was turned off by denominational, doctrinal infighting. So I am really speaking just about my own temperament; I don't believe that you can generalize. What each one does is a matter that is determined by his own makeup, the thickness of his skin, and all these other things over which he has very little control.

INTERVIEWER: You certainly have not shied away from politics in your own novels. I wonder what the reaction was to *Black Thunder* when it was published in 1936. Were you criticized for the obvious revolutionary sympathies in the novel?

BONTEMPS: *Black Thunder* was widely reviewed and favorably reviewed, very favorably. Isabella Paterson complained in the *New York Herald Tribune* that I seemed to be dragging in the word "proletariat." I didn't agree, because actually it was a current expression in the French Revolution in which time the novel is set.

INTERVIEWER: Were you accused by anyone of encouraging violent revolution?

BONTEMPS: Yes and no. There were little hints of that. It didn't keep me from getting favorable reviews from people who were not in the least radical. At the time, actually, there was more tolerance for that kind of writing than there was a few years later. It was published in the depths of the Depression and even conservative people could understand why certain writers could be taking positions that were quite radical.

INTERVIEWER: Would the novel have received severer criticism today do you think?

BONTEMPS: I think so. Two things would happen. I would be accused of advocating violence because everything in the novel was in that direction. On the other hand the people who support the violent approach would pick up the book in greater numbers. And I would have been satisfied (laughing) to exchange one for the other.

INTERVIEWER: Were there contemporary issues which prompted you to write the book at that time which are lost to today's readers?

BONTEMPS: Yes, definitely. I had looked into the Scottsboro case, which was to the 1930s what the Till case was to the Civil Rights demonstrations. The Scottsboro case was a prologue to what happened to my thinking and it encouraged me to go ahead with some such statement as *Black Thunder*.

INTERVIEWER: When you wrote the novel, did you have in mind the kind of effect you wanted to have on your audience? Did you want some change to come about as a result of the novel?

BONTEMPS: I never felt that the kind of change a novel could bring would be instantaneous or explosive; nor did I want it to have an explosive effect. I was most impressed with novels that have a delayed action, and I had hopes that my writing would be of that kind, that it would work almost imperceptibly upon the reader's consciousness. I never felt that I could write the kind of novel I wanted to write and expect it to start a fire.

INTERVIEWER: You said in the introduction to a recent edition of *Black Thunder* that you were discouraged about reaching your generation through novel-writing, so you hoped to influence future ones. Was this the reason you stopped writing novels and turned to children's books?

BONTEMPS: Definitely, that was the transition. I was in no mood merely to write entertaining novels. The fact that *Gone With the Wind* was so popular at the time was a dramatic truth to me of what the country was willing to. read. And I felt that black children had nothing with which they could identify. As a result I tried my hand at writing for children and with immediately better results.

INTERVIEWER: Would today's generation be more receptive to the novels you wanted to write?

BONTEMPS: I think that novel reading is down in this generation and I don't know how long it's going to stay down. There have been some up periods since I wrote my novels but television has reduced the number of people who depend upon fiction for whatever nourishment they need.

INTERVIEWER: Both your fiction and poetry are concerned with themes of history and time. You use the image of the pendulum rather than the river to describe your sense of history.

BONTEMPS: That impressed me a long time ago and I still feel that history is a pendulum that does recur. But in each recurrence there is a difference.

INTERVIEWER: And the image of the river would suggest a sense of completion?

BONTEMPS: That's right. The river is finished, it goes to its outlet. I don't think the river is a very good metaphor for time because we live in a universe that is perpetually revolving. And in our own experience we always arrive at the same point again, but when we get there we find that time has worked some changes in us.

INTERVIEWER: Do you think that in your poetry you look toward the past with a desire to recapture it?

BONTEMPS: Well, there certainly is some nostalgia. I don't know whether I was consciously yearning for the past. I don't think that I ever believed that I could recapture the past. I had a yearning for something, something in my own life. Unlike most black writers I yearned for something in my past because I had something there that I could look upon with a certain amount of longing. A great many writers whom I have known have wanted to forget their pasts.

INTERVIEWER: In the preface to *Personals* you suggest that much of the writing of the Renaissance looked backward and tried to establish a link with the jungle.

BONTEMPS: It has impressed me in black literature that the primitive is often superior to the civilized or educated man.

INTERVIEWER: Of course, in the white Western mind the primitive is usually associated with disorder and perhaps violence. Many black writers seem to see it as a way of tapping some resource in man that frees him from the tyrannical norms of the existing rationalistic culture.

BONTEMPS: That's right. Spontaneity seems quite important in the black culture. The person who can act with spontaneity is the one favored by nature. One of the things I talked about a great deal when I taught at Yale was that Primitivism is often thought of as having no rationale to it. In fact, oftentimes it was actually the result of a long development that had been experimented with and proved. Some African tribes that had no written language—tribes we would take to be the more primitive ones— sometimes had the most sophisticated art. The bronzes of Benin in Nigeria which had such a great influence on modern painters like Picasso, were the work of a tribe that never had a written language. And a tribe in Eastern Africa which has given so many collections of proverbs to us had no written language either until very recently. I have deduced from this that they had some reason for not writing down their language, not that they were incapable. They were capable of things that go deeper than merely writing a language. It was a conscious choice of theirs. So I toyed with the thought that they deliberately refrained from developing written records. Because of the nature of their life, which was very fluid, it may be that tribes that had written languages were more vulnerable. This might have been part of their defense against invasion and oppression. In other words, they must have very carefully considered the disadvantages of writing. There certainly were languages in Africa long before there were Western languages. These languages existed not only in Egypt but down into mid-Africa, into that area in Rhodesia where cities were buried whose languages are known. So, I think the "book" is something they knew all about, talked about, and rejected.

INTERVIEWER: In America there has always been a black literary tradition, but it has not always been a written one.

BONTEMPS: Blacks were the foremost proponents of the tale told for entertainment or instruction. And it was always oral.

INTERVIEWER: This literary tradition is so strongly influenced by music. The structure of McKay's and Toomer's novels was based on musical concepts and critics attacked them for being sloppy and episodic.

BONTEMPS: That's right. They were speaking out of another context, using a different form of notation. They were attempting to free themselves from what they regarded as the limitations of this closed structure which didn't hold what they wanted it to.

Cyrus Colter

Cyrus Colter was sixty years old when his first book, *The Beach Umbrella,* won the Iowa School of Letters Award for Short Fiction. Drawing praise from veteran writers such as Kurt Vonnegut, Jr. and Vance Bourjaily, it was hailed as the product of a major talent, rich in experience and of fertile imagination. Two years later Colter had produced a novel, *The Rivers of Eros,* with others nearing completion. All this was accomplished by a man who did not start writing until he was fifty, and who continued to serve as senior member of the Illinois Commerce Commission. What is most remarkable about his fiction is that Colter matured so quickly, that he did not require one or two books of fiction before finding himself as a writer. A master in both style and theme from the very beginning of his career, his only problem is to find time enough to write. And his plans are very ambitious.

After one phone conversation and the exchange of a few brief letters, I met Colter for lunch at his club on the top floor of Orchestra Hall in Chicago. Much of the talk over lunch was given to discussing his favorite conductors and recent Chicago Symphony performances. They were appropriate subjects in a room that had wined and dined the most celebrated musicians and conductors of this century. By dessert time, Colter was reciting from memory passages from what he considers the three masterworks of fiction—*Crime and Punishment, Moby Dick,* and *Dub-*

liners. He had confined himself of late to re-reading these books again and again. After lunch we drove to Colter's apartment on South Lake Shore Drive, passing on the way the setting for his title story, "The Beach Umbrella." From his penthouse apartment one has a panoramic view of the Chicago he uses as backdrop for all his fiction. On what had turned into a rather dismal and overcast autumn afternoon we began the interview proper, and talked steadily until lights in the surrounding high-rise apartments started blinking on. Except for the weather, it was a most unlikely setting for discussing Colter's pessimistic and despairing fiction.

As the interview reveals, Colter's fiction explores the existential and deterministic nature of man's existence. Disregarding the common myth that naturalistic writers are primarily concerned with the social and environmental dimensions of their characters' experience, Colter in *The Beach Umbrella* relatively ignored the effects of racism on his characters. They are of all ages, economic status, and social backgrounds. They inevitably end in ruin and disillusionment, not because they are black or poor, but because they are condemned to being human. Poverty and racism are merely two forms of determinism that can infect their lives. Colter is more interested in those qualities of experience which affect all people: human isolation, emotional sterility, sexual inhibition and frustration, the indifference of an alien world, self-imposed illusions, accident, and guilt. The protagonist of "A Man in the House" is an innocent eighteen-year-old girl who is abruptly initiated into sexual desire and guilt. In her naïveté she mistakes such desire as evil and ends the story sensing that the rest of her life will be spent in unrelieved guilt and sin. In "A Chance Meeting," an old man meets an acquaintance and is casually informed that the wealthy woman who employed them both had fired him because he once saw her "hugging" another man. The old man had been sustained in life by the sacred and unblemished image he carried of this woman; this new knowledge shatters his belief and prepares him for a bleak and empty future. In "An Untold Story" a character becomes the unwilling cause of a murder because he is emotionally incapable of telling fellow patrons in a bar the personally moving story of *Hamlet* which he had read in college.

Determinism such as this is wedded to a vision which is also existential. Not only are these characters utterly ruled by forces in their lives that they cannot control, but they are doomed to struggle for meaning in an absurd, hostile, and alien universe. The character in "Moot" was betrayed by his wife when he was young and had sought communication in the company of a dog. The relationship, already determined by his past unsuccessful relationships with humans, is one of torment. When the dog dies, he attempts to establish an affinity with the physical objects in his room, but even the television stops working. A short time later he dies. In the closing scene two workmen, agents of the impersonal universe, arrive to clean out his belongings and prepare the room for the next tenant. They judge his remains as "worthless." The protagonist of "The Beach Umbrella" tries to discover love among bathers on 32nd Street Beach in Chicago. After taking every precaution that his questful day will conform to what he has imagined it will be, he arrives on the beach to find it cold, overcast, and scarcely populated. The few people there look on him with suspicion and unconcern. The day ends with him defeated and knowing that love is an illusion.

In his novel, *The Rivers of Eros,* Colter expanded his interest in the purely personal forms of determinism to consider the determining nature of history. In addition to tracing the life of an elderly black woman who slowly goes mad because of her guilt-ridden past, Colter sets into conflict two opposing black solutions for racism: assimilation and nationalism. Ambrose Hammer studies American history to find the true contributions of blacks. He hopes that such discoveries will help to reconcile the two races. Dunreith Smith advocates the violent termination of white supremacy and the creation of a separate black nation. Colter succeeds in reducing both views to the absurd. Just as this woman's life in the novel is determined by her past, so is the racial situation in America. Time and history establish patterns of experience which man cannot alter. Neither violence nor reconciliation can improve or worsen the fate of blacks in America. History has decided the shape of things to come and the hope of change is illusory.

Rather than belonging to an American tradition, Colter is

perhaps most at home in the company of the Russian realists and the Greek tragedians. The conventionality of his prose and story reminds one more of nineteenth-century writers than of anyone contemporary. This conventionality has drawn criticism from a few of his critics who have urged him to formal experimentation in his work. He has resisted such advice and, at the conclusion of the interview, proudly produced a recent essay by Malcolm Cowley, "Storytelling's Tarnished Image," which calls for abandoning the "anti-story" and returning to traditional narrative. After sharing a few drinks and listening to favorite selections from Wagner, Beethoven, and Fauré, Colter dropped me off in downtown Chicago and returned to his Loop office to catch up on work which he must have put aside that day for the interview.

INTERVIEWER: In recent years a great deal of pressure has been exerted on the black writer to become politically involved and to make his own writing a kind of battleground for political issues. Have you personally felt this pressure and has it affected your writing?

COLTER: I've no objection to political involvement at all. I think that if a writer can do it, and can do it with validity, fine. He ought to do it. But I think this thing of writing fiction is something with respect to which we don't have as much liberty and latitude as we think we have. When fiction is true, it tends to be something like an organic extension of oneself. And you're restricted if you're writing truly, just as you're restricted as a human personality. We might like to be like someone else. We'd like to get rid of some of our known faults, but we can't do it. I tend to be a Thomas Hobbes type determinist, or a B. F. Skinner type, and I don't think we have the latitude that some people think we have in what we write and the way we write it. So, I say that every writer better write as best he can according to his own lights. And I don't criticize anybody for writing what they feel they can write, what they want to write about and what they feel they can write about. I think whether a writer writes importantly or not depends first upon whether he's the kind of individual that has the personal chemistry out of which something important can come. If he is that kind of person, then his product will be that kind and nothing else, irrespective of how much he wishes it to be something else.

INTERVIEWER: As a writer are you conscious of a social responsibility, do you feel that your art must be used in some way to effect changes in society?

COLTER: I can't say that I do. That may not be a very attractive position to take but, truthfully, I don't think that I do. What I am trying to do when I'm writing is to get down on paper what I see and feel, and it's very possible that it has no social value at all. I'm not sure, and I really don't care too much actually. I try to communicate what I see and feel in the same way that I see and feel it, and hope that it will impress someone who reads what I've written. I think that's really the way I do it. I'm trying to use a character and an incident to evoke a certain emotion and I feel the emotion myself. The difficulty is in projecting it and you work hard to do it. And, alas, elbow grease alone won't do it. You have to be patient and wait and hope that you'll be vouchsafed the method by which you can attain this artistic goal.

INTERVIEWER: You mentioned that you feel yourself influenced by Hobbesian determinism. Has Hobbes influenced you more than other philosophers?

COLTER: Certainly, Hobbes and B. F. Skinner, those two especially.

INTERVIEWER: Any contemporary philosophers?

COLTER: Well, I think, Camus' *Myth of Sisyphus* has impressed me. It's a sad thing to know, but it's true. I think that's a great book; it's a sad book, but it's a great book. And we must have the courage to face up to what he's telling us.

INTERVIEWER: Is there any conflict between your existential and deterministic views?

COLTER: No, I don't think so. I don't think that there is a conflict between Camus' position that there is no meaning to this life, and that in fact there's such little meaning in it that it's all absurd, I don't think that there is any necessary conflict between that view and the mechanistic or deterministic view that we are here as effects of certain causes about which we have nothing to do, and that these causes determine what we are and what we shall be. In fact, this second view leads to the sense of nullity the existentialists have. We're caught in this bind, and we go inexorably down this course which is willed for us by these causes that we have no control of. It tends to make life more existential, it seems to me.

INTERVIEWER: An example of this determinism would be Mary in "Mary's Convert," where, despite her best efforts at self-reform, she cannot be other than what she is?

COLTER: What I had in mind was to show that irrespective of her trying to improve her life, irrespective of her good intentions, she was unable to overcome certain things in her life. One being her immediate environment, and two being her make-up as a person. Her environment was hostile to her, and her own make-up was insufficiently strong to come out victorious in the end.

INTERVIEWER: Personality and circumstance will not permit her to change?

COLTER: Right. Now the literalist would say that this is because these characters are trapped in the ghetto. Well, that's true. But there is something in addition to that which contributes to their tragedy. I almost said that even if they weren't trapped in the ghetto these things would conceivably have happened to them. And I'm not so sure that's wrong.

INTERVIEWER: Perhaps your existential attitude is most clearly present in a story like "Moot."

COLTER: That's exactly right. Your perception of the story is perfect. And it portrays my attitude toward life. That's why it's a Colter story; it's an existential story. Read *The Myth of Sisyphus* and you'll see why the story had to end the way it does.

INTERVIEWER: Had "Moot" ended with Matthew's death, it would have been pessimistic enough. But you bring on these two cleaning men, agents of an indifferent universe, who dispassionately dispose of all his belongings.

COLTER: That's the irony. Goethe says "all art is irony," and I believe that.

INTERVIEWER: Verna, in "A Man in the House," is another character who is caught in a situation. Is there any way out for her or is she helplessly determined?

COLTER: I didn't intend her to be, but that's how life is, and that's how I saw the facts and circumstances surrounding my characters' lives. Ford in "A Chance Meeting" is a tragic figure because his whole life had been based on his view of this woman. It was his whole life. Seeing this great creature almost enshrined in his fantasy from afar all these years, she was his whole life. And he would have died with this great solace if he had not been out walking that afternoon and if he had not seen Spivey across the street and if Spivey had not seen him. If Spivey had taken some other street or if he hadn't recognized him, Ford would have died with this great vision. That's what the tragedy of the story is. That one fact intervened and sent his life down a course ninety degrees different.

INTERVIEWER: In "An Untold Story" there seems to be something in Lonnie which he cannot control and which prevents him from telling the Hamlet story. Would the murder that takes place have been averted had Lonnie told the story?

COLTER: Possibly not. I think that Ramsey is right, at the end of the story. He's saying, in effect, that it would not have happened had Lonnie told his story. But Lonnie could not tell the story. He couldn't. He was ineffectual in telling the story because there was something in him that he could not understand about what *Hamlet* did to him. So he wanted to tell it, but he couldn't. And as a result of his inability to tell the story, the murder occurred.

INTERVIEWER: Do you think that part of your characters' tragedies is that they are so incapable of articulating their situations, that if they could articulate what was happening to them they would gain some release?

COLTER: Yes, if they could externalize some of these tragic feelings that they all harbor in their breasts . . . what they would like life to be for them, if they could externalize it, you wouldn't have a story. That's the problem. They are people who cannot do it; they cannot cast out these demons. They've got them for life. Some of my friends—not writers, though very literate— have remarked, with some concern, about what they see as the unrelieved tragic tone of almost all the stories. Although I doubt this is entirely true, I may have to admit at least some justification for their feeling. My attitude—and I hope it's a saving grace—toward the tragic in literature is probably quite different from some of the more pessimistic writers. I think all serious writing should have a serene, an aloof, a not-unhappy ending. The tragic story or novel should be evolved and set forth by the writer in such a way that we accept his conclusion almost gladly and would not have it otherwise. And although the conclusion may be outwardly calamitous, or portray the unavoidable fact of life that good people often come to bad ends, or that sometimes the fairest things on earth are the first to perish, the reader must at the end be able to put the book or story down content that this is so. In other words, it's a cool, detached affirmation of life—as life really is—and we are somehow made all the more heroic by understanding and accepting it. For us, then, tragedy should not be an expression of despair, but the means by which we are literally saved from despair. It is a coming-to-terms with life.

INTERVIEWER: You assign great capacity to the writer, then.

COLTER: Yes, I do—I do indeed. Every great tragedy— *Oedipus, Lear, Romeo and Juliet* (for me, the most beautiful, I stress *beautiful*, the absolutely most beautiful tragedy known to the world), *Othello, Ghosts, Desire Under the Elms*—are all, it seems to me, reaffirmations, indeed acknowledgements, of the inexorable nature of life. But we are the better for understanding this—better equipped for what surely lies ahead.

INTERVIEWER: In your writing, there is a preoccupation with philosophical matters that does not frequently concern other black writers. Have you felt this about your own work? Why do you think that black writers are less concerned with so many of the themes that pervade the rest of American literature? Is it related to the social and political position of blacks in this country, that there are other things to be concerned with first?

COLTER: Well, I feel this, that when blacks solve their immediate problem, which is ridding the country of the denial of opportunity based on race . . . when they've achieved that, and they will in time, then they will find themselves on the threshold of other monumental problems of the human condition. And someone would say, "Well, they happen to have those now in addition to the ones they have flowing out of race." But I think that their situation is so painful presently, they're so concerned and involved with the immediate problems of life, that they are less aware of some of the problems that are part of the condition of merely being a human being. Maybe they're less aware of them, but they won't be less aware of them, I think, when some of the strictures they're dealing with today are removed. And I think, since the black writer is writing out of that experience, he is reflecting the present black attitudes.

INTERVIEWER: Perhaps because black writers have not been concerned with many of these metaphysical questions, there is a kind of optimism in black literature which is difficult to find in white American literature.

COLTER: I tend to agree with that. It seems to confirm what you and I both agree on, that blacks and black writers are concerned with these immediate problems—and they can be immediate: where you're going to live, whether or not you're going to be able to get a job by which you'll be able to support yourself and your family, whether or not you're going to be able to live in a decent neighborhood . . . you can't think of things more immediate than that. So that this overtone of optimism that you see through all the turmoil in black writing may flow from the fact that these objectives tend to be more attainable, they're more possible. But they will come—as writers throughout the world who don't have these present restrictions do—to face the really fundamental questions of life. That's what gives rise to the pessimism in my opinion.

INTERVIEWER: It strikes me that there is a similarity between the pessimistic tone one finds in your fiction and in Hawthorne's. Perhaps the great difference is that God is totally absent in your stories. This absence intensifies your characters' isolation.

COLTER: It's possible. I don't necessarily agree or disagree with that. It's difficult, I guess, to keep my agnosticism out of what I write. It's part of what I feel and what I believe. But I'm not an atheist. I think that this great system that we live in, this universe, is so immense that we don't have the equipment even to envision it; it's so infinite that with our finite equipment we can't comprehend it. So I think that any rational individual has got to acknowledge the existence of some power that's far greater than man or anything we see about us. But then to infer from that that this immense power we can call God or the Deity, to infer from that that he has a solicitude about the personal fortunes of each of us is a step not altogether easy to take. So I am sure that is imparted to my characters or what I write.

INTERVIEWER: Your relationship to your stories is a very distant one. You seem to have completely disengaged the writer from the story.

COLTER: Yes, I told you that I am trying to do two things as I write. One is to try to reflect myself as accurately as I can with the tools I have to work with; but more importantly, to keep myself as far away from the story while I'm writing it as I can. I think of myself sometimes as in a dark theater, in a dark movie theater up in the projection booth where that light from the projection booth is going onto the screen, but everything else is dark. And I'm hidden back in that projection booth and what is seen on the screen has not the slightest trace of me as a writer. And I think the farther the writer stays away from his story, the better the writing is.

INTERVIEWER: You have avoided formal experimentation in your writing. Have you ever tried to experiment?

COLTER: Well, I can't write any other way than the way I write. I really don't have any choice. But I'm not against experimentation. I'm not averse to any writing style. I think that style itself is of little importance. It seems to me the crucial thing is whether or not the writer is an artist. If you ask me to define what an artist is or what art is, I can't tell you that. But I have a notion of what an artist is, and experimentation done by an artist can't fail, or seldom fails; it's bound to succeed. But it doesn't succeed, in my opinion, so much because of the singularity or the novelty of the style; it succeeds because we have an artist who's at the helm. Once an artist starts to do something, he seeks the vehicle which will most effectively attain his artistic ends. I think that's how he comes by his style. I don't think a literary artist comes by his style first, and then evolves his content. I think he evolves the content and then seeks ways to project it. His style is modified and is conformed—is made to conform—to the substance and the content of what he seeks to do, more than the other way around. I do realize that there are many pseudowriters who think of style as an end in itself. And it can be, for a short period of time. It will get books published and so on, and he will achieve a sort of coterie supporting him. But I don't think that there are any staying qualities in such a venture as that.

INTERVIEWER: Do you consciously work at certain themes in your stories? For example, there are several variations on sexual themes in the stories and in *The Rivers of Eros*. How conscious of them were you when you wrote the stories?

COLTER: I wasn't conscious of them. I had not that in mind at all. I didn't have much of anything in mind when I used that; it was a natural circumstance of these people that came to me. You see, if I had been trying to do all these things I would have fallen flat on my face. That's what I said to you today at lunch. I wish someone could dream up a better word that would be acceptable because "inspiration" is not acceptable to most literate people today, certainly not to writers, It's corney today to speak in terms of inspiration. And maybe that's not an accurate way to describe whatever happens. But I'm sure that what happens in my case is not arrived at by conscious cerebration. I'm sure of that. I don't try to think up some symbol nor do I try to think up some incident that is going to portray certain traits of character or certain human values. I couldn't do it, I don't see how anyone could do it. Maybe some people can, but I can't do it. There has to be some authentic feeling that I have that this is artistically right. I have never consciously thought up something, or sought to think up something, or racked my brain to think up something that's going to work. It has to come to you. Now what few writers I know, when I talk to them like that, they sort of smile indulgently, but that's been *my* experience.

INTERVIEWER: One of the themes that keeps recurring in the stories is the problem of communication among people. It occurs in a story like "Overnight Trip," where it eventually undermines the marriage. And it is the central theme in "The Beach Umbrella," where Elijah is involved in a desperate search for love and human compassion. Do you think that the sense of community that he creates is a real one or one that can endure for long?

COLTER: Possibly. He was so cut off from life that he was willing to make friends with most anyone who'd spend five minutes with him. And these people whom he took up with on the beach illustrate the extreme position he found himself in. With the exception of Mrs. Green, they were unprepossessing people. And he had a terrific time, even with those people. But they didn't fully appreciate him. In fact, they made fun of him and they were in part derisive toward him. But he didn't notice that in his eagerness to reach out to those people and to seek friendship, or some kind of accommodation with them.

INTERVIEWER: In the hands of another author, Elijah might have gone to the beach that day and fully achieved the kind of human contact he needed. But in your story, illusory communication seems to be the only kind of communication we can hope for in this impersonal world.

COLTER: I rather think that. We can't realistically hope to achieve the kind of company and companions that we would really prefer, and I think that we have to compromise. And, of course, Elijah's compromise here was on a great scale, was on a vast scale. Some of those girls, of course, were girls of pleasure and he even found great rapport with one of those, the girl he went swimming with. He was elated with her. And, of course, she was not giving him a second thought. She was out for an afternoon and there was no one else with whom she could spend any time so she indulged him to the extent of going swimming with him and letting him hold her up in the water. Of course, it was just an experience of greatest elation for him.

INTERVIEWER: Perhaps because your characters realize that they are caught, they have a certain fascination for "unreality." At the end of "The Lookout," the character says that she likes the snow because it seems so "unreal."

COLTER: I'd not thought about that but it may be true. I was trying to show that she would resort to anything, including those strong Manhattans, if it would relieve her of this perennial pain that she suffered from day to day as a result of her unhappy marriage and her unhappy life. And it was exacerbated, of course, whenever she came in contact with these women who had done better in life than she had.

INTERVIEWER: This theme of unhappy marriages, which recurs frequently, is present in "A Man in the House." You seemed purposely to leave vague what Jack Robinson's intentions are for Verna. Are they sexual?

COLTER: I hope that you don't think and that other people don't think I'm kidding or being dishonest when I say that I can't answer some of the questions raised by some of the incidents in my stories. You ask me what was my meaning; I'm not sure that I know myself. Jack Robinson is very dissatisfied with his wife and his life has been empty because of that fact. And here is this fresh, young, nubile girl who is no blood kin to him but who has just really stunned him by her utter femininity, by her beauty, and by her "innocence." So he is really in love with her. Now he tries to keep sex out of his mind; he's a good man. Sex is not uppermost in his mind. Now it's true that if they had been left to their own devices that inevitably would have come, but we don't know what happens after she decides to stay there. Conceivably that comes, and great unhappiness comes to that household because these two individuals are not able to restrain themselves. But he is very much in love with this girl and she is very much in love with him. What happens as a result of that is anyone's guess.

INTERVIEWER: She seems to feel herself fallen at the end of the story.

COLTER: Yes.

INTERVIEWER: Is the guilt real or imaginary?

COLTER: No, the guilt is real. But it isn't because of sex, although she strips naked and gets in bed in her fantasizing. She does feel guilt; she feels guilt about what she's done to her aunt. She's there in the house and she knows she's in love with her aunt's husband and knows he's in love with her and she's a good girl and she feels guilt. And she also feels guilt because she knows that if the barriers were brought down between them, she would engage in sex with him.

INTERVIEWER: In your novel, *The Rivers of Eros*, Hammer is preoccupied with blacks' relation to American history. What is he trying to do with history?

COLTER: Hammer has a hope for this system. He has a hope for blacks in this system and he is doing this research in his ineffective or in his limited way. It's sort of a poignant attempt to gain acceptance for blacks by pointing out to both blacks and whites the great and significant part blacks have played in American history since the days of the colonies. But on the other hand characters like Smith in the novel and like Alexis Potts think that this is a waste of time and they're bitter against anyone who would try to pull off what they would call a specious and ineffectual attempt. They think that blacks have no future in this country and that they have no place to go. They would just like to stay here and cause as much trouble as they can. They're absolutely frustrated and bitter people. But Hammer, on the other hand, has hopes. He's convinced himself that this is the only alternative, that this is the only course that blacks have in this country. To continue to press for acceptance and to continue to point out to the whites in this country the valorous record that blacks have in all American wars.

INTERVIEW: Does Hammer's understanding of the black man come close to that of someone like Booker T. Washington's?

COLTER: No, I wouldn't equate Hammer with Booker T. Washington. Maybe I got too close to that. He is in many ways a misguided man. He is too optimistic, in my opinion. And this tends to make him . . . credulous. He tends to be a credulous human being. A good, credulous human being. And in that way it seems to me he's made more poignant as a character because life is not like the life he describes. Despite the fact that Crispus Attucks was the first black, or among the first blacks to fall in the American Revolution, despite many other examples of black valor in all these wars, that hasn't brought about the black man's acceptance, and I think Hammer's being a little credulous. I don't think that the truth is in his situation nor is it in the situation of Smith and Alexis Potts. I don't think that any of them have the answer. The truth is somewhere in between. In my opinion, Hammer is unrealistic. But we want him to be right because his instincts are so attractive. Would to God this were a world like he seems to see it! Would that there were hope, the hope that he sees. But there isn't.

INTERVIEWER: Is the guilt that Clotilde feels about her past justified?

COLTER: It's entirely likely that to a literate, amoral person (and I think that this is a radical thing for me to say)—and people who know most about this, people who have read philosophers and who have read widely and who know about life, tend to be amoral—to that kind of person, Clotilde has less to feel guilty about than she thinks. You've made that point. But if she really knew about life, she would feel less guilty simply because of the deterministic view I have of life which I think she would have if she were a more perceptive person. She would not feel guilty. She was guilty of an indiscretion, but the laws of determinism set all these other things in motion. As a result of her betraying her sister and going to bed with her sister's husband she begat his daughter, Ruby, who died in these tragic circumstances and brought tragedy on Lester and on Annie, and, therefore, on Clotilde. It was the train of events that was set in motion by this seed and it could happen to anyone. Certainly an amoral person would not agree with Clotilde in her assessment of her own guilt. But because this train of events was set in motion, once it was set in motion it made its way inexorably, and I think that's her tragedy.

INTERVIEWER: That's very much like the Greek concept of tragedy.

COLTER: Michael Anania, my editor, has said the same thing, and he's said it repeatedly.

William Demby

William Demby published his first novel, *Beetlecreek*, in 1950. For the next fifteen years he lived in Rome and worked in movies with such people as Michael Antonioni. In 1965 he produced *The Catacombs*, one of the most original and important novels to come out of the 1960s. In retrospect, one could not have expected such a second novel. *Beetlecreek* is, although Demby himself dissents from this interpretation, a naturalistic novel which possesses all the trappings that go along with that form: a small American town, characters who are the victims of their circumstances and personalities, and even the final scene where the characters both literally and metaphorically cross each other's paths as they move toward their doom. The novel was a fine first novel and established Demby as someone to be heard from. But there was nothing in it to suggest that this same author was capable of or even interested in such an experimental novel as *The Catacombs*. Whereas the first novel is rooted in social and environmental problems, the second takes place more in fantasy than it does the "real" world. It is removed not only from the atmosphere of the American small town but even from the limits of time and place.

Though it is a little pointless to describe the novel in terms of plot, it concerns a writer named William Demby who is trying to write an experimental novel while living in Rome. His problem is that his fictional creations become more real than the real-life

characters around him. A character from his novel is as likely to
show up for dinner as is his wife or a friend. What both William
Dembys are attempting to do is to pattern phenomena, which, it
is decided, may be possible only in art. The author-character
reads several newspapers each day and tries to see how seemingly unrelated events might somehow fit together. He looks not
only at the headlines but at the small items in the back pages in
an effort to piece together an incident that occurred yesterday in
Rome with something that happened last week in an obscure
American town. This thematic interest explains the stylistic methods that Demby employs. In the interview, he remembers having
wanted to write a novel that had the effects of a tapestry, where
the sense of time is most truly captured because it is able to show
so many actions occurring simultaneously. A novel, just because
it requires the reader to turn pages and can deal with events in
sequence, distorts the way time actually works. Demby attempts
to step outside of time and create the sense of simultaneity. In the
process Demby breaks down the traditional narrative method of
the novel.

At the same time *The Catacombs* is a reflection on Western
man's need to keep pace with the changes that surround him, to
evolve into whatever technology and science have prepared for
him. The novel points to the necessity of expanding our consciousness as the only means of survival in a world that becomes
increasingly complicated. Both in art and life man must seek new
forms that release him from the limitations of the past. In former
times, change was necessary for the energetic continuance of a
culture; in our times, though, change is imperative because we
now have the power to destroy both our culture and our world. If
we maintain our past prejudices and our violent efforts to solve
them, we will kill ourselves. We must become aware of the danger that is inherent in our new power. In suggesting this, Demby
creates a new art form to embody this new consciousness. If the
novel is dead, as critics have been telling us for almost thirty
years, then we can either assent to its death or try to revive it by
inventing new ways of writing it. Demby chooses invention both
in life and art.

The interview was conducted in early November, 1971, in
New York City where Demby lives and teaches. He is deceptively

young looking; I thought perhaps it was his son who answered the door and invited me in. He had just moved into a penthouse apartment which did not yet have curtains on the windows. As we talked, outside New York turned into night. Demby speaks slowly and deliberately, carefully choosing his words and pausing to reflect upon what he is about to say. We began the interview by discussing the authors who seem to have influenced him, especially those who have dealt with themes of time.

INTERVIEWER: Are there authors who have affected your writing?

DEMBY: Well, I think that Virginia Woolf did, for some reason.

INTERVIEWER: Perhaps because of her use and treatment of time?

DEMBY: Yes, time. Certainly it came out in *The Catacombs*, the way she was able to slow down time, or stretch it, or treat time as though it were something one touched, and could mold. If I haven't been influenced by her, I at least have a very great affinity for what she was trying to do and was doing.

INTERVIEWER: Are there other writers?

DEMBY: Camus, of course. Of the black writers, only Ellison. I have a strong feeling that the novels of Richard Wright didn't influence me very much.

INTERVIEWER: What about nonliterary influences?

DEMBY: Music. (These are comparatively recent influences. I was writing my first novel over twenty years ago.) But in music, Schoenberg and Berg, everybody who was fooling around with ideas of time. I think that was one influence that really, really profoundly influenced me in ways that I still am not sure of but which certainly influenced the whole structure of *The Catacombs*. I also think that I was influenced very strongly by two extremes of European films, so-called "naturalism," or "realism" as they would call it in Italy, but also other films, experimental films that were being made—at least those dealing with time. Philosophy —oh, I don't know. I was never really strongly influenced by philosophy . . . Kierkegaard, indirectly I suppose.

INTERVIEWER: What about science? There's a great deal of preoccupation with certain scientific problems and theories in *The Catacombs*.

DEMBY: All of us have been influenced by almost everything that has been going on in science. Stretching the consciousness. I suppose it began with Einstein.

INTERVIEWER: Did you read science firsthand or has most of it filtered down somehow?

DEMBY: Most of it has filtered down. I have not studied any of these people whom I have mentioned. My son is reading Marx for the first time. He went on vacation this summer with all those heavy books. But my wife and I laughed because we realized that none of our friends had gone through that type of initiation, yet most of our friends—or at least many of them—are Marxists.

INTERVIEWER: In the last decade there has been a great deal of experimentation in the black American novel by writers like yourself, Ishmael Reed, Charles Wright, LeRoi Jones, and William Kelley. Do you think that the nature of the novel in America is changing? Is the black writer leading the way?

DEMBY: It occurred to me one day in my black literature class that the writing of novels has suddenly become a profound crisis, a crisis which was not only in the black world, but corre-sponded with the crisis of the novel all over the Western world. It's that people—and we have examples of it—broke away from the idea of writing to such a degree that they themselves became characters in a kind of expanded-consciousness type novel. I'm speaking of Malcolm X, Cleaver, Rap Brown. They all seem to have been living a kind of Dostoevskian kind of life. And it may be difficult now for black writers to find exactly what they want to write. . . . I mean that no one could possibly write a novel like the situation of Angela Davis and Poindexter. Or Rap Brown—coming here, being picked-up after being out of circulation for a year at least—being picked-up at three o'clock in the morning down the street here at a bar, claiming to be Clarence Williams, his relatives come and the police make reports. It's not only a novel, but it's a kind of weird novel. The assassination of Mal-colm X, how Dostoevskian that was. It's not clear yet. . . . All this twilight world in which all these things are going on. It must be very, very difficult not to write because there's certainly plenty of things to write, but the whole context of the novel seems to have moved into another ball field. You can do almost anything you want, . . . yet you have to remain in contact with the con-sciousness of your reader at the same time you are seeing things yourself. How much can we feed back, how much should we feed back, and how much does our audience want us to give back? Perhaps what is going on right now is trying to forget what everyone sees.

INTERVIEWER: The achievement of *The Catacombs* is that you are able to incorporate things that are happening in the out-side world, mold them into some artistic framework, and give them some meaning.

DEMBY: That was a deliberate effort on my part. I was speak-ing at Rochester a couple of weeks ago and all this came up. We were discussing all these problems of being bombarded by all these events into our consciousnesses electronically or otherwise, at a fantastic speed, almost the speed of light. How can the novelist give this somehow to . . . how can he recreate this feeling? I was with some Russian writers—I belong to the European Community of Writers—that was in Florence, Italy. We were having an international meeting. Sartre was there; everyone was there. And there was a big tapestry on the wall, and a friend of mine from Iceland and some other people were watching this and saying, "That's the way a novel should be." Not linear, not in a kind of horizontal sequence of events, but as one perceives reality looking at that enormous tapestry upon which any number of things are happening: horses in battle, men being killed, troops lining up. You're supposed to perceive it totally—not look around. This isn't the way we look at a film, which is dependent upon a sequence of images. So that is what I tried to do. First I thought, why not try to start a novel at a certain point and, instead of going forward in time, go backward? Why was it not possible? I never really found out. It was from that idea, that liberating idea, that I conceived of writing a novel, but without any of the controls that a novel usually would have. That is, that I would begin on a certain day and continuously go forward. Every page or every day's work would reflect what has happened to me in my personal life and the lives of the fictional characters who moved around at the same time as the so-called real characters, the people in real life. So each day should reflect all of these things: what I perceived from the newspapers that I was reading, or the things that were happening in other countries, or in the southern part of Italy. Anything. My wife's family. Anything that was going on. All of this was reflected. What astonished me was that there was a real pattern that you perceived. What created this pattern, I don't know. Was it in the consciousness of the author, or was it that any event that you would see happening anywhere, were you to turn your consciousness on it, would fall into some kind of order? I'm not sure yet how it works but I know that it worked in *The Catacombs*. And in that novel there was never any turning back, nothing was ever rewritten. It just went forward from day to day until some instinct told me that that would be the end of it. That went on for two years.

INTERVIEWER: This may raise the question of whether the artist imposes order or whether he reflects it. Is it resolved in *The*

Catacombs whether the order is created by you or whether it exists and you are finding it?

DEMBY: I think that it gets to the deeper truth that there is no such thing as chaos perhaps. There may not be.

INTERVIEWER: The responsibility of the writer then is to find those connections between seemingly unconnected phenomena?

DEMBY: Well, if that is what the author sets out to do. But when you think of it, you see that everyone does that. You're constantly arriving at these kinds of perceptions, otherwise you would go mad if everything is chaotic. When you pick up the newspaper, people have habits of looking and choosing this morsel here and there. Editors do the same thing when the news comes over the ticker tape. They must make some kind of order out of it according to what they perceive as order.

INTERVIEWER: You try to make connections out of everything in *The Catacombs*. You don't just try to create an individual, private order.

DEMBY: I agree with that. I totally agree with that. I mean, that obviously is the function of the novelist. The novelist must have this function of seeing connections. He also has the responsibility—and this may be true of all artists—to make some connection with the past. That is, to illustrate how much of the past is living in the present and how much of the present is only the future and the past. All these things he must bring to life, all the connections, or "myths" if you will, by which people will imagine things to survive. I suppose that may be the artist's function, as you say, to make all the connections, because if we disavow the chronological-progression idea of history, then it must be something like that tapestry, it must be made up at the same moment of the past, present, and future. I suppose that is the only service the literary artist can really perform.

INTERVIEWER: I wonder whether a writer with these ideas about the purpose of the novel is not prevented from being politically involved?

DEMBY: Well, not really, I don't think so. You can see for yourself, you can test it out that when people decide to become engaged politically they do this instinctively at the right moment, if they want to be effective. You do not want to be involved in politics totally. You cannot always do this in a way that has any meaning. Only a professional politician can engage himself in all the hundreds of little battles that make up the fabric of politics in any civilization. That's why before, I said I envied LeRoi Jones, because he seems to have fallen by historical accident into a situation in which he is able to do all these things. Other writers have done it also, but everyone doesn't have these opportunities. Even if one could be involved in a precise revolutionary movement, . . . as an artist, what are the options? What can you do? I suppose the only thing you can do is to go inside yourself, to know precisely when your movement—that is, the movement of the artist—will coincide with other movements so it will be effective. That is, to choose—and I am sure we will all reach that point—when it becomes imperative to act, and not to write. I was very sensitive to that when I was writing *The Catacombs* because there I was in Rome, sitting in front of my electric typewriter, and I knew that things were going on here and that the Third World War was about to break when that ship was on its way to Cuba. In our little corner in Rome we were all frightened. We were as concerned about these things as though we were in the White House. The afternoon the boat turned around we rejoiced. We said, "War hasn't broken out, peace has broken out." That's how sensitive our antennas were.

INTERVIEWER: What effect did your expatriation have on you?

DEMBY: Well, those terms don't have very much meaning— "foreign," "expatriation." They might have had meaning right after World War I. Now nothing could happen—police dogs would attack people in a church in Alabama and we would know about it in Rome immediately. So I don't think any of us were really expatriates. It always embarrasses me when people say, "Oh, you've come back." But you've never gone. You've been there for twenty years, but you haven't changed your language, you haven't changed your personal history. Haven't changed . . . haven't changed . . .

INTERVIEWER: Would *The Catacombs* have been written had you stayed in this country?

DEMBY: No. I don't think so. I was lucky to be in Europe at that time. In Rome you were always at a kind of center for ideas. I might have fallen into the naturalistic novel had I remained in this country. I might have.

INTERVIEWER: Do you think of *Beetlecreek* as being a naturalistic novel?

DEMBY: No. I don't think so. Not *Beetlecreek*.

INTERVIEWER: I think that Herbert Hill made the point that the novel tended toward naturalism, perhaps because of the ending.

DEMBY: Well, the truth is those scenes were written in Salzburg, in Austria. And what had happened was that I had fallen in love with a woman, who was a married woman, an ex-ski champion of Austria. I was living in her house and was having an affair with her while her husband was there. And one night she went out with somebody else and I was pissed-off. So, how do we know where these inspirations come from? I know that it is not a naturalistic novel. I wouldn't call it that at all. The reality of the novel is not naturalistic. The movement that each of the char-

acters has is much more secret than any cause-and-effect relationship. Johnny certainly wasn't reacting to any . . . it wasn't that
he wanted to be in a boy's gang or anything like that. I think that
it was the imperative to act, to do anything. I think that all the
characters came into something like that. Everyone did something and we say how these doings had a pattern and I suppose
you can do that with any group of people. But it is only when
they do something, when they move, and the movement is on the
level that is perceivable, then I guess at that moment it is worthwhile to write about it. What happened in the novel? Not very
much.

INTERVIEWER: Would you accept a term like "existential" to
describe the novel?

DEMBY: I was always a little wary of that until two weeks
ago. I was up in Rochester reading and talking. A young lady
who had been my classmate at Fisk University and worked on
the literary magazine I edited, showed me a number in which I
had written a review of Camus' *The Stranger,* in which I was also
discussing existentialism. Now I had thought that I had been interested in existentialism in Europe at the time when it was fash-
ionable. I know now that I had been interested in it in college,
though I had forgotten about that. It appealed to me very much,
though I was not quite sure what existentialism meant, and I am
not sure I am now. All of our friends were talking about it, and
my wife, for example, is very interested in Kierkegaard. In fact, I
was never able to pin down intellectually what existentialism is,
except the idea seems so beautiful, so real, and so true to what I
was feeling that I had to say that I believed it, although I
wouldn't be able to defend it on any technical level.

INTERVIEWER: How do you think that existentialism affected
the novels?

DEMBY: What has always astonished me was how little minor
movements on that great tapestry or landscape there, how minor

things are interconnected—this is the sense in which the characters in *Beetlecreek* were moving existentially—the things they did seemed in themselves of no importance and yet they moved or touched other lives. And I suppose we look at reality like that, and relationships. We don't always see the small movements of people. And certainly it must be the small movements that give any movement to, for example, a revolutionary movement. Not the big gestures. The big gestures must be the fruit and the tool of many millions of gestures.

INTERVIEWER: Is there any hope for the characters at the end of *Beetlecreek?*

DEMBY: Well, . . . hope. I think the only movement in my novels, and the novels I will be working on, will be more and more a trying to understand the relationships between small movements. That is, people think they move in a meaningful way, that they have come to a decision: they get on a bus. That is only movement without any real . . . I don't know why people expected that in the novel there should be something resolved. In life there's nothing to resolve. There's just death. What is there to resolve? What is hope? Well, hope means that you still have options of movement. I suppose that this is the only thing hope can be. You cannot conceive of yourself changing, because you cannot change. Not only will that character who went North on the bus bring with him the experiences in Beetlecreek, but all his life he'll carry that bag around with him. I think that is what life *is*. Even if the movement, the particular movements, are just like shadows. In revolutionary periods, for example, people think that a revolution happened when the cannon knocked over a certain wall, when the troops ran in. This is not true. That gesture was the fruit of who knows how many gestures. And I think more and more I will be exploring that idea. The danger, of course, of the period in which we are living is that, because of television I suppose, there is an illusion of movement going on. Possibly because on television every evening something has to happen. Every day on the radio, something has to happen. The newspapers have to have a headline. But they might as well put in the newspapers that "Joe Doakes Builds A New Shit House And Took His First Shit In It." Hope? I don't know. Is it desirable for the characters to change? I don't know.

INTERVIEWER: Are you suggesting that all events are of equal importance, that we only choose to give one event more emphasis than another? Is Kennedy's death in Dallas equal in importance to any other death that might have occurred at the same time?

DEMBY: That is a good question. Many people asked that at the time it happened. Asked it of me.

INTERVIEWER: It seems like the kind of thing that Virginia Woolf was often interested in also.

DEMBY: Yes. Small Movements. Yes. Yes, I guess that we have to believe that everything is of equal importance.

INTERVIEWER: Another example might be in your fiction where an event taking place in your wife's family is as important as any of the world events taking place.

DEMBY: I think that there are some things, though, that are of moral importance. That is, there must be some things which verge on evil. If we can conceive of order in our perceptions, that each of our acts contributes to a kind of beehive type of movement, there must be some acts which break away from our perceiving the whole. They are a real example of disorder. Disorder in the sense that they are actions which are outside some kind of moral order. There is some tremendous evil in the assassination of Kennedy because whoever committed that act of assassination believed that it would cause something to happen. I think that is evil. Not so much the act in itself, but the fact that some people thought that this act . . . they were so presumptuous as to think that this would force something to happen or not happen. I think that type of presumption is evil. If the assassin, or the people who were behind the assassin, . . . if some madman cut down their child or killed their dog, they would probably have a different idea as to the importance of an act like that.

INTERVIEWER: Who does the determining, either in life or literature, as to what is to be designated as evil?

DEMBY: Oh, I believe in a moral universe. That is, a universe in which there is movement, where people are born and they die. These are basic things. The world we must live in has a kind of intrinsic order to it. And occasionally there will be gestures which are presumptuous in that they pretend to make things happen when the truth probably is that they are only acting in accordance with something over which they have no control. People today, for example, talk about revolution. But it always seems to me that the revolution has already happened and we are speeding to try and catch up with it or at least to explain it to ourselves. If this is true, then it means that a lot of the movements, the revolutionary movements, are just expended energy. They are not leading to anything that will be a change. In one period—at least the period I try to demonstrate in *The Catacombs*—there is no change. There is only the illusion of change. It's an idea I will have to think about in the future.

INTERVIEWER: I'm interested in the structure of *The Catacombs*. You said before that you wrote it day by day and that it sort of structured itself.

DEMBY: I came back to this country to go to the March on Washington. I went to that, and before I left, there was the Kennedy assassination. I went back to Italy on a very slow boat. Then I wrote the rest of the novel. What was the question again? I was thinking about something else.

INTERVIEWER: About the structure of the novel . . . whether
the events forced themselves into the novel without your choice.
Had other events taken place, would they have worked themselves into the novel and influenced the outcome?

DEMBY: I think so. It's a weird experience. But, yes, all these
things were included. And it seemed to me that sometimes I
would be sitting down and it seemed to me that events—this is
real paranoia—were being dictated to fit in with the novel, when
of course, it is the other way around. But using this technique
creates paranoia. You begin giving attention to things which
didn't merit all that attention. But it occurred to me that anytime
that anyone gives attention to certain things . . . you get unbalanced by placing too much . . . you know, you really could.

INTERVIEWER: I guess now that you could write a novel
about how that novel was written.

DEMBY: In writing it, I think I said this at one point or another in the novel, I felt as though I were boxed inside the novel
and would never get out. And I remember, I think there is a Zen
story of a painter who painted a picture and couldn't get out of
the painting. I really felt boxed in.

INTERVIEWER: Is that why the real-life characters worked
themselves into the novel and why your fictional characters came
out of the novel and became real?

DEMBY: There's a lot of that. Sometimes people who knew
. . . some nutty girls who knew how I was working on this novel
would try to invent things so that they would get into the novel.
But of course I would put them in, or not put them in. One of
these girls committed suicide, so she was in the novel. There were
a lot of suicides at that period too.

INTERVIEWER: I think that it was Joyce who had a great fear
of the written word: that once it was written it would occur in
real life.

DEMBY: Yes. And I was sensing that too. On the other hand, if you are going to assume that type of magic, you could go to the other extreme and say that just by writing it down, it will not happen. But—there are ideas of magic there.

INTERVIEWER: *The Catacombs* is a very open-ended novel because there are so many possibilities of what could happen, so many things, for example, going on in science, which might change the whole direction of human life. Or even small events which might have as great an effect.

DEMBY: Yes, this is true. And those are the things that should be in history. But probably the things that get into history are reflections of the other things. That is, it is probably not given to us to know which little action or which little gesture, or which movements, are the ones which are going to push things over.

INTERVIEWER: What are you doing in your third novel?

DEMBY: This is another thing which I am doing some heavy thinking on, since I can't write until my apartment is completely moved into and I can get a desk. It's called, *The Journal of a Black Revolutionary in Exile*. And this requires a lot of thinking. It seems that everytime I get an idea it happens in reality.

INTERVIEWER: Is it going to be as different a novel as the second one was from the first?

DEMBY: I guess that it will. I'm going to investigate what is a black revolutionary, what kind of character would he be? And whether he has the real possibility of starting a revolution—revolutionary activity—or whether he is just becoming aware that the breed no longer has any historic function. It will be that kind of story.

INTERVIEWER: Are you experimenting with . . .

DEMBY: So far I haven't. It's narrated in the first person. And it may be that something will develop at the beginning of the next draft. But I don't think so. It's a straightforward story. Everything depends upon what I understand about such a character. He's a young man. The age of Cleaver, or something like that. It seems that all the revolutionary figures are romantic, that is, that they are outside any contemporary context. Their type of revolution doesn't seem possible. Maybe there are any number of people in the world who are "revolutionary," but who are condemned to live out a role for which they are not really prepared, since revolution isn't like that anymore. We are past the point I think where individuals can lead a large group of people into anything important. There can be leaders, for example, who express the longings of a great number of people, but that is not revolutionary.

INTERVIEWER: I wonder whether you are aware of any contemporary writers who are doing similar things to what you did in *The Catacombs?*

DEMBY: No. I've not really read very many novels by contemporary writers.

INTERVIEWER: You mentioned earlier that you are teaching a black literature course. Is it necessary to be black in order to teach such courses?

DEMBY: I've been asked that question in the past, but I don't think it's a cosmetic problem. I think that black teachers should teach the new literature; that is, they should teach about all the young writers working outside the context of the contemporary literary world, which is dominated by certain critics. I know that all the young writers are not paying any attention to those values, the values of the professional critics. And I think rightly so. Their literature should be taught by . . . But it is not necessarily true that a black person will understand black literature just because he's black. I think it's a lot of nonsense that black people have to teach black literature. There's a political factor in black students possibly wanting to have a black person sitting in front of them, but it does not mean that there is any greater insight. I think it all has to do with the politics of teaching and it comes down to campus power in politics. Black Studies programs are funded, and there is money, and I am sure a lot of people want some of the money. But sincerely, as a teacher and a writer myself, I think it's a lot of nonsense to say that only a person with black skin can teach black literature. I don't think so. I don't think it's true that only a black person can or should be the one to teach it. The teacher's function is to illuminate, and even a teacher with an extremely reactionary point of view could give the class some perspective that the class would revolt against. It's not the idea of a black teacher sitting up there, and out of his mouth comes words of gold—No—the whole function of the learning process is a back-and-forth kind of skirmish. That's when good teaching and good learning are taking place. But I am sure that all the hubbub has to do with jockeying for professional . . . I don't think the black people take it very seriously. The only thing it means is that a black teacher is getting a good salary. This is the level that it is all taking place at. In spite of it being said that it is a life-and-death struggle to—no, I don't think so.

INTERVIEWER: Then you wouldn't think that only black critics can write about black literature?

DEMBY: I don't pay attention to that. There might be a problem—not between black and white, but between the middle-aged and the young. Some critics, I am sure, just aren't with it. That's all. And maybe some black critics are like that too, but that wouldn't have anything to do with being a black critic or not being a black critic. Even the idea of a black scholar is a kind of funny idea to me. Certainly, what is going on doesn't need scholars, at least on a certain level. I don't like the idea of dissecting black literature, smelling under the arms, and seeing if they have lost their teeth, seeing if they are clean between their toes.

INTERVIEWER: When was the last time you were back in
America for any period of time?

DEMBY: For the last ten years I have been back and forth
constantly.

INTERVIEWER: Has your traveling given you a certain
perspective that you would not otherwise have had about things
that have been happening in America?

DEMBY: No. I was always back and forth. But I'm more at
ease in America than ever before. I think that anything that's
happening is happening right here. You feel vibrations of something very powerful going on, but you can't pin it down. And
part of the problem there is that the media gobbles up every shift
in taste before any movement has a chance to mature.

INTERVIEWER: Was there any particular time when you came
back to this country and felt that some great change had occurred?

DEMBY: The youth thing, not so much in this country. But in
all the travel I was doing in the late fifties, either in Hong Kong,
or Japan, or Thailand, I would always see the same thing happening among the kids. And of course it was very exciting to be
coming back here in the sixties. But what it is that is happening
is too difficult to say. Not so much that the country has changed.
It is looking at itself with a lot more realism. I don't think the
country has changed very much. It may be becoming more American, more of what it really is.

INTERVIEWER: Will this new "realism" have positive effects
on the racial situation?

DEMBY: I don't think that there is anything that is really American that will get better or worse. That's because of the dynamics

of our society. . . . Will they get better? But what would that mean? We will always have tensions—in this country—between groups. Now it's between young and old, black and white. We might be going through a period in which all of these relationships between the races will become more and more polarized. But I don't see anything wrong with that, if that is what our reality is. We cannot come to grips with it by pretending that it doesn't exist. It will force liberal people—who have always been kind of self-protected from events—to test their attitudes, and this is healthy. We will probably have a resolution of racial conflicts in the South before we do in the North. But even if racial conflicts should be resolved . . . then of what importance is that, if for some reason the country is deteriorating in general? I suppose the total effort now must be to save the country, to get it together somehow, to make it a viable social, historical unit, because there is nothing in the books that says that America has to be eternal.

Owen Dodson

Owen Dodson's poetics come from those of Countee Cullen and Langston Hughes, and his themes come from the tension between what he instinctively wants to believe and the facts of his experience. So while he desires to praise the heroes of black history and the God who has shaped this wondrous universe, he is forced to stare at both the injustice of God and man. In "Rag Doll and Summer Birds," Job-like patience only seems to insure doom: "We sit in our cabin corners waiting for God/And the stove goes out,/The newspapers on the walls, telling of crimes,/Curl away from the walls." The wait for God and the hope of change are illusions because "In the blackness the stars are not enough!" In his verse drama *Divine Comedy*, the search for Christ leads to the discovery that "We need no Prophets," that "we are the earth itself."

Perhaps Dodson's most accomplished work can be seen in his series of poems dedicated to his dead brother, "Poems for My Brother Kenneth." Here, it seems to me, his lyrical inclination is perfectly styled to his elegiac subject. Although "His voice has gone to talk to death," Dodson struggles to envision a new relationship of life to death which will permit his brother's continuance. Like Donne and Dylan Thomas, he attacks death as a weak and illusory master whose domain is conquered by the living: "The resurrection is now,/in Memory/Ringing all her jester bells;/Is now and for the ever of all my days."

The interview was conducted at Dodson's New York apartment in November, 1971. At the time he was convalescing from a recent illness and tired after about the first hour of conversation. A year later he agreed to expand on some of his previous answers, which he did by mail. Dodson has published widely in several different *genres*. Along with his poetry, *Powerful Long Ladder* (1946) and *The Confession Stone: Song Cycles,* he has written one published novel, *Boy at the Window* (1951), as well as one which never found a publisher. He has directed and staged his own plays, and served as the head of Howard University's Drama Department. Like several other black writers of the 1940s, his work has been largely ignored for its lack of narrowly defined racial concerns.

INTERVIEWER: I know that you wrote a sequel to your first novel *Boy at the Window*. Why wasn't it ever published?

DODSON: I had proposed to do a series of novels, the first one of which was *Boy at the Window*. What I wanted to do was to follow the life of a little boy from his birth on. I started with *Boy at the Window*. Then I got a Guggenheim Fellowship and wrote the second novel which I now have in manuscript form. But I was told that the novel was not "black enough." Part of it won a prize in *Paris Review* and was put in *The Best Short Stories of* THE PARIS REVIEW. Of course, writers from all over the world were represented there, not just black writers. In *Soon One Morning* the first chapter of the novel, "Come Home Early Child," was published. So the second novel is here, but it ain't "black." It's about the growing up and fulfillment of a little boy, and that's why it has not been published. The book of poems which I have here and which I will read to you from later is not "black enough" either. They want Nicki Giovanni poems now. You know these poems. You can make them up in a minute. You can say: "Look, man, I am black/Don't you see how black I am?/I'm black as my fingernails/and I'm black to my toes/and if you smell me/I am black/And now I want you to give me a job/because I am black." That's the end of the poem. You can make them up by the minute. I myself have a sense of humor about the whole thing.

INTERVIEWER: Then you have personally felt pressure to write certain kinds of novels and poems?

DODSON: Any writer has got to write about what he sees and what he feels, his total observation. The black writer is no different from any other writer. White writers or Chinese writers walk along the same streets and they observe what they observe. Then they put it down on paper. The black writer has no obligation to "blackness." He's got an obligation to what he sees and what he feels and what he knows. They sent me a letter from Bates College where I had received my undergraduate degree and asked me to join the Black Alumni Association of Bates. I wrote one sentence back: "Did I learn black Latin?" That was the end of that. Yale did the same thing. I didn't answer them at all. I think we have to begin to realize that people are people, they're not black or white or anything. They're themselves. People. And they have their own worth. That's the only thing that we can consider. If we try to do anything else, then we're lost.

INTERVIEWER: Do you have positive feelings about the work being done by young contemporary black writers, writers like LeRoi Jones and Ed Bullins?

DODSON: Well, I think that the strength and power of a work like Jones' *Dutchman* is tremendous. He had a drama there, he knew about conflict, knew about all the things that were important, that make drama work. So I have a great respect for what he has written in drama but not for what he has written in poetry. I had to lecture recently on Mr. Bullins and other black writers, mostly dramatists. I had a whole week at Lincoln University to prepare, so I read all of Bullins' things that I could get ahold of. Two weeks ago I read in the *New York Times* that Ed Bullins is one of the greatest dramatists in the world. And I said, "Bullshit!" That's what I said to myself, and that's what I meant. Here was a man who is presenting or thinks he is presenting a whole race and that race is doing nothing but cursing, fucking, and farting. And that's what he writes about. I don't see any spire of meaning, any richness of hope. I just came across a quotation which says that if you don't see any hope in the theater then flee from it. The people have fled from the New Lafayette Theater where Mr. Bullins is Playwright-in-residence. They have fled from it because there is nothing there. What he is doing is feeding garbage to people when that's what they've been brought up on. Garbage. And I know now that playwrights and writers like Richard Wright know that even in the degradation there is something golden in everybody's mind. There is gold even in those people, as you see them walking along Amsterdam, Broadway, and Lenox Avenue. They want to be something else. Richer in their spirits. But they don't know how to do it. The playwrights must say that it can be done. When people talk about praying at the table and all that, that's not important. God has given everybody an intelligence, a mind. That's what we work from. We don't work from God because God has given us what we need and we must use those gifts. You think of people like Richard Wright and Margaret Walker coming out of the depths of the South. They made themselves do it. I just wrote an article about Richard Wright and I tried to say something about this man. What education did he have? He didn't have any education at all. He educated himself. When he got to Brooklyn he wanted to know how to grow vegetables in his little yard, so he got all the books on it (laughing). I think it's ridiculous, but it's kind of wonderful too. Books about seeds and about growth and about how to make the earth fertile. And then he took up physics. And why would he do that? That man was after something. We can't excuse society but we can't excuse ourselves either. Never. We can't excuse ourselves for our behavior.

INTERVIEWER: In your poetry and plays a recurrent theme is religion and history. You have an apocalyptic sense of both. Do you think this characterizes what your central concern is in your writing?

DODSON: I have written three books of poetry. The first was —I would say—somewhat propaganda, but the third was filled with stories, diaries, and remembrances of Jesus. They are really framed in diaries by Mary, Martha, Joseph, Judas, Jesus, and even God. This, I believe, is my most dedicated work. But I have also been interested in history. A record company asked me to write some kind of history of black people from slavery to their entrance into the United States and now. I did this in *A Dream*

Awake. It is illustrated and spoken by James Earl Jones, Jose-
phine Premice, Josh White, Jr. and others who are dedicated to
the mainstream of making the world a wide world, a blessed
world, a step-in world where all races hold hands and bless God.
I have written and fought somehow in my writing, but I know
now that the courage and forthrightness of writers and poets will
change something a little in our dilapidation.

INTERVIEWER: When did you first start writing?

DODSON: Once, at Bates College, my teacher asked me "What
do you think of this sonnet of Keats?" I said, "I don't think nothing of this sonnet of Keats." He said, "Oh, it is considered one of
the great sonnets of the world." I answered, "I don't think so."
And he said, "All right, Owen, you will write four sonnets a
week." (He didn't even laugh.) He meant what he said. So for
four years I wrote four sonnets a week. Toward graduation he
had a conference with me on all of them and summed up his criticism: "You have written about the rape of Africa, the terror of
the first years in America, and Owen, you have put them in sonnet form. Your form and idea must collide. Your form broke
through your idea. That is the lesson of the day." The experience
of writing those sonnets was an exercise, however. I know now
that form and experience are one. Terror cannot be contained in
a cool form!

INTERVIEWER: And then you went to Yale after Bates?

DODSON: I went to the Yale University Drama Department,
and there I wrote my first play. It was called *Divine Comedy* and
was written about Father Divine who had become a prophet and
an influence in the world of the thirties, a little man with a strong
force of character. He could not be ignored. He had followers,
black and white, who believed that the human spirit would never
die. This play was produced at Yale and was received, I would
say, with raptures of pleasure. The following year I wrote *The
Garden of Time*. It was about Medea and her struggles with
Jason and Creon—a black woman in a white world, bewildered

but with power, shaping her destiny. I had written songs and hoped for dancers in this drama that embraced what I wanted of drama—song, dance, and music.

INTERVIEWER: Have you written other plays since then?

DODSON: Yes, one that I am very proud of: *Bayou Legend*. Its inspiration came from Ibsen's *Peer Gynt*, but now reading it again, I know that it is my own creation, just as Anouilh's *Antigone* is really not attached to Sophocles' *Antigone*. We will be presenting this at the Harlem School of the Arts Community Theater in the early fall of 1973. *Bayou Legend* is filled with fantasy, love songs, and the beauty of a mother's love for her son who is a vagabond, filled with the son's love for his mother who has made his life full of fairies and phantoms and quicksand.

INTERVIEWER: I know that you were acquainted with many of the writers from the Harlem Renaissance. Did any of them have a direct influence upon your work?

DODSON: One writer is Langston Hughes. He presented the whole idea of Negro life. He said, "These are my people and I love them and I will live on 127*th* Street and I will grow flowers there." He wrote poems that had such thrust. Langston had a beautiful perception about people. In his will he wanted two things. He said, "Do nothing until you hear from me." And, of course, I've been writing and hearing from him. Second, he wanted a combo at his funeral. And he had a combo—ain't that nice? A combo. The combo was on a little stage. But when the combo came in, Langston had to get out because his coffin was too large for the combo. So they moved him out. Countee Cullen was another influence. He was black and lost because he made— or rather we did—his dedication to society. He wanted to be a lyric poet; that's what he wanted. He didn't want to write all these things about race, but he did. He was pushed into death. They say he died of some blood disease. No! That man was made to die, by himself and by us, because we did not recognize the universal quality of what he wanted to say. In one of his poems he wrote, "Wake up world, O world awake." That's what he wanted to write. He didn't want to write about rioting in old Baltimore. He wanted to write about the lyrical quality of life.

INTERVIEWER: Did you know Claude McKay and Jean Toomer?

DODSON: I didn't know McKay. However, I know that he came late to his own funeral. In fact, he came late to every appointment. At his funeral he was in Chicago and we were in New York. The train was late, and so he was late. It was really strange because all the pallbearers just left. We were at Dade's funeral parlor and we kept going into Small's Bar right next door. He still didn't come so there were only about four people left. Walter White made the eulogy. I never knew Jean Toomer. I think the only thing to say about Toomer is that he evaporated. I don't know when he died. He just disappeared.

INTERVIEWER: Do you like talking about your novel *Boy at the Window?* It has been about twenty years since it was first published.

DODSON: It's really difficult for me to remember specific things about the novel. Characters take over when you are writing a novel. They tell you what to do. It's very strange. It is no longer your writing. All you have to do is to sit down and begin to put things down on paper. If you want to know something about one of my characters, ask them. Of course, you will never find them. It's like when somebody asks me whether they can use such and such a poem. I say, "What poem?" They tell me the poem and I say, "Well, I didn't even remember it." It is especially difficult to talk about the protagonist, Coin, except to say that he has worked something out for himself when the novel ends. But I can't say where he will go or what he will do. Richard Wright in talking about Bigger Thomas could say a great deal, because Bigger Thomas is such a direct character and he has a direct ending. But Coin is just starting.

Ralph Ellison

Ralph Ellison has acted as a pivotal figure in the development of the concept of black American literature. He was the first black American writer to be taken seriously by critics. His first, and so far only novel, *Invisible Man,* was credited as not only being the most important piece of fiction by a black writer, but also as being one of the great novels of twentieth century literature. As a result, Ellison has been pointed to by critics as a model for other black writers, as an example of what could be done with the "black experience" if it were handled with imagination and control. This role, which Ellison talks about with some degree of amused irony, has caused unfair criticism from more militant black writers.

In addition to a great novel, Ellison has written some of the most stirring and perceptive essays in recent American criticism. Collected with a few interviews and book reviews in *Shadow and Act,* the essays analyze trends in American literature in the light of America's racial conflicts. In one essay Ellison suggests that it was the nineteenth-century novelist, such as Melville and Twain, who attempted to come to terms with what Ellison sees as the central moral dilemma in America—racism. In the figure of Hemingway he saw the refusal of the twentieth-century author to forge a vision that would address itself to the relationships between blacks and whites. Instead, he points out, Hemingway went to foreign and distant forms of rituals of violence rather than choosing those of America. Ellison interprets this as the effort of the American writer to turn from social to personal concerns as the drama of his fiction.

Although Ellison has published parts of his second novel, which has been rumored to be three volumes long, his reputation rests upon *Invisible Man,* despite the fact that it was published almost twenty-five years ago. It has never been out of print and continues to be widely used in American literature classes. The stature that the novel has achieved is well deserved. Breaking loose from the limiting notion that racial themes could be handled only in a naturalistic novel, Ellison molded a style which moves, as he has suggssted elsewhere, from naturalism, to expressionism, to surrealism. And as with other American classics, the novel endures because it locates and brilliantly explores truths of the American experience.

The interview was conducted in December, 1972. We met on a Saturday afternoon in Ellison's New York apartment which looks out onto the Hudson River. We talked steadily for almost three hours. Unlike most of the other interviews, I avoided asking him specific questions about his novel and essays because he has in other places already addressed himself to these matters. Instead I hoped to have him develop some of the informing ideas of his work which might help to illuminate his fictional concerns.

INTERVIEWER: I have been re-reading your essays recently, especially "Twentieth-Century Fiction and the Black Mask of Humanity." In that essay you explain all of American literature in terms of racial attitudes and conflicts in America. It is a very original and very perceptive essay.

ELLISON: That essay was written but wasn't published for a number of years. Then an editor of something called *Confluence* up at Harvard asked me if I had something for them and I sent them that essay. That editor (laughing) turned out to be Henry Kissinger.

INTERVIEWER: Had you tried to get it published before?

ELLISON: I don't recall but I suspect that I did. I suspect that I wrote it for something but that it was turned down. The essay itself is very vague in my mind. I *do* know that I wrote it (laughing).

INTERVIEWER: You interpret American literature by applying your own moral framework.

ELLISON: There is a moral obligation for the critic to recognize what is rich and what is viable in criticism and then apply it and play it back through his own experience, through his sense of what is important not simply about criticism, but about life. I look at criticism as a corrective, as a moral act, as well as an act of appreciation. The critic should try to give as much as he has gained. In doing this, of course, you run the risk of making a fool of yourself. For instance, I was told, "You're out of your mind, Ellison. This had nothing to do with what you're saying." But I always felt that if it didn't have anything to do with what I was saying, then something was wrong either with me or with criticism.

INTERVIEWER: There is a certain amount of daring in your essays. Because you are concerned with large trends you often are forced to speak in sweeping generalities. I don't think that this invalidates what you say but it certainly makes it easy for other critics to attack you.

ELLISON: Well, (laughing) that's the advantage of being outside the academy, at least in my training. Also, it's the advantage of not being primarily a critic and of having written such an essay at a time when I had nothing to lose. I could say any kind of thing that I felt was valid. I had no board of examiners asking me to substantiate it. I did have friends, however, who said I was a damned fool. But there was no problem of advancement. I was just trying to make as much from the insights I had gained from reading good criticism and trying to say what American literature looked like from where I stood. Whatever is valid in it comes from that particular freedom and whatever is invalid comes from the same source.

INTERVIEWER: One of your points was that a writer like Melville was consciously aware of the American democratic ideals and was looking forward to the time when they would be fulfilled. It seems to me that such a writer necessarily feels alienated from the society about him because it has not yet reached that point in the future. You argue that Melville did not feel this tension between himself and his society.

ELLISON: No, he was not writing about a future but about a futuristic society, a society that was always moving toward the materialization of ideals that were stated in an ideal document. That's what I mean by futuristic. Tragedy always involves making the ideal manifest in the real world. The whole drama of man against nature in *Moby Dick* is a tragic story because Ahab is using the resources of technology and his great courage in a misdirected way. His enemy was not nature but his own wild ambition, his own uncontrolled obsession which made him pick a quarrel with a whale. You can call the whale evil, or call it nature, or even call it good. It amounts to the same thing. Americans are called upon to regulate themselves. God is not going to stop us and no foreign enemy is going to stop us. We have to stop ourselves. We have to define what is human and see that we live within it without creating a stultifying atmosphere, and see that within it human ingenuity will not be discouraged.

INTERVIEWER: Then you would read a novel like *Moby Dick* and feel that Ahab acts as an example to us of what must be avoided?

ELLISON: What must be done and what must be avoided. We need an example like Ahab. Ahab was a philosopher, Ahab was a man who was determined to define his humanity against all of the dangers of nature, and he went to his death doing so. But it was the role of the writer within the book to record in a meticulous way all of the nuances of that drama.

INTERVIEWER: You see, I don't think that the heroes of the great American novels act as a warning to us as much as they show us what is inevitable in our American experience. And that experience is almost always one of defeat. You can think of Young Goodman Brown, Ahab, Hemingway's heroes, Jay Gatsby, and—though I am sure he wouldn't agree—Faulkner's heroes. This experience of the hero seems to me to be opposed to that of the hero in many novels by black writers. For instance, the hero at the end of Toomer's *Cane*, although he has not fully realized himself, is about to gain his manhood and enter life. The hero of *Invisible Man* suggests the same thing. Then in a novel like LeRoi Jones' *Tales* you have a character who triumphs over his experience, masters environment, and is ready to begin living. On the other hand, the hero in most American novels, and perhaps even in most Western literature, ends in either alienation or death.

ELLISON: I don't think that I can go along with your analysis. Oedipus is defeated and Christ is defeated; they're both defeated in one sense, and yet they live. Raskolnikov is defeated; he's found out and sent to Siberia. But there's a promise of redemption. So, just take those instances. You've got an ambiguous movement from defeat to transcendence in those works. Ahab is defeated but Ishmael isn't. Ishmael brings back the story and the lesson; he's gone to the underworld and has returned. Gatsby ends up dead but the narrator does not; he gives us the account. So, you don't have absolute defeat or absolute victory. You have these ambiguous defeats and survivals which constitute the pattern of all literature. The reason for that is that literature is an affirmative act, but, being specifically concerned with moral values and reality, it has to deal with the possibility of defeat. Underlying it most profoundly is the sense that man dies but his values continue. The mediating role of literature is to leave the successors with the sense of what is dangerous in the human predicament and what is glorious. That's why we must judge literature, not on the basis of its thematic content or its technical innovations, but on its vision of the human condition.

INTERVIEWER: Then you would say that the heroes of Hemingway's later novels reached such an affirmation?

ELLISON: Well, I would even think that about his earlier novels. Jake Barnes survives, precisely because Jake Barnes is the writer of *The Sun Also Rises*. Ball-less, humiliated, malicious, even masochistic, he still has a steady eye upon it all and has the most eloquent ability to convey the texture of the experience.

INTERVIEWER: It is what they survive with that interests me. I think that our real concern in the novel is with what happens to the protagonist, with whether or not he will be able to handle his experience. I can't understand why the American novelist, with the exception of certain black writers, appears unable at most times to show transcendence or triumph. The narrators who are left behind will not be any better able to tackle the moral problems that faced the protagonists.

ELLISON: I think they will. They shared the experience and their moral sense interprets the story. This is where their moral thrust comes in. You can say that's having it easy, but after all, a novel is only a novel, and the characters in novels have to go by the conventions of novels. At that point we have to leave the characters in the novels and look at the creator of the novel. And there again you have to come back to asking how much reality did he make us feel and what was the breadth of his vision of life. And that's something that changes as we come back to a book as we grow older, and as times change.

INTERVIEWER: Would works like *The Odyssey* and *The Aeneid* represent to you what literature should be?

ELLISON: Yes, yes, yes, indeed.

INTERVIEWER: Do you find that there is a preoccupation with evil in American literature as a whole that is not as pronounced in the works of many black American writers?

ELLISON: I think the difference is how people from these two backgrounds designate evil. One of Faulkner's labors, as was true of some other white Southern writers, was to redefine evil. And when you redefine evil you redefine human quality. That's why Lucas Beauchamp is one of the heroes of Faulkner's work. Faulkner had to see Lucas Beauchamp through the lens of the stereotype. When Lucas first appears in Faulkner he's a lecher. He's always goosing and feeling the maids in the kitchen and he's eating ice cream and collard greens, which is a terrible way of pointing out that this is a negative son of a bitch. But when he ends up Lucas is one of the great examples of humanity. So, how you define evil has been a major preoccupation of American literature because in the larger political context the symbolism of evil has always been racial, and basically the evil within the American body politic has been designated black. That's where the difference comes and that's why there's this conflict between blacks and whites over the nature of reality. I carry on the fight to get us to see reality in a more realistic manner and to designate evil in terms of human unpredictability rather than in terms of racial prejudice.

INTERVIEWER: *Invisible Man* comes down strongly on the side of the ideal of democracy and that in the future the ideal may be fulfilled. But I wonder whether there isn't something in the American experience which necessitates that we have someone as a victim—to designate someone as evil—whether or not he be black. I see no reason to believe that we will ever come any closer to living the ideal than we have in the last few hundred years. We change in superficial ways but remain essentially the same.

ELLISON: I see what you mean. I would suggest that all societies are hierarchal either through the inheritance of wealth and authority or through genetic inheritance of talent or intelligence. By the nature of things you are always going to have those inequities, those ills in society that can be ameliorated but never cured. Some people are going to have less than others whether it's in a democracy, a socialistic society, or a communistic one. Some people are going to have more talent or more ambition than others. This also involves the values of the society. You are going to have people who feel guilty because they have more, and you're going to have people who feel guilty because they have less. In order to have a human society you are going to have to have some form of victimization. Somebody is always going to be designated as the symbol of evil. They may be lynched in a realistic rite of scapegoating, or scapegoated verbally, or scapegoated in terms of where they can live, how high they can rise in the society. This is the human way. I suspect that as this society matures we're going to find ways of designating the scapegoat on a basis other than race. We no longer designate him on the basis of his late entry into the society, as with the Irish migrants in the late nineteenth and early twentieth centuries. Just as the Irish are no longer designated as scapegoats and have even become a cult because of the Kennedys, you are going to have other modifications. And I am hoping as this society matures that whatever the scapegoat is going to be, he's not going to be black and it's not going to be based upon race. And I think that as that happens we are going to come to grips with the fact that we are a class society but that the possession of culture is much more important in the scheme of things than a man's skin or his background.

INTERVIEWER: But rather than this natural kind of hierarchy, we have always had an irrational method for deciding how the system of power should be put together.

ELLISON: What do you mean by natural?

INTERVIEWER: The possibility of ascendancy because of the innate abilities of the individual would seem to me to be a natural hierarchy as opposed to one in which race was used as the criterion for who would get what, and where.

ELLISON: Well, I think human life is a move toward the rational. Whatever man must do in order to bring order to the society is what he considers rational. For a moralist, the problem is to point out that such order is not imposed by nature and it is not imposed by God. It's a human thing. Some of the most moral men supported slavery. They rationalized it and in rationalizing it they accepted the most vicious practices and the most brutal forms of violence in order to keep the structure going. But this happens in France, it happens in England, it happens all over. What is significant in America is that at some point a group of men said that they were going to do something about this, they were going to change it, at least idealistically. So, now we have a Constitution which gives all of us a ground to fight on. And it works, though it doesn't work fast enough.

INTERVIEWER: What I wonder is whether, even if we do manage to stop using blacks as the scapegoat in this country, we will not simply replace them with another. Perhaps our scapegoating will go on internationally. This does not appear to me to be a movement toward the ideal.

ELLISON: Well, that's a whole other thing. I know of no country that has been less involved internationally, and we certainly have been involved. It started with taking over this continent from the Indians.

INTERVIEWER: But we have been less involved?

ELLISON: I think we've been less involved. Certainly less involved than the French and the British. We never colonized Africa. We haven't colonized Southeast Asia. We have had people fight in these places but we were never over there to colonize. We certainly have exploited these countries, but I don't think that these wars come about as a solution or a stopgap measure for our problems here. They come about because we belong to a family of nations and we are a very powerful and influential one. And we will continue to be involved no matter what we decide as a part of national or international policy.

INTERVIEWER: It's that I don't see why—because we live with this myth of democracy—we should assume that we will ever really become a true democracy. We have the myth on the one hand and the reality on the other. They move along side by side, and we don't really seem to care.

ELLISON: But all societies have scapegoats. You're scapegoating right now; I'm scapegoating right now. That's the way language works; it's built in. The moment you begin structuring values, some are going to be ideal and some are going to be less ideal. If you extend it, you are going to end up with God on the one hand and the devil on the other, or a term for God and a term for the devil. And in a political system you are going to end up with some form of inequality. But in just the very nature of things there are going to be some who are more equal than others and some who are less equal. The human challenge is to moderate this and you can only do this by consciously keeping the ideal alive, by not treating it as a folly, but by treating it as Thoreau and Emerson were treating it, as a conscious discipline which imposed upon you a conscientiousness which made you aware, every hour and every day. To impose a human vision upon the world . . . but it's so easy to drift. All right, we don't have the stability of an England, but England isn't as stable as it used to be. In England, the grandeur of language and the grandeur of ceremony, both of the state and the church, have been geared to impose values upon the populace and to make the system work. These are human systems. They work at a cost. America's works at a cost. What standards you view them with determines your judgment. I'm stuck with democracy.

INTERVIEWER: There are a few questions I want to ask you about *Invisible Man.* According to the way you define blues, in your essay on Richard Wright, as "an autobiographical chronicle of personal catastrophe expressed lyrically," would you say that your novel is a blues novel?

ELLISON: I think of blues as a tragi-comic form. Stanley Hyman has said that it's a blues novel. I'm not able to judge. I just wish that it were as resonant and elegant as some of the blues. I tried to use blues elements as well as I could.

INTERVIEWER: Jonathan Baumbach has suggested that the novel is structured according to episodes of death and rebirth. At the end he argues that the invisible man may be metaphorically returning to the womb by his descent into the basement.

ELLISON: I certainly structured it on patterns of rebirth. That is a pattern that is implicit in tragedy, in the blues, and in Christian mythology. But I didn't think of his going underground as returning to the womb. That's imposing (laughing) Freudian symbolism without thinking too much about what a womb is. After all, that novel is a man's memoir. He gets out of there. The fact that you can read the narrator's memoirs means that he has come out of that hole.

INTERVIEWER: I guess that I understood that he was writing it while he was still underground.

ELLISON: The fact that you can read it (laughing) means that he went out to mail it to a publisher. You couldn't read it if he were still in there. But that's a form beyond the form.

INTERVIEWER: The image of history that you use in the novel is that of a boomerang. How does this differ from other geometric figures that are used to explain the shape of history?

ELLISON: Vico, whom Joyce used in his great novels, described history as circling. I described it as a boomerang because a boomerang moves in a parabola. It goes and it comes. It is never the same thing. There is implicit in the image the old idea that those who do not learn from history are doomed to repeat its mistakes. History comes back and hits you. But you really cannot break down a symbol rationally. It allows you to say things that cannot really be said.

INTERVIEWER: When I read Reverend Barbee's speech I was reminded of the sermon that Stephen Daedalus hears when he's on retreat in *A Portrait of the Artist as a Young Man.* Did you perhaps have Joyce's satire in mind when you composed Barbee's speech?

ELLISON: Sure, I had read Joyce. I had read *Portrait* any number of times before I thought that I would write a novel. But I was also concerned with the problem of heroism and with the mythology of the hero. I had read Rank's *The Myth of the Birth of the Hero*. I wasn't using these things consciously, but they are just a part of my sense of how myth structures certain human activities. Barbee's speech had a great deal of irony in it but it was not simply a projection of irony. Barbee believed in certain things and I believed in certain things. Myth has a viable function in human life and I don't think that we can escape it. But what I was trying to show was that this is how Barbee saw the Founder, who was by now idealized and whose influence was shaping the pattern of the narrator's life. And, of course, the hero was not going to deal with the myths; he was going to deal with the realities of growing up. He was not going to deal with abstractions of literature or theology, but with the real obstacles in the real world.

INTERVIEWER: I am interested in the assumption you seem to make in the novel about identity. Unlike what I find in many contemporary novels where characters must invent their identity, you seem to suggest that the invisible man must find the identity that was always there but hidden from him.

ELLISON: I think it has to be created too. However, man does not pick his parents or the place in the world where he begins his journey. His problem is to recognize himself through recognizing where he comes from, recognizing his parents and his inherited values. This is a very active, self-creating process. The way to create a false identity is to think that you can ignore what went before.

INTERVIEWER: I think it's valid to ask why he doesn't settle for an identity that will be less painful.

ELLISON: I suppose he had to go through it because (laughing) I had to write a novel. I feel that a novel should contain joys and sorrows and that an encounter with experience is important for readers, especially those who want to compromise. It's like asking why Oedipus decided to have a fight with that old bastard on the road, why he didn't just move aside and let him go. He might well have done this but then you wouldn't have had this great tragedy.

INTERVIEWER: Maybe that's just my point. Why shouldn't a person avoid those things that seem to cause him pain? Why doesn't the invisible man find a way of life that will not result in alienation from his society?

ELLISON: But what else was there to settle for? Being embittered like Clifton? Consciousness is all! The reason that the hero cannot settle for less is, as he says, that the mind didn't let him. He says that explicitly. The mind kept driving him.

INTERVIEWER: Yet Bledsoe seems to understand all that the invisible man does and he is not driven to do the same things. Is it just that Bledsoe was able to be cynical about all this?

ELLISON: Bledsoe is cynical, but Bledsoe never lied to this guy. And Bledsoe's acceptance was based upon rebellion too. He bawled out the invisible man because he had allowed Norton to get a glimpse of the chaos of reality and the tragic nature of life. Bledsoe expected him to be a man who could equivocate because Bledsoe looked upon equivocation as, what we now call (laughing), the "credibility gap." Bledsoe lived within and manipulated the credibility gap. But this young man is an idealist. He went through the agony of "the battle royal" because he wanted to go on following an ideal, wanted to become a leader; and this experience is an initiation into the difficulties of an heroic role, especially given his background and place in society. Finally, if there's any lesson for him to learn, it's that he has to make sense of the past before he can move toward the future. Now, if people feel that this wasn't worthwhile, I have to accept that. But then I would have to ask whether they found it an interesting book. Did they read it through?

INTERVIEWER: And his sense of himself as an individual is tied to his sense of the past?

ELLISON: His problem is to create an individuality based upon an awareness of how it relates to his past and the values of the past. He's constantly puzzled by his grandfather, puzzled and angered over Bledsoe and his various compromises, bewildered by Trueblood. His experience is a warning against easy abstractions and easy individualism because no one was allowing him to be an individual. Everybody was giving him a name, telling him what to do. He finally exhausted that and got down to the bedrock where he had to come to grips with himself and with his past.

INTERVIEWER: I   also   wanted   to   ask   you   about   the lobotomy . . . . .

ELLISON: It wasn't a lobotomy, but I left that purposely vague. Some people say lobotomy, some people say shock treatment. It's probably closer to shock treatment, but I deliberately did not make it definitely one or the other.

INTERVIEWER: It seems to be the reason for the great change in the invisible man that immediately follows his experience in the hospital.

ELLISON: No. You have to take these things in sequence. It happened after he had gone North, after he had gone through certain experiences there, after he had been introduced to the world of technology and labor unions. It's a metaphor for a new birth, wherein assumptions that he had about the North and assumptions that he had about himself had to be reversed.

INTERVIEWER: What bothers me, though, is the method of the change. Perhaps what I am asking is whether or not the metaphor implies things which you really did not intend. After the hospital he is very much changed and one is forced to wonder whether this operation did not cause it.

ELLISON: Well, he could have accepted the effects of the lobotomy and have become a vegetable; but he didn't. He continued to press on toward his ideal of becoming a leader.

INTERVIEWER: The last question I wanted to ask concerns the novel you are working on. In an interview with James

McPherson that appeared about two years ago, you said that it was nearing completion. Do you want to say anything about it now?

ELLISON: (laughing) The only thing I'll say is that in the next issue of *New American Review* there will be a section of the work-in-progress. I am very pressed now because I will have to start working with my editor on my novel. It's not quite finished, but it's getting there.

INTERVIEWER: You seem to have had the misfortune of having written a classic American novel the first time out.

ELLISON: That's something other people decided; I didn't (laughing). It was just a book I wrote. I didn't have anything to lose. I didn't think that I was writing a classic. I didn't think the book would sell. I hope that this new book will be good. I've published some sections which I like very much, but the problem is to make a total functioning whole. If I make it function, it should be an interesting book.

Ernest J. Gaines

The fiction of Ernest J. Gaines is often compared to that of William Faulkner. The initial similarities are apparent: Gaines' mythical creation of a locale in Louisiana in which all of his stories originate or take place, his oral narrative, his preoccupation with themes of change, stasis, and time. But unlike many other writers who demonstrate the influence of Faulkner, Gaines has taken these Southern literary materials and made them his own. Although Gaines is careful not to dwell too long in conversation on how he relates to other writers or how others have influenced him, and even hesitates to make daring statements about what departures he has made from his predecessors, he has learned from them.

But unlike Faulkner, who was enamored of the past because its strict social order at least offered man stability, Gaines in his fiction labors to escape the immobile past and to view change as necessary in sustaining life. This effort has been long and arduous. Many of his earlier characters broke from the past at the expense of alienation and death. So, although Marcus in *Of Love and Dust* resists the racist and unjust plantation system into which he was born, he also becomes its victim. It was perhaps not until the concluding story in *Bloodline* that Gaines was able to create a character, Aunt Fe, who is in tune with an order of nature which demands a respect for the past as well as a realization of the need for growth. At the same time that she is ready to accept her impending death, she also assents to the social upheavals that are about to occur.

It is in his much praised recent novel, *The Autobiography of Miss Jane Pittman*, that Gaines discovers and convincingly portrays a character who works harmoniously with time. Miss Jane Pittman learns that time itself is change and that it is only by accepting it as such that man can order the present. Otherwise he becomes a slave to history and a stifling social order that blindly repeats the evils of the past. Whereas in Faulkner the characters are usually trying to upset the natural order of things by stopping time or making it move backwards, Gaines, with some remorse about the loveliness of certain qualities of the past, reaches toward a future that can potentially shape the world in a more humane way. Death is not the ultimate enemy that man submits to out of despair and frustration, but is part of a natural process which in itself is good and in which man must take his place.

Gaines' first novel, *Catherine Carmier* (1964), concerns the return home of a young man who has left the South and, by so doing, left behind the cultural values of the plantation life. He is unable to understand and reconcile the old and the new, and fails to persuade Catherine Carmier to leave with him for the North. The second novel, *Of Love and Dust* (1967), continues many of the same themes, as Marcus attempts to usurp the plantation system by revolting against the landowner. Although his attempt assures him of personal honor, he is killed. *Bloodline* (1968) consists of five long stories which are very closely related. The first is about a small boy who experiences his first painful encounter with the real world when his parents separate. He goes to bed that evening, only partially educated by the events of the day. The last story in the book treats a young man who has traveled away from the South and has now returned to change it. Gaines' most recent novel *Miss Jane Pittman*, is narrated by a centenarian who tells her version of "history" to a young naïve history teacher. Because of Miss Jane Pittman's age and vast experience, Gaines is able to portray someone who undergoes and transcends the dilemmas that faced the characters of his earlier stories. Despite the imminent danger involved, she, at the end, is preparing to attend a protest march in the South and thus help initiate the social and political reforms that took place in America in the 1960s.

The interview was conducted in November, 1972. I sent Gaines tapes and a sheet of questions. He continues to live and work in San Francisco where he is now completing his fifth book.

INTERVIEWER: I wonder to what extent you have felt the influence of Hemingway and Faulkner? Jerry H. Bryant in his critical article on your work argues that there are both stylistic and thematic similarities between your work and theirs. For instance, he points to the stoicism of Hemingway's characters, found also in characters like Proctor Lewis in "Three Men" or Marcus in *Of Love and Dust.*

GAINES: Of course I was influenced by both Hemingway and Faulkner. I think all of us who were trying to write during the fifties have been influenced by them. But I was not conscious of Hemingway as I was writing the story "Three Men" or the novel *Of Love and Dust.* I should point out that Proctor Lewis and Marcus Payne are the same character; I wanted to show what would have happened to Proctor Lewis had he gotten out of prison, the chances he would have taken to attain his freedom. The stoicism in these two characters was not because of Hemingway's influence on me. I was writing these stories during the time when young blacks were standing up against the establishment. They were no longer doing what everyone thought they ought to do, whether it was the white man, or the law, or their own black people. So that was an influence. Then I also knew a guy on whom I based Proctor Lewis. This guy had been involved in a killing; three men had jumped him and he had killed one with a knife. He had been working as a mechanic for a white man and when he was thrown into jail his boss came to get him out. But he told him that he would serve his time. So these characters were not necessarily influenced by Hemingway at all.

INTERVIEWER: Bryant goes on to suggest that when your own distinct style emerged in *The Autobiography of Miss Jane Pitt-*

man, so did your own vision, which no longer shared Faulkner's sense of the past or Hemingway's sense of defeat.

GAINES: I don't know whether my characters have ever accepted defeat. Proctor Lewis does not accept defeat; I think he rises above defeatism. When he asks himself where is his own father now that he needs him and the father is not there, he then turns to the boy and he becomes the father of the boy. That to me is not defeatism. As far as sharing Faulkner's sense of the past goes, I don't know whether my sense of the past is exactly that of Faulkner because I don't know how to interpret Faulkner. I don't think that *Miss Jane Pittman* marks a departure from my other work. I just think that I was doing something different from what I had done in other books. I could not have possibly written *Miss Jane Pittman* the way I had written *Of Love and Dust* or the *Bloodline* stories. Miss Jane's interpretation of life is quite different from the way Jim Kelly saw life in *Of Love and Dust* or the way the characters see life in *Bloodline,* especially the characters in "Three Men." I don't know whether I have actually broken away from the Hemingway and Faulkner influence. I don't know whether that's possible to do, just as I don't think it's possible for me to break away from the influences of jazz or blues or Negro spirituals or Greek tragedy or James Joyce or Tolstoy. Perhaps what is happening now is that I've been writing longer and I have developed my own style, whatever in the world that may be. But I don't think that I've broken away from anybody's influence, because I don't think I tried to imitate anybody in the beginning.

INTERVIEWER: In another interview you mentioned that the Russian writers, especially Tolstoy, Chekhov, and Turgenev, as well as Greek tragedy, had strongly influenced you. Could you say what exactly those influences have been, how they appear in your work?

GAINES: Well, when I first started reading I wanted to read about my people in the South, and the white writers whom I had read did not put my people into books the way that I knew them.

When I did not find my people in the Southern writers, I started reading books about the peasantry in other places. I read the John Steinbeck people of the Selinas Valley, the Chicanos as well as the poor whites. This led me to reading the writers of other countries. Then in some way I went into the Russians and I liked what they were doing with their stories on the peasantry; the peasants were real human beings, whereas in the fiction of American writers, especially Southern writers, they were caricatures of human beings, they were clowns. So, initially I read the Russians because of their interest in peasant life. Then I began reading everything that they wrote because of their styles. I read Chekhov's stories, plays, and letters; from there I went to Tolstoy, Pushkin, and Gogol. I think that the Russians are the greatest writers of the nineteenth-century. No other country produced names like Gogol, Tolstoy, Turgenev, Dostoevsky, and Chekhov. And when you think of it, these men were all living at about the same time.

INTERVIEWER: And what about Greek tragedy?

GAINES: The Greek tragedies were always limited in space and time. Most of my work, at least before *Miss Jane Pittman,* if it did not take place within a few hours it took place within a few days. But I must also go back to Hemingway and Joyce to explain this, because I think they were doing the same thing. Their stories did not go over a long period of time, they were usually confined to a few hours. So I was not only influenced directly by the Greeks, but also by the influence they had upon other writers whom I was reading.

INTERVIEWER: One of the recurring themes in your fiction is the conflict between the past and the present, between change and stasis. Many of your characters are victims of the past—Tee Bob in *Miss Jane Pittman,* who, despite his own willingness to change, cannot overcome his racial and cultural past, and Jackson in *Catherine Carmier.* Other characters seem quite content to have the past control them, even though it may be a past which is corrupt. Do you see your work as involving this great struggle to discover how or when man can escape the past which tries to hold him captive?

GAINES: There will always be men struggling to change, and there will always be those who are controlled by the past. In many cases, those who are controlled by the past can be just as human and sometimes more human than those who try to change things. Yet, there must always be those who try to change conditions; there must always be those who try to break out of the trap the world keeps going in. Man must keep moving. In the case of Tee Bob and Jackson, they were victims of the past. They tried their best to escape the influence of the past, and I think their attempt to do this can lead to someone else picking up where they left off. This is the kind of thing I am doing in all of my work. These characters make an attempt toward change, and some other character might continue where they left off. But to break away from the past, from one philosophy to another, is a burden that one person cannot endure alone. Someone else must pick up from there and go on.

INTERVIEWER: Has there been a change in your own views, as they're expressed in your novels, about how this conflict will be resolved?

GAINES: I don't know how this conflict between the past and the present will be resolved. I don't think I am talented enough to explain that kind of thing in my writing, I'm not philosophical enough. There will be someone else, later, who can do this much better than I.

INTERVIEWER: Well, as Bryant's article convincingly argues, I think that your philosophical concerns are more than you may admit. But I wanted to ask you about the concept of manhood in your fiction. All your male heroes are possessed of a need to prove that they are men, and their attempts—which seem to be lifelong ones—always end in death. For Ned and Jimmy Aaron in *Miss Jane Pittman* that testing involves declaring their freedom in the face of those whites who have other plans for them; for Joe Pittman it means trying to break in a horse. Raoul Carmier must prove his manhood by exercising complete control over his land and his daughter. When Miss Jane visits the hoodoo she suggests that men test their manhood in the most "foolish" of ways. I wonder whether you think that Jimmy and Ned have found the proper basis on which to prove themselves?

GAINES: You must understand that in this country the black man has been pushed into the position where he is not supposed to be a man. This is one of the things that the white man has tried to deny the black ever since he brought him here in chains. As Joe Pittman says in *Miss Jane Pittman,* a man must do something, no matter what it is, he must do something and he must do that something well. My heroes just try to be men; but because the white man has tried everything from the time of slavery to deny the black this chance, his attempts to be a man will lead toward danger. The hoodoo lady and Joe Pittman both say that man has come here to die. So whenever my men decide that they will be men regardless of how anyone else feels, they know that they will eventually die. But it's impossible for them to turn around. This is the sense of Greek tragedy that keeps coming back in my writing, that men are destined to do things and they cannot do anything but that one thing. Whatever that one thing is, it is to be done as well as the man can do it.

INTERVIEWER: Jackson in *Catherine Carmier* is one character who is trying to establish his manhood, but the ending is somewhat ambiguous as to whether he has been successful. Do you think that Jackson has been successful in his usurpation of Raoul but that he himself will not reap the benefits of his action? Should this ending be seen more in mythical terms?

GAINES: I think that you have already answered the question. This is what I meant before, when I said that Tee Bob or Jackson might be victims, but that someone else will pick up where they left off and will continue the effort to escape from darkness to light, or from the past to the present. Perhaps, however, some people do not find the present much better than the past, even though they know how bad the past was.

INTERVIEWER: Do you think the ending of that novel suggests that there is no solution for Catherine? She seems unable to separate her love for Jackson from her loyalty to her father. Is she fated to a situation from which there is no escape?

GAINES: People who have truly deep feelings are always tragic. They just cannot change the way that so many of us can. Definitely, she is a tragic figure, and she has no control over her condition. We go right back to Greek tragedy again. People like Catherine Carmier cannot determine their way of living, it is fated that they must live a certain way. But without those kind of people I am sure that this world would be a much more unpleasant place to live in.

INTERVIEWER: Jackson also seems to be trapped. By leaving the plantation when he did, he is not able to adjust now that he has returned. This theme of the black becoming alienated from his own culture is a common theme in many black novels and short stories. Were you aware of DuBois' treatment of this theme in *The Souls of Black Folk* or of Toomer's, in *Cane?*

GAINES: No, I was not aware of this theme running through black literature. I've never really read all of DuBois' *The Souls of Black Folk* and I did not read Toomer's *Cane* until long after I had written *Catherine Carmier*. But just as in any race of people, when a young man leaves an area to go to a more enlightened area it is hard for him to come back to his home. Thomas Wolfe said it, and it's been said since the beginning of time. Once I left the South, which I did when I was fifteen years old, it was hard for me to go back and act the same way with my friends and people. Oh, I could drink and talk with them, but when it came down to accepting certain things as they did, it was just about impossible for me to do.

INTERVIEWER: Is Jackson the last hope that Catherine has of escaping the past?

GAINES: I may hit myself later for saying this and other people may not like it, but I don't think that Catherine could exist outside of the South, I think that she would die like a fish out of water. As long as there is one other person left, she would want to be there. I know many women like Catherine who wanted to leave and did leave, but many of them went back. Many of them have left and stayed away, but I don't think they were happier once they did.

INTERVIEWER: Is there an implicit condemnation of Jackson for lacking compassion toward the old tradition? Should he, like Catherine, be willing to sacrifice his life for this dying culture?

GAINES: Jackson cannot be like Catherine again. Jackson had gone North and had received an education that was quite different from the way he was brought up. It's impossible for him to go back. I've had men in other situations, like Ned in *Miss Jane Pittman,* who did go back, but of course he went back as a grown man. He went back after he had seen the world and felt that he should go back in order to teach others. Jackson does not have that kind of feeling about others at that time in his life. He was still searching for himself. And though he did not find himself in California, he knew that he could not do it back home even with someone as beautiful and who loved him as much as Catherine Carmier.

INTERVIEWER: Why was the book named after Catherine Carmier when Jackson is really the central character?

GAINES: The answer is really almost a joke. I had been writing this book for a very long time and I had no title for it until the day I sent it off to the publishing house. I had called it several things, including some titles I don't think should be put on paper (laughing). I had been trying to write this novel for about five years. I didn't know anything about writing a novel when I first started, so it had given me a lot of trouble. So I simply ended up calling it *Catherine.* When I sent it to my editor, Hiram Haydn, he told me that I should give it a second name; so I simply called it *Catherine Carmier.* The book was much longer in earlier versions and it had much more to do with Catherine and her family than it did with Jackson. Though Jackson was the central character, much more of the action concerned Catherine, her background, and her family.

INTERVIEWER: Do you think that Catherine's decision to stay with her defeated father is noble or cowardly?

GAINES: I don't know whether it's one or the other. It was fated that she stay there; I don't think she could decide her fate. Even if she had gone with Jackson, which she really wanted to do, she probably would have turned around and come back. It's almost impossible for Catherine to have left the South, especially at that time. Perhaps, as Della says, twenty years hence Catherine may have been able to do so, but not that night. I've been back to the South several times and I have seen girls much like Catherine who wanted to leave their family's tradition but who could not. Of course, there are others who could leave, but Catherine had to stay there.

INTERVIEWER: In *Of Love and Dust* Jim Kelley acts as a kind of moral guide to the action, much like Nick in *The Great Gatsby*. But as with Nick, it is suggested that Kelley's worldly wisdom is short-sighted and may actually help in producing evil. Isn't this the realization that Kelley himself comes to at the end, when he decided that he and Aunt Margaret are very much alike? Each helps to sustain an evil social system, though each in his own life tries to avoid doing evil.

GAINES: I don't know whether I agree with you that Jim is helping to sustain an evil system. I don't think that Jim knew he could change anything at that time. What he found out at the end was that there had to be people like Marcus, that people like Marcus existed and that they had as much right to do what Marcus did as did people like himself. But he himself was not in any position to change the system. When he said that he and Aunt Margaret were alike he was just saying that he was not like Marcus. But I don't think that he or Aunt Margaret could have done anything else. After being influenced by Marcus, all Jim could do was what he did in the end—pack up and leave.

INTERVIEWER: Do you think that Marcus's rebellious action produces any real change? He succeeds in displacing Bonbon, but won't Bonbon simply move on to doing something similar somewhere else?

GAINES: If there's any change it is the influence that Marcus has had on Jim. Jim leaves the plantation, and perhaps after thinking about Marcus some more he will be a different person. I really don't know. As far as I am concerned, he is a great person here at the plantation where the action of the novel takes place. As far as Bonbon goes, I don't know. I think I state in the story that Bonbon was determined by society and his environment. I suppose that the idea that man is determined by society runs through most of my work. Whenever my heroes decide to rebel against this condition, physical death usually results. In the case of Marcus, though, something else takes place too. Marcus is very noble at the end when he refuses to run because running would destroy his manhood. Jim's awakening is due as much to Marcus' death as to his life. But all this is after the fact. After I end a novel I am no longer concerned with what my characters do. That's another story.

INTERVIEWER: Especially in this novel you do not seem to share Faulkner's nostalgia for the past. The past in this novel, though ordered, is usually evil and is the single greatest obstacle to change.

GAINES: I don't know that the past is usually evil. There are some very beautiful things in the past. The people are beautiful; Aunt Margaret is as beautiful as anyone in the present. Though I don't long for the past, I don't see the past as basically evil, any more than I see the present or future as necessarily good. What we experience now or in the future can be just as terrible or worse than what we experienced in the past. But I find the differences between the three, dramatic, and something that I like working with. I find good and evil in all of them. The young to me are not necessarily good, any more than the old or the past is necessarily evil.

INTERVIEWER: With the exception of Marcus and Louise, all of the characters in the novel are controlled by their conceptions of the past. In fact, they insure that the past will be repeated because they refuse to recognize the possibility of change.

GAINES: You have got to understand that Marcus and Louise are in love, and with them anything is possible. It's the same story you find in *Romeo and Juliet*. They feel that they can get away with it and that there's nothing to harm them. Whereas the people who have lived longer cannot conceive of any other life than the one they have been living. But after the lovers have died, then—and only then—can the others see a future that permits change. There has to be this kind of tragic action before they can see things differently. This is why all the characters except Marcus and Louise feel that whatever is will continue to be.

INTERVIEWER: Why was Kelley unable to keep his wife? Here is a man who was always so wise and practical, who always knew how to stay out of trouble. Does this suggest a flaw in his "wisdom"?

GAINES: Kelley couldn't keep his wife simply because his wife wanted things that he couldn't afford to give her. She wanted a good time, she wanted—what is it he calls it—"silk drawers." So Kelley just has the problem that any husband might have.

INTERVIEWER: Can you recall how the image of "dust" evolved in *Of Love and Dust*? The image seems to oppose what is suggested by "love."

GAINES: You're absolutely right that dust is the opposite of love. I think that the dust is death. When a man dies he returns to dust. If you lived on a plantation you would find that there's no value to dust at all; it's just there. Dust is the first thing Jim sees when he's sitting out on the porch at the beginning of the novel. When the dust finally settles, Marcus is walking toward the house. So the dust brings Marcus to the plantation. The dust is always there. Whenever Marcus goes by Louise's place the dust rises, or whenever Marshall Hebert moves around in his car, the dust starts flying. Louise realizes at the end that it is the opposite of love. It is a symbol of death.

INTERVIEWER: What went into arranging the five stories in *Bloodline?* I know that they do not appear in the order in which they were written, so I wonder whether you intended a thematic development. Do you think that there is a sense of growth and maturation in the characters of the later stories that is not present in the earlier ones?

GAINES: The first story is told by a six-year-old child. The second story is told by an eight-year-old child. The third story is by a nineteen-year-old. The fourth story is by someone in his earlier twenties. The final story is told by many characters. I definitely arranged these stories in this order because there is growth. In the first story, "A Long Day in November," a six-year-old child can only see a certain amount of things, he can only interpret a certain amount of things. That's why his story is limited physically to the plantation. By the time he's eight years old in "The Sky Is Gray" it's time for him to get out of the quarters. He ends up in a small Southern town where he sees a little bit more. Though he does not understand everything that is going on, he can understand much more than the six-year-old. In "Three Men" the boy is nineteen and has committed murder. Of course, his experiences are much broader than the first two boys'. From there you go to "Bloodline" where Copper Laurent has traveled much more than Proctor Lewis in "Three Men." He has not seen just the brutality that the young black can suffer in the South, but he has seen what the world has done to men everywhere. By the time you come to the last story there is much more experience to interpret. You have both older women and older men. You have the point of view of the white woman. There are many different experiences coming into the story. So there is a constant growth from the first to the last story.

INTERVIEWER: I saw the child's returning to bed at the end of "A Long Day in November" as a refusal to change, an acceptance of defeat.

GAINES: I don't think it is the most significant thing about the story. The most important thing is his waking up in the morning and going outside because, you might recall, he didn't want to get up. He had a hard time getting up. When he finally goes back to bed that night he feels quite good. He feels good being under the covers and he feels good that his mother and father are back together again. And he feels that tomorrow will be a better day for him.

INTERVIEWER: Christianity and "the Christian" are often satirized in your fiction because they are often hypocritical and seem to represent one more institution that does not permit change, especially social change.

GAINES: Yes, I suppose I agree with you that Christianity is an institution that does not want to recognize or permit change. But you must remember that most of my work has been written in the last eight or nine years. Most of the things I write about happened before the Civil Rights demonstrations. At that time the Church was only concerned with sending someone to heaven rather than with creating social changes. It was not until Martin Luther King came along that the Church really became involved in social and civil injustices. The people whom I felt actually lived the Christian life were not necessarily Christians, as is the case in "The Sky Is Gray," where the old couple takes the mother and boy out of the cold. That particular incident was based upon people I actually knew.

INTERVIEWER: Why did you choose to have an "Introduction" to *The Autobiography of Miss Jane Pittman*? Would the novel have been greatly different without this note that the book is the editorialized reminiscences of Miss Jane?

GAINES: I think that the Introduction was very important. It was the first thing I wrote. I couldn't see the novel any other way except with such an Introduction. I put it there because I could not see how a person who is a-hundred-and-ten years old could actually tell the story, and I wanted to use the whole community to help Miss Jane tell her story. When I first started writing the novel it was a short biography of Miss Jane Pittman. Then there were many people after her death who talked about her. After I had gone so far trying to tell it from that point of view, I changed it because I didn't think the other characters could get to those intimate thoughts that I wanted. Once I started to tell it from this personal point of view, I wanted this Introduction to show how these other people helped her tell the story. I've seen this kind of storytelling many times before. One person may be the main narrator but there were these other people around to help her along if she could not remember or if she got tired talking. I also used the Introduction because I wanted to explain some things about my writing. I said that Miss Jane used the simplest terms and that she believed in repetition. These are characteristics of my own writing. Another reason for the Introduction is that the book covers a hundred years and I wanted the reader to know exactly how all this came to pass. I wanted it there as an explanation for when Miss Jane started rambling from one episode to the next. I suppose I also put it there to make the story seem credible. It is hard for people to believe somebody like Miss Jane actually exists.

INTERVIEWER: Do you think that this fictive editor of yours is naive? He says that he teaches history and hopes that Jane's narratives will help him to explain history to his students. Yet there is the suggestion that he may be missing the most important and subtle things about what Miss Jane tells him. For instance, he complains about the episodic form of her stories which appear to him to be going in ridiculous directions. He wants her to tell him about facts and events; she succeeds in explaining "how" history works.

GAINES: Yes, I think he's naive in a way, just as we all are naive about the true history of blacks in this country. We have DuBois, Douglass, and Booker T. Washington, but we don't have the story of the average black who has lived to be that age. After Miss Jane starts to ramble he does see that she is not going in any definite direction. I suppose that until we started editing the tape we would have felt the same way. But Miss Jane has not read all these books on what a narrative should be and she could only narrate history the way she saw it.

Michael Harper

Michael S. Harper is one of the most remarkable poets in America. He possesses complete mastery over the tools of his language and utter joy in the rhythm and sounds of words, as well as a sense of image that reminds one of such poets as William Carlos Williams and Gilbert Sorrentino. Much of his early poetry is an imitation of forms that come out of black American culture—black speech, jazz structures, and the rhythms of black music. In his first two books of poetry, *Dear John, Dear Coltrane* and *History Is Your Own Heartbeat,* he specifically imitates the sounds and vision of black musicians like Coltrane and McCoy Tyner. His success lies in his ability to capture the colors, mood, and physical reality of the past, both personal and racial.

A preoccupation with history and the past mark Harper's themes. He attempts to find a thread that will tie past experience into a meaningful whole. At the same time he seeks release from the controlling influences of the past by inventing new myths that will give the future openness and possibility. The personal and the historical become one as he discovers the patterns of history in the individual life ("history is your own heartbeat"). He roams over the great historical and mythical forms that shape Western conduct and beliefs, in an effort to uncover their basic tyranny and danger. The myths he tries to invent stand in opposition to those which govern the West: myths rooted in a schizophrenic approach to experience. Even in the language he is forced to use, Harper finds this dangerous sense of duality that is present as much in our political and social structures as in our religions, and our psychology. Rejecting this dualism that has been with us since the inception of the Judeo-Christian tradition (God and the devil, good and evil, body and soul, emotive and cerebral), Harper, by reordering the shape of history, works for what he calls a "wholistic" vision.

Harper's unique personal experience has served him well in his training for writing poetry. His formal study of medicine, which he gave up to pursue poetry, has lent him an extraordinary system of metaphors. His wife's mother in "Blue Ruth: America" suddenly becomes a metaphor for America as she lies in her hospital with "the tubes in your nose,/ in the esophagus, in the stomach." A wounded Vietnam soldier is the subject of "Debridement: Operation Harvest Moon: *On Repose*," which details the surgery to remove damaged tissue and suggests Harper's own effort to bring life to the damaged history of black Americans. Similarly, his wide knowledge of jazz and his love of the rural life of Minnesota afford him images and analogies to explore history and myth.

His first book of poetry was issued in 1970. Since then he has published four others. The interview was conducted by mail in February, 1972, and was carefully edited by Harper a few weeks later. He currently teaches at Brown University where he is an Associate Professor of English.

INTERVIEWER: In a review of *Dear John, Dear Coltrane* that appeared in *Saturday Review* you are quoted as having said that the poems are "rhythmic rather than metric, the pulse is jazz, the tradition generally oral." Could you expand on that?

HARPER: That statement came from a comment on the book's jacket. It was taken completely out of context. As I remember, the review thought I was kind of silly and unprofessional. The point I was trying to make is that there is a difference between a metronomic approach to language and a human, intuitive feeling for the language. The best equivalent I could think of was jazz idiom. When I say "oral" I mean that to me poetry is to be spoken or sung. In any event, the comparison between music and poetry is not always one to one, and the reason I was speaking about it in terms of music rather than poetry was because I felt my influences were more musical than poetic. This doesn't mean that I haven't read a great deal of poetry. I have. But I think in terms of music I've been most heavily influenced by Charlie Parker, Miles Davis, Bessie Smith, Billie Holiday, John Coltrane, and Thelonius Monk.

INTERVIEWER: John Coltrane has obviously influenced you in a very special way.

HARPER: I loved John Coltrane and I loved his music. I loved the kind of intensity he brought to his playing and I loved his commitment. There are lots of levels on which one can look at the poem "Dear John, Dear Coltrane." Its aim is redemptive both in terms of black experience and in terms of the painful private life of black musicians. The suffering is both personal and historical and when it's internalized in the music of Coltrane, for example, it becomes a kind of cultural process. The poem begins with a catalogue of sexual trophies for whites, a lesson to blacks not to assert their manhood. Black men are suspect because they are potent, and potency is obviously a great part of Coltrane's playing and of the music of contemporary black musicians.

INTERVIEWER: Is the form of the poem influenced by Coltrane's music?

HARPER: I think the most important thing here to remember is that jazz and blues are open-ended forms, not programmatic and not abstract. They're modal. And by modality I mean some very complicated perceptual and moral things. Modality assumes many things which society really has not fully understood, although there are singular members of the society who do accept them. Number one is that man is basically spiritual. Second is that one has a "wholistic" concept of the universe. This means that the universe is not fragmented, that man has a place in it, that man is a reflection of the environment, and that the environment is a reflection of man. John Coltrane was a modal musician. One of the things that is important about Coltrane's music is the energy and passion with which he approached his instrument and music. Such energy was perhaps akin to the nature of oppression generally and the kind of energy it takes to break oppressive conditions, oppressive musical strictures, and oppressive societal situations.

INTERVIEWER: Does your sense of myth come out of your feelings about modal music?

HARPER: For most people, myth refers to Jung's concept of myth. That's not what I mean by myth. The point about myths is that they are open-ended. They are open-ended *when they are true* in that they suggest new arrangements of human essentials based on contingent human experience, not on historical, systematic experience. Human beings are capable of all kinds of possibility, combination, and diversity. But if one has a vision of history as myth as lie, one has a closed, reductive view of things. Of course the fantasy of white supremist America with its closed myths has always been a fantasy of a white country. Out of that kind of fantasy came genocide, Indian massacres, fugitive slave laws, manifest destiny, open-door policies, Vietnam, Detroit, East Saint Louis, Watts, the Mexican War, Chicago and the Democratic Convention of 1968. So one ought to be careful about myth as lie, when it's stereotyped, when it's reductive, when it freezes experience and denies freedom. Myths are true when they suggest new arrangements of human essentials confirmed by past experience, when they invoke modes of connotation and implication, when they are open-ended.

INTERVIEWER: Have any poets influenced you?

HARPER: I never imitated because I wasn't interested in writing poems which I had seen. I was interested in talking about things which I didn't think were represented in the poetry I had read. Of course, I had read other black poets such as Langston Hughes, Countee Cullen, Sterling Brown, Robert Hayden, Dunbar, and Gwendolyn Brooks. I think my poetry began to be distinctly my own, as I conceive it, when I was teaching and able to look at poetry as something I loved to do and probably could do all my life. But I think the most important thing having to do with thematic influences is the need I have to connect my work with a tradition which I came out of and which I understood. And that tradition was the black musical tradition.

INTERVIEWER: How do you know when a particular poem is finished, when everything is there that should be?

HARPER: I'll give you an example. I wrote a poem called "Deathwatch." When I got to the end of the second stanza I knew that the poem was uncompleted but I didn't know how to finish it, and didn't know what else to add. Then one day I was in the San Francisco YMCA (I used to go to the "Y" so I wouldn't grab people on the street at a certain time in my life). There was a guy there who shined shoes that I used to periodically talk with. He had lots of photographs of athletes, particularly black boxers. He had been quite a well-traveled man and had been in jail. And he had a favorite saying: "America needs a killing." One day he said that to me and it just clicked. I went home and finished writing this poem. "America needs a killing" just clicked in my mind. (The point of the last three lines in that poem has to do with violence and contact as humanizing processes. The poem refers to what has already taken place and is not a prediction. Black suffering isn't considered material for poetry outside of the spiritual.) Most of the time, poems I write are very difficult to finish because I have high standards and there are things I want to do with them. Sometimes poems complete themselves. That's rare but it happens. A poem takes on a life of its own and finally gets to a point where one can't do anything with it to control it.

INTERVIEWER: Could you explain how you start working on a poem?

HARPER: Poems begin with me in many ways. I remember an idea, something I've been thinking about for a long time and something perhaps which I haven't been able to deal with. Then finally I get the right kind of circumstances to begin to write it out. There are poems which I don't seem able to get down on paper but I've ceased to worry about them. If I'm going to write them, they'll get written because they must be important enough in my life for me to handle them. Oftentimes sheer time prevents me from working on a poem but I really don't worry about it. It's a brewing process. I realize that all things can't be done and things which don't get done I have to feel aren't really important to me.

INTERVIEWER: Could you say something about the structure of *Dear John, Dear Coltrane?*

HARPER: This is kind of difficult. First of all *Dear John, Dear Coltrane* is a compilation of ten years' work. The book was originally entitled *Black Spring*, from a poem which is in the first book. I was advised to change it by my publisher because of a conflict with Henry Miller's book. I hesitated about naming the book *Dear John, Dear Coltrane* because the book is not only about John Coltrane or only about music. And I didn't want to take advantage of a man whose playing, whose whole way of looking at the world, influenced me so much.

INTERVIEWER: Structure in your second book, however, is much more important in understanding the book as a whole.

HARPER: *History Is Your Own Heartbeat* is divided into three sections because I wanted to make a kind of testamental statement. It begins with a poem called "Ruth's Blues." This particular poem is in twenty parts. It's historical and mythic. And it's a kind of introduction into the blues using contemporary modes of speech and metaphor. At the same time it's psychic and literal in its anatomy of a midwestern family. It's also about a woman who rises above her condition of personal and cultural anemia to love, connection, and contact. And strangely enough, this happens in America. It's a very complicated poem and one which I still don't fully understand. Of course, the hospital is both literal and a metaphor for America as a way-station of the wounded. And it's about this woman's and all women's unfulfilled nature in this world and in this land. So it's about one's own emotional landscape while it's also historical and mythic. It's about family tradition and about institutions. There's a kind of bridge in the second part of the book, "History as Personality." "Here Where Coltrane Is" is about different kinds of commitments. First of all it states the kind of eternality of music, color, race, and culture. And it's a statement of reconciliation between black tradition in the family and natural history. And finally it's about the necessity of creating a continuum for children, a dynamic, personal, and aesthetic process which presupposes human interaction and contact. And it must be open-ended in order to revivify people. So the poem seeks to reconcile the disease of intolerance with love. It seeks to unify. That's what the poem seeks to do. And it also suggests that Coltrane is ever-present, just as blacks have been in this country since the country's inception. Almost every one of the poems in the second part is dedicated to somebody. They can be seen as kinds of commitments to many people who have been good to me or who have been important to me in terms of making me see things conceptually. Another poem in that section is "Dance of the Elephants," which I wrote after an anecdote told to me by John Callahan's wife, Susan Kirschner Callahan. It comes from a story told to her by her mother who was escaping from the Germans and had to get through the Gestapo who were searching people getting on the trains. Her mother was pregnant and was carrying all she could with her. One of the things she was carrying was this toy elephant which one of the Gestapo grabbed and slammed to the ground. This toy elephant gave this extraordinary human squeal which made the people laugh who were waiting to get on the train. It brought momentary relief. Of course, this woman was then ushered into the train, survived, and came to America. And there's a poem in that section written for Gwendolyn Brooks, "Madimba: Gwendolyn Brooks." This poem was written after a piece of music by McCoy Tyner which he played on an album called *Time for Tyner*. Madimba is an African instrument that has no middle parts. There's a refrain line, "Double-conscious sister in the veil," which recalls DuBois' *The Soul of Black Folk* and his insight into the kind of double consciousness that black people have in dealing with this white supremist culture.

INTERVIEWER: And Part Three?

HARPER: Part Three of *History Is Your Own Heartbeat* is perhaps the most complicated and is one which most people chose not to deal with. I think one of the reasons why it's difficult is that it's a ritual poem in nine parts. It's about a black painter named Oliver Jackson. Jackson and I went to the University of Iowa's Graduate School together. He was a painter and I was in the Writers Workshop. Anyway, the poem expresses a modal myth in language. It attempts to transform classical myth into modal myth. Of course it invokes the titans of black music and its history. It assumes a lot of complicated things. It assumes—number one—that there's an African continuum. That means that there is an unbroken continuity of beliefs and concepts of the black people who have an unbroken African residual in their lives and are essentially connected to Africa. This concept involves a world-view which has always been antithetical to America, with its concepts of manifest destiny, slavery, westward expansion, and so on. And the poem has to do with language and dominion. Articulation is one way of saying what the world is, what its components are, and finally, who is human and who is not. The reason the larger poem is in nine parts is that it's based on a myth about Zeus and how the arts and sciences got into the world. In the Greek mode, cultural fusion is always suggested through an annunciation, the relationship between divinity and morality. In the text I read there was Zeus and the nine maidens. At the same time I am trying to do some things with experience, with morality, and with the testamental process. The larger poem is about Jackson, Jackson in personal terms trying to work out a cosmic problem having to do with race and what the artist must do with the creation of images. He must become his own god through contact with other people and make his own images which reflect his world-view and not his oppressor's.

INTERVIEWER: A number of the poems in *Dear John, Dear Coltrane* concern Mexico. Did you spend much time there? How did it influence you? Did it affect your style?

HARPER: Yes, I've been in Mexico. I spent a summer there. I used to live in Los Angeles and would commute down to Ensenada and places south of there. On this particular occasion I spent a summer there with my wife and oldest son. I'm not sure whether it affected my style or not. What it did do was make me understand how to write about painting. This was something I wanted to do and did do in the "High Modes" poem where I talk about Jackson's painting. Two particular sections are "Apollo Vision" and "Zeus Muse."

INTERVIEWER: In "Three O'Clock Love Song" you make certain observations about the failure of language. In one part of the poem a photograph seems better able to capture what it is you see; later, silence is the best expression or form of love. Why do you work in an art form that is "all" language? Why not photography?

HARPER: "Three O'Clock Love Song" represents a great commitment that I had and still have to my wife. It's a poem about being amazed. It's also about visiting a place, Sutro Park, above the Cliff House in San Francisco where I used to take my wife almost daily before we were married. It's about being inarticulate and having certain things happen to you or certain perceptions about the world which you really can't articulate fully. But you don't worry about them. It's a funny thing about your reference to photography. I just finished a book, which will be a limited edition, called *Photographs, Negatives, History as Apple Tree*. I guess my answer to "why not photography" is . . . I heard a man say recently a very profound thing: "The dream of every poem is to become a myth." And in many ways that is what I think about poetry, language, and articulation. It's my responsibility to articulate. And that's what I do. It's not that other forms aren't equally as important. It's just that this is what I have to do. I think too that articulation is all that we have in certain situations. But a man's deepest feelings are really inarticulate. Feelings don't go unexpressed, it's just that they don't translate very well. They certainly don't translate into a dualistic, schizophrenic language such as English.

INTERVIEWER: When you began the poems that are collected in *History Is Your Own Heartbeat*, did you know that they would have the close thematic relationship they have? In other words, did you have the book as a whole in mind before you started individual poems?

HARPER: I knew that *History Is Your Own Hearbeat* would be the title of the book after I wrote "Ruth's Blues." And that was a very personal thing because I felt that this woman, who happened to be my mother-in-law, was an extraordinary woman. Her story had not been fully told. The goodness, her kind of human power, the will, and the love she represented hadn't been told. She came out of a kind of Gothic world. At the same time she was able to rise above it and was much better than all the things which supposedly explained her. And she had done much of this through tribulation and personal suffering. But she was still able to survive and grow. I watched her beautify other people's lives, oftentimes at the expense of her own, but never with the thought of self-preoccupation. She was extraordinary in terms of her sacrifice, and sacrifice, in my estimation, is akin to love. Anyway, I knew that *History Is Your Own Heartbeat* had to be organized around a particular principle and the last poem in the book is about many of the same things. It's about a man who is a friend of mine and whose wife died by her own hand; she took poison. I could say a lot of things about what the book means in terms of its title. But I would be very suspect about taking me too seriously simply because it came upon me before I ever really thought about it. I knew that it was going to be the title of the book. But I think some of the things I am trying to suggest is that there is a relationship between the single beating heart and all hearts beating. And there's a relationship between a single historical story and all the stories which are modulated on their own heartbeats.

INTERVIEWER: There are a few poems in particular which I would like to ask you about. If you can, I would like you to recall the circumstances in which you began writing them. The first is "We Assume: On The Death of Our Son, Reuben Masai Harper."

HARPER: The poem "We Assume" is strange. Reuben was my second son. We had a great deal of difficulty with my oldest boy, Roland. He had a number of problems and almost died just after his birth. Anyway, I was sitting in the front room of our house in San Francisco; my wife was on the couch having checked out of the hospital earlier that day. And the second boy, Reuben, was still in the hospital in the intensive care unit. We knew that he was going to die. We were watching the fog roll in at three o'clock in the afternoon, and I was waiting for the telephone to ring—that the boy had died. And I began to scribble some notes and discovered these notes sometime afterward, perhaps a month or so afterward. I changed very little of what I had written. And I am sure had I not scribbled down those notes and lines at the time, I never would have written the poem.

INTERVIEWER: What about "Near Colorado"?

HARPER: "Near Colorado" is a poem which isn't very hard to explain. It kind of represents some of my travels. I had taken many trips across the country driving on Highway 40, on Highway 30. I was thinking about a girl I had left on the West Coast. I had been in touch with her, had something in mind of an intense relationship with her, and was thinking of returning to her. At the same time I knew full well that the contingencies might make it very much other than what I thought it was. I knew for instance that she was involved with another man; that kind of clarifies the last line: "human, woman, sometimes mine." It's a long time ago.

INTERVIEWER: And "The Journal"?

HARPER: "The Journal" is a poem that I wrote for and about my wife and her relations with her family. It's about a young girl who keeps a journal I was reading and the details in that poem are details from that journal. My wife's from Minnesota. The poem's kind of my introduction into her family, into her life, into her problems, into the complexities of her background, into all the kind of pain and beauty which I was obviously attached to, that had become my own.

INTERVIEWER: What about "Zeus Muse: History as Culture"?

HARPER: "Zeus Muse" is based on a legend about Zeus and the nine maidens. "History for us begins/with murder and enslavement/not with discovery" comes from William Carlos Williams' *In the American Grain*. But essentially this poem is about the making of grids, the relationship between horizontal and vertical axes, and dominion. Essentially it's about imperialism. And, of course, Apollo is mythic in origin also. He supposedly brought up the sun in his chariot. But there is also a statue of Apollo staring out into space with no pupils in his eyes. I suppose I meant to suggest a kind of eternity or spacelessness. And to me it represents a gaze over all things, dominion over all things. But black people can't function in that particular vision of the grid. They're expendable, they've been annihilated; and not only black people but nonwhites or pagans or Indians or anyone or thing in the way of this particular vision, with its armies, navies, and its technological system. And I'm also trying to integrate this with Oliver Jackson's own vision in his painting, with his creation of his own metaphors which come out of an African residual. Jackson's vision is opposed to Renaissance humanism and a Greek-oriented, finally schizophrenic vision of the rationalist mode.

INTERVIEWER: Has the fact that you are black influenced your poetry? Is it perhaps that critics and publishers will not permit black writers just to function as writers?

HARPER: America—I mean the people who are in influential positions and who know something about literature and letters— always ask silly, redundant questions. They're always running around asking people who've been kicked in the teeth how it feels. And this country has a way of asking people who've been oppressed how it feels to be oppressed. They have a way of asking backward, asinine questions. What we've got to do as poets and artists is to ask the correct ones, ask them uncompromisingly, and not be worried about the ramifications. Art is always the product of artistic *vision,* and that demands cosmology or worldview, or its lack—some totality larger than man, in which he can focus his being in conjunction with an environment he is but a part of. My recent books of poems, *Song: I Want A Witness* and *Debridement* direct themselves to the concept of fragmentation resultant from a reductive vision of complexity in a historical context. Dominion has functioned as aesthetics through the modicum of a specialized, reductive language without the reactive imagery connected to a true picture of history, national and personal. The first act of liberation is always to destroy one's own cage.

Robert Hayden

Robert Hayden best describes himself when he says that he is a romantic who has been forced to be realistic. The subjects of his poetry—religion, the past, nature—lend themselves to treatment by the romantic. But Hayden's importance as a poet lies in his ability to explore the tension between the ideal and the actual. In a poem like "October" he glories in autumn's beauty, celebrates it as the time of his daughter's birth, and is reminded by it of "God in/the saint's mind." Yet in "Electrical Storm" he knows that it is the same nature and God that unsuccessfully conspire to kill him and his wife; only chance intervenes (Arna Bontemps calling to him from across the street to warn him that the electrical wires are down) to save their lives: "Who knows if it was heavenly design/or chance/(or knows if there's a difference, at all)." God is holy, one, and all loving; but he is also capricious, obscured in the world's madness, and oftentimes silent.

Hayden's religious commitment does not free him from the frightening realities of the contemporary world. In fact, it throws him into the center of them because he must try to see them as part of a divine plan, one which very often seems to have lost its direction. His faith is tested and purged in the fires of his doubt, made clean in the struggle that arises between belief and the condition of the modern world. Even the past does not afford the solace that he longs for in it. His brilliant memories, which capture the sounds and colors of his childhood, are filled with bitterness and self-reproach. In "Those Winter Sundays" he is reminded not only of his father's love for him but also of his own ignorance and indifference: "Speaking indifferently to him,/who had driven out the cold/and polished my good shoes as well. /What did I know/of love's austere and lonely offices?"

To cite his themes, however, is to point to only a part of Hayden's triumph as a poet. His chiseled language, his precision, and economy control his themes and give them their enduring quality. At the same time, his symbolism, allusions to classical and religious literature, and his delight in using the obscure word or phrase sometimes make his poems difficult. Some of them are highly personal and reveal their meaning gradually as one becomes familiar with the rest of Hayden's work. Hayden uses language to establish a distance between experience and art. Unlike the "confessional" poets, he purposely maintains and works for a detachment from his materials. Even in his most personal poems he remains hidden behind carefully sculptured form and language that do not allow him to bare his soul. He creates a poem that works as a whole, rather than trying to effect a single memorable line or image for which the rest of the poem is sacrificed.

The interview was originally conducted in December, 1971. We lunched in a downtown Ann Arbor restaurant whose walls were covered with memorabilia of Michigan's football heroics. One proud forty-five-year-old man with his wife stood over us for ten minutes recounting his and his father's football days. We went to Hayden's home for the interview itself, which lasted for about three hours. The next day I discovered that the recorder had malfunctioned and that I had several cassettes of blank tape. Hayden kindly agreed to go through the ordeal again the following month in Chicago. There we talked for another three hours in his hotel room. His contagious energy seems to mark everything that he does, though he admits that he is forever behind in his work. He is warm, comic, and very articulate despite his frequent fears that he is making little sense. He presently teaches at the University of Michigan and has mentioned that he is planning a biography.

INTERVIEWER: We've been talking about the recent death of John Berryman and then more generally about the relationship between neurosis and art. Do you believe that there is a connection between the two?

HAYDEN: No, I really don't. I don't think art grows out of neurosis. One doesn't have to be neurotic in order to be creative. When artists are neurotic I believe the reason is that the very thing that makes them creatively aware, that makes them respond to life in the particular ways they do, is also the very thing that makes them vulnerable. They're unable to throw off what I call the "burden of consciousness." And they have to make use of what hurts them. Art is not escape, but a way of finding order in chaos, a way of confronting life. I think the artist, in having to cope with the demands of life, of society (whatever *that* is), as well as with the unsparing demands of art, is often involved in ways that other people are not. An occupational hazard, one might say. A matter, also, of a certain kind of sensitivity. Or, perhaps, sensibility. One is reluctant to use the word "sensitivity," because if often connotes a sort of delicate and finespun temperament that just can't bear the realities everyone has to face. And this is not true. Most artists are tough, and if they weren't they'd never accomplish anything. Neurosis can thwart creativity. If you become too involved with the self, the ego, if you're too unhappy, you're liable to be so blocked you can't work. Hart Crane killed himself because he just couldn't cope with his problems. So did John Berryman. I suppose there's no denying, however, that sometimes art does originate in neurosis. Emily Dickinson's poems, for instance, and Sylvia Plath's. But weren't they poets *first?* Isn't such poetry an attempt to transcend neurosis—to find liberation from it through the creative act?

INTERVIEWER: Are you sometimes struck by the mystery of your art?

HAYDEN: I've always felt that poetry and the poetic process are pretty mysterious. What is it that makes one a poet? What are you doing when you write a poem? What is poetry? The feeling of mystery is no doubt intensified because you can't deliberately set out to be a poet. You can't become one by taking courses in creative writing. You are born with the gift, with a feeling for language and a certain manner of responding to life. You respond in a particular way to yourself, to the basic questions that concern all human beings—the nature of the universe, love, death, God, and so forth. And that way of responding, of coming to grips with life, determines the kind of poetry you write. Once you discover you're a poet—and you have to find out for yourself—you can study the art, learn the craft, and try to become a worthy servitor. But you can't *will* to be a poet. This is an age of overanalysis as well as overkill, and we've analyzed poetry and the poetic process to a point where analysis has become tiresome, not to say dangerous for the poet. And for all our investigations, mysteries remain. And I hope they always will.

INTERVIEWER: Do you see a progression in your work? Do you realize that you are writing poetry today that you could never have succeeded with ten years ago?

HAYDEN: I've been very much aware of that. Yes. I think I'm now writing poems I couldn't have written ten or fifteen years ago. But I should add that some of my best-known poems were written back then. But there've been changes in outlook and technique since, and so I'm able to accomplish, when I'm lucky, what I once found too difficult to bring off successfully. I didn't know enough. Still, there are elements, characteristics in my work now, that seem always to have been present. Certain subjects, themes, persist, and—perhaps—will continue to give my work direction. My interest in history, especially Afro-American history, has been a major influence on my poetry. And I have a strong sense of the past in general, that recurs in much of my work. I don't have any nostalgia for the past, but a feeling for its relationship to the present as well as to the future. And I like to write about people. I'm more interested in people than in things or in abstractions, philosophical (so-called) ideas. In heroic and "baroque" people especially; in outsiders, pariahs, losers. And places, localities, landscapes have always been a favorite source for me. I once thought of using *People and Places* as the title for one of my books. Despite changes in outlook and technique over the years, the qualities I was striving for as a younger poet are the same ones I'm striving for today, basically. I've always wanted my poems to have something of a dramatic quality. I've always thought that a poem should have tension—dramatic and structural. And I've always been concerned with tone, with sound in relation to sense or meaning. I sometimes feel that I write by the word, not by the line. I'm perhaps oversensitive to the weight and color of words. I hear my words and lines as I write them, and if they don't sound right to me, then I know I'll have to go on revising until they do. I revise endlessly, I might add.

INTERVIEWER: Did you ever fear that you might stop developing as a poet, that perhaps in another year or two years you would have exhausted yourself?

HAYDEN: Oh, yes. A year or so ago—before I'd completed *The Night-blooming Cereus*—I was afraid I'd never be able to write a new poem again. In the back of my mind, I suppose, I knew I would. But I didn't see how, what with all the demands on my time and energy—teaching, poetry readings, all sorts of responsibilities. I went stale, felt I was repeating myself, had nothing more to say. I've been through all this before, many times in fact. *Cereus,* which Paul Breman published, was a breakthrough for me, and no doubt that's why it's my favorite book up to now. Writing it released me, also confirmed ideas and feelings I'd had before, but distrusted. I began to move in a new direction and to consolidate my gains, such as they were.

INTERVIEWER: When you first started writing, were there poets that you tried to imitate and hoped you would be as good as, some day?

HAYDEN: When I was in college I loved Countee Cullen, Jean Toomer, Elinor Wylie, Edna St. Vincent Millay, Sara Teasdale, Langston Hughes, Carl Sandburg, Hart Crane. I read all the poetry I could get hold of, and I read without discrimination. Cullen became a favorite. I felt an affinity and wanted to write in his style. I remember that I wrote a longish poem about Africa, imitating his "Heritage." All through my undergraduate years I was pretty imitative. As I discovered poets new to me, I studied their work and tried to write as they did. I suppose all young poets do this. It's certainly one method of learning something about poetry. I reached the point, inevitably, where I didn't want to be influenced by anyone else. I tried to find my own voice, my own way of seeing. I studied with W. H. Auden in graduate school, a strategic experience in my life. I think he showed me my strengths and weaknesses as a poet in ways no one else before had done.

INTERVIEWER: How do you know when a poem is completed? What tells you that it doesn't require another stanza or another image?

HAYDEN: That's a hard question to answer. Sometimes I'm not sure, and I lay the poem aside, hoping I'll be able to come back to it with a fresher eye and ear. The time always comes, after I've written many drafts, when I know I've met the requirements, solved the problems. I feel I've realized the design. But this sense of having fulfilled my contract, so to speak, only comes after much rewriting, many, many revisions. And I must say that I rather incline to the belief that, as another poet once said, no poem is ever finished, only abandoned. There are poems, though, that I can't do anything further with. I can't get back into the mood, the frame of mind that produced them originally.

INTERVIEWER: I know that your religion has greatly affected your poetry. Have your religious views changed since writing "Electrical Storm," where you recorded a near encounter with death? There seems to be a skepticism in that poem, absent in your most recent volume of poetry, Words in the Mourning Time.

HAYDEN: No, not actually. I'm only suggesting the skepticism I might have felt earlier in my life. This wasn't a factor at the time I wrote the poem. I've always been a believer of sorts, despite periods of doubt and questioning. I've always had God-consciousness, as I call it, if not religion.

INTERVIEWER: Do you think that there is a religious dimension to the work of the poet? Is there a special role that he must play in a century like ours?

HAYDEN: Being a poet is role enough, and special enough. What else can I say? I object to strict definitions of what a poet is or should be, because they usually are thought up by people with an axe to grind—by those who care less about poetry than they do about some cause. We're living in a time when individuality is threatened by a kind of mechanizing anonymity. And by regimentation. In order to be free, you must submit to tyranny, to ideological slavery, in the name of freedom. And, obviously, this is the enemy of the artist; it stultifies anything creative. Which brings me to my own view of the role of the poet, the artist. I am convinced that if poets have any calling, function, *raison d'être* beyond the attempt to produce viable poems—and that in itself is more than enough—it is to affirm the humane, the universal, the potentially divine in the human creature. And I'm sure the artist does this best by being true to his or her own vision and to the demands of the art. This is my view; it's the conviction out of which I write. I do not set it up as an imperative for others. Poetry, all art, it seems to me is ultimately religious in the broadest sense of the term. It grows out of, reflects, illuminates our inmost selves, and so on. It doesn't have to be sectarian or denominational. There's a tendency today—more than a tendency, it's almost a conspiracy—to delimit poets, to restrict them to the political and the socially or racially conscious. To me, this indicates gross ignorance of the poet's true function as well as of the function and value of poetry as an art. With a few notable exceptions, poets have generally been on the side of justice and humanity. I can't imagine any poet worth his salt today not being aware of social evils, human needs. But I feel I have the right to deal with these matters in my own way, in terms of my own understanding of what a poet is. I resist whatever would force me into a role as politician, sociologist, or yea-sayer to current ideologies. I know who I am, and pretty much what I want to say.

INTERVIEWER: There's an impersonal tone in almost all of your poetry. You're removed from what you write about, even when a poem is obviously about something that has happened to you.

HAYDEN: Yes, I suppose it's true I have a certain detachment. I'm unwilling, even unable, to reveal myself as directly in my poems as some other poets do. Frequently, I'm writing about myself but speaking through a mask, a *persona*. There are troublesome things I would like to exteriorize by writing about them directly. One method for getting rid of your inner demons sometimes is to be able to call their names. I've managed to do so occasionally, but not very often. I could never write the confessional poems that Anne Sexton, Robert Lowell, John Berryman have become identified with. And perhaps I don't honestly wish to. Reticence has its aesthetic values too, you know. Still, I greatly admire the way Michael S. Harper, for example, makes poems out of personal experiences that must have been devastating for him. He's a marvelously gifted poet. I agree that poets like Harper and Lowell do us a service. They reveal aspects of their lives that tell us something about our own. One of the functions of poetry anyway. I think I tend to enter so completely into my own experiences most of the time that I have no creative energy left afterward. I'm thinking now of distressing or unpleasant experiences, obviously. And of course, everything is an experience and has meaning for me. But this is a tangential observation. To get back to the original idea, let me say that perhaps the detachment you mention is a matter of aesthetic or psychic distance. By standing back a little from the experience, by objectifying to a degree, I'm able to gain a perspective not otherwise possible. Maybe. How do I really know? Whatever I say about my poems is tentative, and certainly after the fact.

INTERVIEWER: Do you think of yourself as belonging to any school of poetry? Do you place yourself in a romantic tradition as well as a symbolist?

HAYDEN: I don't know what to say to that. I suppose I think of myself as a symbolist of a kind, and symbolism is a form of romanticism by definition. I've often considered myself a realist who distrusts so-called reality. Perhaps it all comes down to my being a "romantic realist." How would I know? Leave classification to the academicians. I do know that I'm always trying in my fumbling way to get at the truth, the reality, behind appearances, and from this has come one of my favorite themes. I want to know what things are, how they work, what a given process is, and so on. When I was writing "Zeus over Redeye," for instance, I studied the booklets I picked up at the Redstone Arsenal so I'd learn the correct terminology, get the facts about rocket missiles. I scarcely used any of this information, but it gave me a background against which my poem could move. But to return to your question: let me answer it finally by saying I hope that however I'm eventually classified, I'll still be considered a poet.

INTERVIEWER: There are a few poems for which, if you recall, I would like you to describe the circumstances in which they came into being. I have tried to choose poems which might have had quite different beginnings. The first is "October."

HAYDEN: Well, what started the poem was a long walk Erma my wife and I took through the woods one day in October. When we returned home, I jotted down a few impressions, maybe an image or two, and then several weeks later began working on the poem in earnest. October has a special meaning for me, because my daughter Maia was born on a beautiful October day. I wrote the poem as a birthday present for her, although in the early versions I didn't refer to her by name. I worked on the poem for several years, off and on. I thought it was going to be much longer than it is, but now it's more concentrated, possibly more suggestive.

INTERVIEWER: And "Lear is Gay"?

HAYDEN: The title is from Yeats. When I was writing this, I had in mind my wonderful old friend Betsy Graves Reyneau, who is dead now. It's dedicated to her. Betsy was an artist and a gallant human being, in many ways years and years ahead of her time. Nothing human was alien to her. She'd endured much physical suffering but had had a rich and exciting life nonetheless. She had a delightful sense of humor and could laugh at herself as well as at the world—at pretentiousness and old-fogeyism dressed up to look new. Although I was thinking mostly of Betsy, I was writing for other people too, who were old but not defeated, who weren't going to give up and retire from life, no matter how rough it became for them. And ultimately this poem is for myself. I've reached old age, and these days I hope the poem will be a sort of talisman for me.

INTERVIEWER: What about "Middle Passage"?

HAYDEN: That grew out of my interest in Afro-American history during the forties. It was to be part of a long work—a series of poems—dealing with slavery and the Civil War. I'd read Stephen Vincent Benet's poem, *John Brown's Body,* and was struck by the passage in which he says he cannot sing of the "black spear" and that a poet will appear some day who will do so. I hoped to be that poet, and I also hoped to correct the false impressions of our past, to reveal something of its heroic and human aspects. I was fascinated then, as I still am, by Civil War history, the African background, the history of slavery. I spent several years reading, in desultory research. I wrote "Middle Passage" and several other sections during the forties. But, I'm sorry to say, I never achieved my total design, owing to the fact that it was next to impossible for me to find enough time for sustained work on the book. I've discussed the composition of "Middle Passage" and other poems in the series at some length, in a book published last year, *How I Write.* Suffice it to say that "Middle Passage" was to be the opening poem in my book, which I, at first, entitled *The Black Spear,* after Benet, later, *Fire Image.* It rather amazes me to realize I wrote it nearly thirty years ago. Not much happened after it was first published, but today it's become almost a standard anthology piece.

INTERVIEWER: And the poem "Those Winter Sundays"?

HAYDEN: An intensely personal poem, one that I still react to emotionally. Written in memory of my foster father. I realized late in life, years after his death, how much he'd done for me. The poem was written during the fifties, but I can't remember how I got started on it. All I can say is that during that period I seemed to be looking back at my past, assessing my life.

INTERVIEWER: Except when you are dealing with an obvious historical situation, you depend upon the present tense in your poems.

HAYDEN: I've made a superficial—very superficial—analysis of the recurrence of the present tense in my poems, and I think I may be using it to achieve dramatic immediacy and because in a sense there is no past, only the present. The past is also the present. The experiences I've had in the past are now a part of my mind, my subconscious, and they are there forever. They have determined the present for me; they exist in it.

INTERVIEWER: There appears to be a progression in your long poem "Word in the Mourning Time." The first few sections catalogue the madness of our age, particularly that of the 1960s. Yet love enters in the last section and restores what appeared to be a hopeless condition. I'm not sure how you move from the vision of the evils to one of love. Were you suggesting that love comes after the violence and killing, or perhaps because of them?

HAYDEN: The final poem is the culmination, the climax of the sequence. For me, it contains the answers to the questions the preceding poems have stated or implied. If I seem to come to any conclusion about injustice, suffering, violence at all, it's in the lines about man being "permitted to be man." And it's in the last poem, written originally for a Baha'i occasion. Bahá'u'lláh urged the absolute, inescapable necessity for human unity, the recognition of the fundamental oneness of mankind. He also prophesied that we'd go through sheer hell before we achieved anything like world unity—partly owing to our inability to love. And speaking of love, I try to make the point, in the elegy for Martin Luther King in the section we're discussing, that love is not easy. It's not a matter of sloppy sentimentality. It demands everything of you. I think it's much, much easier to hate than to love.

INTERVIEWER: I wonder about the poem "Sphinx," which begins *Words in the Mourning Time.* You refer to the riddle that man must answer as a "psychic joke." Could you say something about that?

HAYDEN: Not man, but an individual. I'm unwilling to explain the poem or the joke. Various people have come up with interesting ideas of what it is. I'll tell you this much, however: the poem revolves around the psychological, deals with some tic or block, some inner conflict you may have which gives you your particular inscape, makes you what you are. You may come, in time, to accept your condition as the definition of yourself. And the poem implies that something fundamentally negative, or apparently so, may be used in a positive, a creative way. I think that's all I need to say.

INTERVIEWER: Are there poems of yours which you like very much but which have not gained attention, have not been frequently anthologized?

HAYDEN: Oh, there are several of which that is true. The poem we've just been discussing for one. And "Mystery Boy Looks for Kin in Nashville" has never received the attention I feel it deserves, and there are several others I could mention. I can't complain, though. I consider most of the poems to be close to my ideal of what a good poem is, most of these have become fairly well-known and been anthologized.

INTERVIEWER: Could you answer a few questions about "The Peacock Room"? What is the Peacock Room? How is the question you raise (Which is crueller?) resolved?

HAYDEN: I find it extremely difficult to come up with coherent answers to these questions. I have complex feelings about the poem. I wanted very much to write it, felt, indeed, impelled to do so. I don't know how, quite, to put into prose statements what I struggled so hard to make the poem say. I consider it one of my most important poems; important to me, if to no one else, and to my development. And the fact that it was written in memory of Betsy Reyneau, whom I've already talked about, makes it very special to me. But let's begin with something about the Peacock Room itself. It's in the Freer Gallery at the Smithsonian, where Betsy's paintings are now exhibited. It was originally in the home of a rich English connoisseur who commissioned Whistler, the American artist, to decorate it. This was during the late nine-teenth-century. Whistler painted golden peacocks on the walls and doors of the room, and it therefore came to be known as the Peacock Room. It was the cause of much bitterness, even of trag-edy. A younger artist had first designed the room, but the results had not satisfied the owner. Whistler undid all the work of his predecessor, and the younger artist was so appalled that he went insane. My poem, you may recall, refers to this. Whistler subse-quently quarreled with his patron over his fee. There's a beautiful portrait of a young woman in the room today that Whistler painted for a Greek ship-owner. It's rather exotic, Japanese. Well, that picture led to still other quarrels, because the ship-owner re-jected it, and when Whistler insisted that it be hung in the Pea-cock Room, his patron objected. The room was dismantled after the owner's death and sold by an art dealer to Freer, a rich De-troiter and friend of Betsy's family. He had it installed in his mansion, and Betsy told me that on her twelfth birthday Mr. Freer gave a party for her in the Peacock Room. I think I'd read something about the Peacock Room but hadn't the vaguest notion of what it was like until Betsy told me about it a few years before she died. I came upon it quite by accident one day when I wan-dered into the Freer Gallery. Seeing it for the first time was a tre-mendous experience for me. I stayed there as long as I could that day, observing its details closely, my mind full of Betsy. I bought a booklet giving its history, and I got the armature of my poem partly from that account. I knew it was going to take a long time for me to write anything that even approximated the feelings I had—the sensuous enjoyment, the sadness. Perhaps the biggest difficulty—and here I'm theorizing, speaking after the fact again —perhaps the biggest problem was that I knew what I felt and I had all the background material I needed, but I didn't know how to organize, how to make a coherent whole. I learned how as I wrote. I began to see relationships. As regards the questions about art and life, let me say here that I'm aware that they are clichés, but they're still fundamental. They're archetypal. And, at my age, they're no doubt inevitable. I hope the context, the setting I've given them, redeems them, and I'm inclined to think it does. I suppose the "cruelty" of art is that it outlasts those who make it. That's simplistic, though, and doesn't begin to suggest what I mean in the poem. When I visited the Peacock Room after Betsy's death, my second and last visit, I couldn't help thinking, "Well, here are these peacocks, just as they were before, here is this room, and Betsy's dead. Whistler's dead. A whole generation's gone, but these artifacts remain." And I found myself also thinking: "What is art anyway? Why does it mean so much that it can determine one's whole life, make a person sacrifice everything for it, even drive one mad? What is it?"

INTERVIEWER: How do the peacocks function in the poem?

HAYDEN: On second and third thoughts I'd say they're necessary to convey some impression of the room, and they help to unify the poem. And, yes, they're a dramatic device, and they help to make a transition that's both emotional and thematic. They enable me to modulate from the past to the present, and from horror to serenity. The lines describing their descent "with shadow cries" and so on is rather surreal. This part of the poem cost me an agony, as Frost used to say of his poems, because what is presented there is painful to me. The peacocks lead me into this pain, and they also help me get away from it.

INTERVIEWER: In "Monet's Waterlilies" you refer to "the world each of us has lost." Is it a world of innocence, of childhood?

HAYDEN: I'm absolutely cold to the voguish and over-used theme of "lost innocence." Maybe I'm just too pseudo-Freudian. I might have been thinking about childhood, though surely not about innocence. But no, I can't honestly say I was even thinking about childhood. I grant you the poem could be so interpreted without doing too much violence to its meaning. Certainly, children, as we all know, live in a fantasy world, in a realm of the imagination that's forever lost to them when they grow up. But each of us has known a happier time, whether as children or as adults. Each of us has lost something that once gave the world a dimension it will never have again for us, except in memory. A botched answer, to be sure, but the best I can offer at the moment.

INTERVIEWER: Is it through art that one is able to recapture it or at least become highly conscious of it?

HAYDEN: Sometimes. That particular Monet helps me to recapture something—to remember something. I would say that one of the valuable functions of all the arts is to make us aware, to illuminate human experience, to make us more conscious, more alive. That's why they give us pleasure, even when their subjects or themes are "unpleasant."

Clarence Major

Clarence Major is the author of two novels, *All-Night Visitors* and *NO*, several books of poetry, and a soon-to-be-published collection of short stories and essays. His most remarkable accomplishments have been in fiction where he demonstrates a preoccupation with experimenting with the form of the novel. *All-Night Visitors* is both a daring innovation in form ("the universe is not *ordered*, therefore I am simply pricking the shape of a particular construct, a form, in it") and an experimental perspective on self-identity. Fragmented, disengaged, and terrified, Eli Bolton tries to reshape the chaos of his experience by affirming his body ("This thing that I am—it is me. *I* am it. I am not a concept in your mind, whoever you are!"). His immersion into sex, however, can lead him in two directions: it can bring him back into the "ancient depths of myself, back down to some lost meaning of the male," or it can lead to more depersonalization and separation. The novel, loose and episodic, catalogues the gestures of violence that occur without warning and threaten even the rudimentary pockets of meaning that Eli Bolton can discover. The novel ends uncertainly, as he makes his first real contact with people by inviting a mother and her dispossessed family into his apartment ("*Her* dispossession was my responsibility.").

Major's second novel *NO*, is even more radical in its experimentation than was the first. Whereas the first novel adhered to a chronology of events and rather well-defined characters, *NO* tries to destroy and at the same time gain a new perspective on language, time, and personality. As Major points out in the interview, he purposely mingled and confused the slang from various decades of the twentieth century in order to break down the limits imposed by realistic fiction. He also merged characters so that it is sometimes impossible to recognize whether it is the hero or his father. The purpose of all this is to help him in tracing an awakening mind as it moves through its earliest sensual awareness in childhood and finally blossoms into full consciousness at a bullfight, where the hero faces mutilation and death. And in following this mind, Major is not concerned with whether or not the "action" of the novel takes place in the imagination or in the real life of the character because, for Major, the two are inseparable.

Imaginative experiences have as much and perhaps more influence upon personality than do things in "actual" experience. It is of little importance whether the character at the end of the novel is confronting a charging bull, or whether he is sitting in a New York apartment imagining such an experience. The point is that the imagination can make it real.

Both novels are linked in their essential preoccupation with defining the "I," its elusiveness, its fragility, how it is threatened, how it comes to be. *NO* moves beyond the first novel in insisting that the self is a phenomenon of language and the imagination rather than of actual experience, time, and place. The self is created by and emerges as the product of an imagination that can give it meaning and direction through language. As with Stephen Dedalus, the first problem is being able to give names to things, which is the first step in gaining control over them and oneself. By placing his fear of death in a ritualistic story about a bullfight, the character transcends that fear. At this point art and life make contact; art becomes a vehicle through which life can be ordered and given significance. The artist does not reflect life but rather gives it meaning as he fictionalizes it. The "self" then becomes the artifact of whatever the imagination has been able to create and is limited only insofar as the imagination itself is limited.

At the time of the interview Major was living and teaching in New York. He has completed two other novels and is at work on more. In the interview Major was careful to note that his ideas about his work and the writing of fiction are tenuous and temporary; his ideas change as he writes more. He re-reads his own work very critically and is anxious to point out what he thinks are its weaknesses. The interview represents about four hours of telephone conversation that took place in early winter, 1973.

INTERVIEWER: In your essay, "A Black Criterion," you call for black writers to break away from Westernized literary strictures. Do you think of *All-Night Visitors* as being an example of a "non-Western" novel?

MAJOR: I've changed since writing that essay in 1967. I now find repulsive the idea of calling for black writers to do anything other than what they each choose to do. A lot of blacks grew up in the United States and became writers. They are different because of the racial climate and because of this country's history, but they still are part of this common American experience. They may speak black English and use Afro-American slang, and eat black-eyed peas and corn bread, yet they are not African. And certainly they are not Chinese. So what do we have? We are Americans. We work in English; it may be black English, but at its roots, it's English. This does not mean that there are not several very unique black writers. If you look at Cecil Brown, Al Young, William Demby, Ron Fair, and Charles Wright, you'll see how original the contemporary black fictionist really is. But as far as some kind of all-encompassing black aesthetic is concerned, I don't think black writers can be thrown together like that into some kind of formula. Black writers today should write whatever they want to write and in any way they choose to write it. No style or subject should be alien to them. We have to get away from this rigid notion that there are certain topics and methods reserved for black writers. I'm against all that. I'm against coercion from blacks and from whites.

INTERVIEWER: Then you did not intend that your first novel be seen as working against a Western idea of what the novel should be?

MAJOR: No. *All-Night Visitors* was not a non-Western novel. I was struggling against a lot of Western concepts when I wrote it, but it is still an *American* novel. I once said that it was not a Christian novel. Christianity is something with which I have been at war almost all my life. When I was a kid I believed the things I was told about God and the Devil. I think that in the West, Christianity's great attraction is that it offers life after death. It's something that people can lose themselves in because they can say that everything is going to be all right. Eastern religions don't have that built-in escape, nor do they have the tremendous self-hatred that's at the center of Christianity. These feelings about Christianity are in my work because I agonized with these things in my own experience of growing up, these problems of good and evil and sex. I think that's why there's so much sex in *All-Night Visitors*. Here was a man who could express himself only in this one natural way because he had absolutely nothing else. Christianity's view toward sex exists because of the great self-hatred that's so embedded in Christian teaching. Look at Saint Paul's doctrine of Original Sin. I can see it in everything around us: sex is something that's nasty and something to hide. *All-Night Visitors* was a novel I had to write in order to come to terms with my own body. I also wanted to deal with the other body functions. In *NO* I was trying to exploit all the most sacred taboos in this culture, not just sexual taboos, but those related to the private functions of the body, and that's where they all seem to center.

INTERVIEWER: Sex in *All-Night Visitors* is used in many ways. As you say, it is the only means that Eli Bolton has of expressing himself, but it also reminds Eli of death and is sometimes quite violent and brutal. At the same time I don't think that sex is used in a metaphorical way to imply the changes Eli undergoes.

MAJOR: Eli's attitudes about sex reflect the crisis of the 1960s. In speaking of the novel, John A. Williams said it is a sad book that gives off a kind of gentle helplessness and anger with no place to go and that it shows the discontent of the "death-wait" in our society. Now sex features very large in *All-Night Visitors*, and so does violence. I wanted it that way because this society is preoccupied with both. All kinds of negative stigmas concerning sex have been imposed on black men by both black and white people, and Eli doesn't escape this kind of psychological warfare. Some people feel that by showing Eli's sex life I'm playing right into the hands of white myths about black people. And white liberals have expressed pretty much the same sort of reaction to the novel. All I can say is that certain people have no interest in the human body and even hate it. These people seem to have no sex life.

INTERVIEWER: Why does Eli see the relationship between sex and death?

MAJOR: When you ask about sex and death in the same breath you really hit on something in the book, something most people concerned with the sexual aspect of the book never get to. And fiction that tries to deal with sex in an open and honest way and attempts to get beneath the purely physical is bound to come to terms with the link between sex and death. I don't mean that sex is here at the beginning and death there at the end. They are interchangeable. The expression of one can be found in the act of the other. I think that the French word for orgasm can be translated "little death." And I think that you are right when you observe that sex isn't meant to correspond with anything that Eli's going through. It is, rather, a kind of alternative to the brutality around him. That's one of the last natural things he has in a world where he cannot assert himself. It is a means of expression and, at times, a weapon.

INTERVIEWER: Eli keeps complaining about how "unreal" the world about him has become. I wonder whether his search for some new reality, a search which begins with discarding old sexual myths, requires that he question all the "realities" that his culture lives by? Perhaps it also calls into question what the author's relationship with reality is. Does he reflect it, as the traditional realist supposedly does, or does he invent it, as the fantasy novel, begun by Sterne, does?

MAJOR: I really don't like either idea. The novel is an invention in itself, which exists on its own terms. It has its own reality
and I don't think it's designed to relfect reality in any kind of logical sense. It's not a way of showing reality and it's not really a
fantasy. But then I'm simply talking about what the novel means
to *me*. The kind of novel that I'm concerned with writing is one
that takes on its own reality and is really independent of anything outside itself.

INTERVIEWER: In some very real and practical sense, though,
a writer is forced into relating himself to the outside world. He
may choose to ignore it or try to see it in a new way in his fiction, but he must always be reacting to it in some way.

MAJOR: But in a novel, the only thing you really have is
words. You begin with words and you end with words. The content exists in our minds. I don't think that it has to be a reflection
of anything. It is a reality that has been created inside of a book.
It's put together and exists finally in your mind. I don't want to
say that a novel is *totally* independent of the reality of things in
everyday life, but it's not the same thing. It's certainly not the
kind of reflection that's suggested by the metaphor of the mirror.

INTERVIEWER: Well, I think then that you are ascribing to
the tradition of the fantasy novel. Rather than life, it uses the
imagination and the novel itself as its primary subject.

MAJOR: Its subject-matter is the novel itself? Yes. I think
that's closer to the truth. At the same time I know that my fiction
has been directly influenced by other things. I regret, for instance, in my haphazard education my exposure to Freudian psychology because it has left its effect on my thinking. Since I finished *NO*, I found myself weeding out so much of it. I can't reject
it all, because we live in a technological world where we have
certain ways of dealing with reality. But that's one thing I regret
about *NO*. I noticed the Freudian influence there and it's very
disturbing. That whole sensibility is probably present in my earlier work too, and it's a sensibility that I want to forget. I don't

want to get trapped in terminology. I worry that, despite the fact that *NO* came from the gut level, a large part of it seems to be caught in the sensibility of Freudian psychology.

INTERVIEWER: One might also question what psychology's relation to reality is.

MAJOR: I think that you should stop when you use the word "reality" because reality itself is very flexible and really has nothing to do with anything. I don't think reality is a fixed point around which theories adjust. Reality is anything *but* a fixed point. So it seems strange to me that a work of art could be an interpretation of *the* reality.

INTERVIEWER: I agree with that, but we usually do not take that approach to a system like psychology which is really just as fictional as literature. Psychology is only an attempt to impose an artificial order on the chaos, but the chaos remains. In literature, we most often make a distinction between literature as an imaginative act and as a truthful picture of the way things are; but we don't make that distinction with philosophy, or with psychology, which really has no relation to anything except itself. I agree with you that reality is no fixed point, yet someone like Freud imposes his pattern and says, "Here it is. Here is the truth." Perhaps we should look at psychology as essentially an imaginative act.

MAJOR: Yes, right. You're absolutely right. Freud was inventing. He was doing the same thing a novelist would do. He was creating his own reality. It was an invention just like Darwin's, despite the correspondences to what we call "facts." They are still inventions. That may have something to do with the nature of writing and thinking, thoughts relating to words.

INTERVIEWER: I see so much of your fiction as an attempt to break away from the myths men have invented, which now tyrannize them. Sometimes those myths are Christian ones, sometimes psychological, and sometimes racial. I see very much the same thing going on in Ishmael Reed's fiction and Michael Harper's poetry.

MAJOR: I see them in Ishmael's work. He was exposed to pretty much the same kind of background as I was. He handles this in a different way; we all do. And it isn't just Christianity in my work. There's the whole racial thing which I try to handle not as a psychologist or a sociologist, but as a writer who tries to integrate these things into a novel. This, by the way, is what I have against a lot of black fiction. So much seems designed to preach racial, or political, or sociological sermons.

INTERVIEWER: At one point in *All-Night Visitors* Eli reflects that "I suppose we have all gotten used to it. Our dislocation is so complete." Do you think that the unifying theme of the novel is the various forms of dislocation Eli experiences?

MAJOR: Yes, I'd agree with you that the dislocation can serve as a kind of unifying theme. I like the sense that you get from the novel. Not many people came away from it with the feeling that the story—if I can say story—is a nightmare in which a whole series of strange things happen. But that was the impression I wanted to create.

INTERVIEWER: In the "Basement Rite" chapter you slip into a surrealistic style. It's interesting because the story up to this point has been very bizarre, but it isn't until this chapter that you break away from a naturalistic treatment of your materials. When it occurs, one hardly notices the shift in style because it seems like such a logical extension of what's been going on.

MAJOR: Real and surreal are two tricky words, but I know what you mean. I can't think of a term at the moment that would be better. The entire novel is meant to have that surreal quality. Many people, unfortunately, missed this in the book because, I suppose, they were too concerned with the surface reality.

INTERVIEWER: Why was the novel written in rather short episodic chapters? There's really little or no plot. Were you purposely breaking away from the traditional realistic narrative?

MAJOR: I discovered early that what I was trying to do in *All-Night Visitors* could not be done in a smooth symphonic fashion. I needed short broken chapters, little twisted episodes. Omitting traditional plot and other kinds of traditional devices was dictated by the same need to capture all the elements of this "unreal world" into a form specifically designed for it.

INTERVIEWER: What went into structuring these episodes?

MAJOR: The arrangement of the chapters changed quite a bit in the several drafts preceding the final one. I followed my feelings with very little conscious planning. In other words, the writing itself was the discovery of what the novel was.

INTERVIEWER: Unlike the rest of the novel, there's a lyrical spirit in the chapter "Week-End Away." It seems to clash with the tone of the novel and to suggest certain qualities about the character of Eli that are not present in the other chapters.

MAJOR: What Eli feels and expresses in that chapter is very real. He would be a quiet peaceful person if his world permitted him to be. That chapter is one of my favorites in the book. I think it shows a side to Eli that one has to see in order to understand the other sides.

INTERVIEWER: The novel ends with Eli helping a destitute Spanish family, and he feels that "I had become firmly a man." I am not sure how seriously to take all this, whether or not to believe that a change has taken place. All the evil that he has seen and felt does not seem to be balanced by this one moment of light.

MAJOR: No one ever says, "Now I have become a man." That moment is never so clear. It happens slowly and in so many unseen ways that there isn't likely to be a moment as dramatic as the one Eli experiences. I had him stand in a doorway with rain falling, thinking this. It works all right in a novel, but I am not so sure that it works as well in what we call "reality." One person told me that she did not believe the ending. It was not credible that he could have given his apartment to a helpless woman and her children. Others have felt that the ending explained everything and gave the novel its point, if it has a point. Yet I wasn't trying to make any point when I wrote the novel. I was simply trying to describe Eli's life and what it was like for a black man in the 1960s. Ron Welburn in *The Nickle Review* said that the book had no overt message. That was the way I wanted it, because Eli's life really had no point.

INTERVIEWER: One recurring concern in both novels is that of the "self." One way of looking at your characters is that they lack a sense of who they are and they must discover that. But seen in the way I think you intend it to be, the self is really a nonexistent thing, or something that is in a constant state of becoming. Moses in *NO,* for instance, *is* all the things that happen to him and all the ways that people look at him. In this sense, one cannot say that his problem is that he doesn't know who he is. The point is that he isn't one thing, but many. Is the self something that is created, rather than found, or uncovered?

MAJOR: The notion of self in *NO* is dealt with in a superficial way. The narrator says at various times that he thinks the idea of a self is ridiculous. He's called by many names. This might be a clue to just how artificial or shifting this whole business of self becomes. (The search for freedom is another artificial thing in the novel. That's deliberately artificial. There's no such thing as freedom, in the sense in which it's used in that novel.) At one point he's called Nicodemus, which is something out of Negro folklore. And he's called C. C. Rider.

INTERVIEWER: And at times "the Boy."

MAJOR: Right. And Ladykiller, the Inspector, and June Bug. And there's a play on Nat Turner; the narrator is called Nat Turnips. And, of course, the name he usually goes by is Moses. Did you get the sense that there were two Moses?

INTERVIEWER: Yes. One is the narrator and the other is the father figure.

MAJOR: One is definitely the father image. And although it wouldn't be the wisest thing to do, you could substitute "God" for "father." It wouldn't be too far off either. . . . But to get back to your question about the notion of self. I was trying to show all the shifting elements of the so-called self. One way I did it was by giving the narrator all these names. The other Moses, of course, is not concerned with problems of who he is. He's a doer, he's a hard-hitting, physical type; the narrator is more reflective and spiritual. The father is really the "ladykiller."

INTERVIEWER: Yes, literally.

MAJOR: He's a sort of pimp, and he's a hustler. He's deadly and yet he's gentle. I tried to make his character difficult to penetrate.

INTERVIEWER: I wanted to ask you about the bullfight scene at the end of the novel in relation to this question of the self. Does it suggest something along the lines of the Hemingway idea of the moment of truth?

MAJOR: I hope that it's not that corny, but it may be.

INTERVIEWER: What is it that happens there? Must he have this encounter with death before he can be free of these terrible things in his past?

MAJOR: He must come to terms with an ultimate act. He has to have that look into the endless horror of things in order to get beyond the whole petty business of worrying about it.

INTERVIEWER: I wonder why you did not write *NO* as a naturalistic novel. In some ways it is merely a story of a boy growing up.

MAJOR: Why do you think that he is young?

INTERVIEWER: I assumed that he was now looking back on the things that happened to him as a boy.

MAJOR: Right. That's what I was trying to do. I was trying not only to construct a chronological story but one that was psychologically unrestricted by time. You notice that there are elements from the 1920s, the 1930s, and the 1940s. And there are qualities out of the 1970s and the space age. I was trying to bring all of this together and blend it into a kind of consciousness that was not restricted. I wanted a landscape in language that would give me the freedom to do this. I felt that this freedom could not be achieved in a naturalistic novel.

INTERVIEWER: Yes. You would not have had the range you needed. You move through all different states of mind and ages. The narrator not only sees the action and events of the story the way a child would, but also as a grown man reflecting on and shaping those experiences.

MAJOR: You also probably noticed that I was grabbing at every useful reference that I could get my hands on: magic, mysticism, Judeo-Christian religion, philosophy, witchcraft, American superstition and folklore, black terminology, and black slang. But I didn't start out with any conscious notion of doing that; it just developed in a very organic way. It was only after I finished the first draft that I saw what I wanted to do. When I got that finished I started making out elaborate charts with the names of the characters, personality sketches, and their possible ages. I worked hard at inventing names that would really work with the characters, names like Grady Flower, Lucy Nasteylip, Grew . . . and B.B.—a name little black boys in the South are often given.

INTERVIEWER: There are many Southern elements in the novel. At times I was reminded of Faulkner.

MAJOR: It's very definitely a Southern novel. I tried to capture the flavor of the South as I remember it. There was also a sub-

dued treatment of the relationship between the country and the
city, but it wasn't fully developed in the novel. The paradox of
the country and the city is very deep in me because I know both.
I was born in the city, but shortly after that I lived in the country. It's been that way on and off ever since.

INTERVIEWER: Was it difficult getting through the first draft
of *NO*?

MAJOR: What I am doing right now, very consciously, is to
outline a novel and it's very difficult because I am watching what
I am doing too closely. I didn't have that problem with *NO*. With
NO I got teletype paper, put it on a spool, made a little platform
with a stick, adjusted the typewriter, set the paper into the typewriter, and wrote it on this endless sheet of paper. It was a very
spontaneous thing. I would write until I ran out of steam. It was
very easy to do, because it was a story that I had been trying to
write since I was twelve. It was the story I needed to write most.
I wrote it in 1969, when my personal life was really tossed around
in many ways. But I had finally reached the point where I felt
that I could finally do it. Although it's not an autobiographical
novel, its roots are very deep in my emotional life. So, though it's
fictional in its design, the energy that holds it together is very
real. This is true of any fiction.

INTERVIEWER: You and I have talked before about the relationship between your poetry and fiction. What do you see as the
relationship between the two?

MAJOR: Much of my poetry is purely fictional. I sincerely believe good poetry should be fictional. I work hard to make all my
poems work as fiction. My newest book of poems which hasn't
been published yet, *The Syncopated Cakewalk*, is pure fiction. I
think that it was Carson McCullers who said that poetry should
be more like fiction and that fiction should be more like poetry. I
am working very deliberately to break down what I think are the
false distinctions between poetry and fiction.

INTERVIEWER: Is there an essential difference, though, that still exists? Does it have to do with the use of language or with the fact that fiction is still narrative in nature?

MAJOR: No, I don't see the difference. But I am really in a state of transition with all of this. It is rather difficult for me to abstract theories about what this means and where I'm going with it.

INTERVIEWER: I know that you attended the Art Institute in Chicago for a while. Has painting affected your writing in any way?

MAJOR: The Art Institute experience has often been misunderstood. It didn't involve any academic classes. I was there on a fellowship to sketch and paint. I learned a lot in those days, but mainly on my own, upstairs in the gallery and in the library. I was very serious about painting. I almost painted my mother out of house and home actually. We nearly ran out of space, but my mother always encouraged me to paint. She wanted me to become a painter. I think my experience with painting, the way that I learned to see the physical world of lines, color, and composition, definitely influenced my writing.

INTERVIEWER: Can you describe your work habits?

MAJOR: They change all the time because they depend on the thing I'm doing. If I'm writing a group of short stories, I might work exclusively on one each day. If I'm writing a series of poems I might do one or two a day.

INTERVIEWER: How much revision do you do?

MAJOR: I revise endlessly. Even after publication. I am not one of those writers who sees publication as a cut-off point.

INTERVIEWER: Eli in *All-Night Visitors* says something very interesting and I wonder whether or not it describes your reasons for writing: "the universe is not *ordered*, therefore I am simply pricking the shape of a particular construct, a form, in it."

MAJOR: I don't know. I suppose writing comes from the need to shape one's experience and ideas. Maybe it assures us a future and a past. We try to drive away our fears and uncertainties and explain the mystery of life and the world.

Julian Mayfield

Julian Mayfield was born in Greer, South Carolina, in 1928 and was raised in Washington, D.C. He has written and directed plays, published three novels, several literary and political essays in such magazines as *The New Republic, Commentary,* and *Nation,* and had a truncated acting career as a co-author and co-star with Ruby Dee in the movie *Up Tight.* In addition he edited *THE WORLD WITHOUT THE BOMB: The Papers of the Accra Assembly,* and founded *The African Review,* a political monthly begun in Ghana where Mayfield worked in the office of the President from 1962 to 1966. In our correspondence before the interview he indicated that he was "more interested in responding to questions which have to do with politics and power than with literature and aesthetics." He considers all art political, though it was not until his third novel that he became overtly concerned with exploring political activity in the bounds of his own fiction.

His first novel, *The Hit* (1957), depicts the efforts of a black building-superintendant to secure his version of the American dream by winning big at the number's game. He has an indomitable belief that equality has arrived for blacks and he criticizes other blacks for abusing their freedom. Although he is moved when he hears a street corner orator advocating black nationalism, if he "had been blessed with fairer skin he would have crossed the color line and never returned." He plans to escape Harlem and his stifling family life by betting the month's electric and gas money on the numbers. The "dream" is all but fulfilled when his number wins but the number's man skips town with his money. Although he ends defeated and disillusioned, his son is forced to realize that the dream, symbolized in the person of the number's man, " 'never really comes.' "

The Long Night (1958) is an initiation story of a "very black boy" into manhood. The novel echoes old myths, though Mayfield disparaged the notion that he was aware of any of them. On the night in which the story takes place, the boy is in search of both his real father, who has left home, and a spiritual father who will engender in him a sense of his racial and cultural past. His father realizes that unless a black boy has such a cultural and historical image, he cannot "see himself in the future." By the time he finds his father that night, he has passed from the ignorance and inexperience of childhood into the knowledge of the world with its contradictions and evils.

The apparent optimism of the first two novels, which both suggest that the generation coming into being will be better able to discard the illusions of the past, turns to pessimism in Mayfield's political novel, *The Grand Parade* (1961). The book deals with the attempts of a young, ambitious reform mayor in a Southern town to bring racial harmony to his city while still fostering his political future, and ends with his assassination and a racial riot. The novel's success is perhaps limited to affording insights into the complex forces at work in the racial and political issues of the 1960s. Mayfield's critics complained that the novel lacked a focus, that parts seemed to lapse into reportage rather than fiction, that it was mechanical in its effort to represent every element of the social and political spectrum, and that the author employed melodrama at the end. Most of the criticism may be quite accurate and suggests the dangers of the political novel when it is conceived and written from too narrow a perspective.

The interview was done in the Fall of 1971. Mayfield was planning to move to Guyana and we decided it best to conduct the interview by letters. Our correspondence was completed just as he was finishing teaching a two week seminar course in Black

Techniques of Survival at Cortland College in Upper New York State. He typed his responses and carefully edited in pen what he had said, avoiding questions which he felt required more time and thought than he could give them. A few days later he was scheduled to leave the country. At present Mr. Mayfield continues to write fiction and is at work on his autobiography, *Which Way Does the Blood Red River Run.*

INTERVIEWER: Were there writers who impressed you when you were younger and perhaps ones whom you wanted to emulate?

MAYFIELD: At school the writers I admired most were the obvious ones: Hemingway, Dreiser, and Steinbeck. The one I wanted to write most like was Thomas Wolfe, because of his lyrical gifts. I suspect all writers are failed composers—at least in their own minds—and they want their prose to come as close as possible to achieving a spiritual whole, in the way that the greatest of symphonies satisfies. Wolfe never brought it off, but he wasn't quite forty when he died. On the evidence of his major works, I think he might have managed it if he had lived a few more years, and had achieved the serenity to discipline his tempestuous nature.

INTERVIEWER: What about black writers?

MAYFIELD: In the early years there were no black writers who influenced me because I don't recall that I knew of any (other than the poet Paul Lawrence Dunbar). I don't believe a single black writer was ever mentioned in any of my classes. I discovered Richard Wright by accident, and read everything of his I could find. But I was already nearly eighteen, and I don't think now that the influence could have been very great. If the United States can be said to have a group of literary giants, Wright has to be among them. Speaking of later influences, certainly the work of W.E.B. DuBois has been the most important

influence on me. It is, I hope, spiritual as well as literary and political.

INTERVIEWER: Your novels are preoccupied with social and
political themes. In fact, your most recent novel, *The Grand Parade,* is overtly concerned with politicians and the dynamics of
political life in a society like ours. Do you see any possible conflicts for a writer who is concerned with such themes and who, at
the same time, must fulfill the demands of his art?

MAYFIELD: I have never seen a conflict, and have no use for
writing which is deliberately an exercise in the use of
language. All writing is political in the sense that the author
makes choices—of character, plot development, social setting.
Some, as with Dreiser, are more overtly political. The delicate
strokes of Virginia Woolf illuminate the inner life of people of a
particular time in a nation where people of that class took it for
granted that God was an Englishman. I think your question probably exaggerates any conflict between social responsibility and
the necessities of art. Virginia Woolf writing in comfortable England in the twenties can afford luxuries which a James Baldwin
(who strikes me as similar in artistic style) cannot. Baldwin, like
it or not, belongs to a people who face problems which may be
genocidal in character. I suspect from his earlier work that he
might like to experiment in areas which are not so urgent or political, but he also would not like to get shot, or to finish his work
in a concentration camp. But, make no mistake, I'm still afraid of
Virginia Woolf.

INTERVIEWER: Have you ever found a conflict in your own
writing between meaning and form? In other words, have you
ever realized certain things may be demanded artistically, but
that you might sacrifice meaning were you to do them?

MAYFIELD: I really don't know how to answer this. I think I
am more concerned with communicating my meaning, which, of
course, means using the most effective art form. Weird as it may
sound for one who has never displayed any musical ability, my

ambition is to develop a musical form to get what I have to say across to a people who respond readily to music, but until recently were discouraged from reading, largely because most that was written had nothing to do with them.

INTERVIEWER: Do you have a particular audience in mind when you write? For whom do you write?

MAYFIELD: For black people, in the same sense that whites write primarily for whites, Russians for Russians, Spaniards for Spaniards, although I never met or heard of a writer who wanted to confine his work to his own group. A special problem for black American writers has been that until recently they have had to have the quality of their work approved by white publishers, and all too often they have had this circumstance in their mind as they worked. Writing may be—in some cases—an art, but publishing is a business which has as its main objective the making of a buck. All writers know this, whether or not they admit it.

INTERVIEWER: Do you think that the relatively recent interest in black literature signifies a radical change in literary tastes in America?

MAYFIELD: I don't care about the critical interest from whites —except as it helps to sell books—for their view of life is bound to be different from blacks, and we have no common frame of reference. It is good that black writers are being read more widely, especially the poets. But it is a mistake to think that a revolution in literature has taken place. Blacks are not being published as widely as it appears. It is simply that there were so few published before now, and the appearance of *two* in the *New York Times* on a Sunday, where only one had been before, makes it look like a flood. As with television.

INTERVIEWER: Some critics have argued that if black literature is concerned only with the so-called "black experience" it is not important.

MAYFIELD: That's just plain silly, but it probably pleased the precious souls in certain academic circles.

INTERVIEWER: The ending of *The Grand Parade* is strikingly pessimistic. The endings of your first two novels were just as striking in their optimism. What happened to alter your views, or was this just a different story that demanded a different ending?

MAYFIELD: Remember what was happening in the late 1950s. Little Rock. Ole Miss. White mothers spitting on black kids. Et cetera. It became clear to many of us that the goal of integration was based on an incorrect assessment of reality. That white racism was so deeply inbred in our society that for our survival we had to take this fact into consideration and base our strategy on it. We could not agree with the great Dr. M. L. King, not because he did not always have our respect—he did—but simply that his philosophy of passive resistance and nonviolence had no application to the reality of the U.S.

INTERVIEWER: It seems clear that integration in the novel is brought about as a political move. In fact, it is finally used to incite a riot which is thought necessary by one of the reactionary political groups. Do you think that integration in America was used just as a political weapon by people who were not really concerned about integration?

MAYFIELD: It is difficult to talk about how integration has been used, because—except for public facilities in many places —it has not been achieved in many meaningful areas. And now there is a growing opinion among both black and whites that it is not desirable. (I'm speaking here of social integration.)

INTERVIEWER: Do you think of American politicians as being as disinterested in what is "right" as the politicians of your novel?

MAYFIELD: I believe that U.S. politicians are even more disinterested in "good" and "right" than I believed in 1961. They might have "good" and "right" impulses when they get up in the morning, and they would do good and right if they could push a button and do them. But nearly always they must compromise between powerful forces. And because blacks have so little power, they get the short end of the stick. I said "nearly" always they must comprise, but I can think of no exceptions.

INTERVIEWER: One reviewer of the novel called Douglas Taylor a "reform" mayor and suggested that his motivations were honorable ones. It seemed to me that he was as ruthlessly selfish as the others.

MAYFIELD: Douglas Taylor fits into this pattern . . . begins as an innocent, learns to be ruthless if he is to stay in the game. Though I don't agree that he is selfish, as you say, unless you refer to his personal ambitions.

INTERVIEWER: Is there some sense in which Patty Speed is the most "virtuous" of all the characters in the novel? She seems to be the only one who does not hide behind deceptions and social pretenses, and perhaps the most dedicated to helping other blacks.

MAYFIELD: Yes. She has no illusions. She understands the workings of power.

INTERVIEWER: A few of your reviewers, Saunders Redding in particular, said that the novel lacked a focus. I guess what they mean is that there were so many characters and that you went into such great detail in creating each of them. Perhaps, though, the town itself should be seen as the focus or "hero."

MAYFIELD: My friend, and indirectly my teacher, Saunders Redding has always been very straightforward about *The Grand Parade*. At dinner one evening he asked me what the new book was about and I told him, whereupon he replied that he didn't think he would like it. In his view, politics and literature were seldom compatible bedfellows. Therefore, his negative review in the *New York Herald Tribune* came as no surprise. Even now, a decade later, I find it hard to react to because I am not certain how much I agree with his basic premise. When a man of his distinction speaks, I listen. Besides, it is uncomfortable to be put in a position of defending your own work, of a long time ago, because you are yourself dissatisfied with it. I do know this. I believe now, as I believed then, that all writing is political. Or, if it is not, it ought to be. That black people in the United States are economically obsolete, except as consumers, and this places them in a dangerous position. The black writer addressing himself to various aspects of this problem may not always achieve high art —that depends upon the extent of his individual genius. But even if it is only good propaganda, he may help to create a world where—even if he himself is quite dead—art can flourish.

INTERVIEWER: Langston Hughes, in his review of *The Hit,* said that it is concerned with the pursuit of "the dream," the American dream. Is the dream in this novel the same as it is in so much of American literature, or is the "American dream" for blacks in general different from that of whites?

MAYFIELD: I suppose so because he has never really wanted very much. Just decent treatment, and humble opportunities. Things which were denied him by a thoroughly racist society. Millions of whites are poor and exploited. For a variety of reasons they just can't cut it, can't better themselves. But—and this is important—they are never kept down because they are white. The most brilliant black American is up shit's creek the moment he is born because of white racism.

INTERVIEWER: Did you intend in *The Hit* that, although Hubert Cooley seems hopelessly lost in his false dreams, James Lee will act upon the realization he comes to at the end of the novel?

MAYFIELD: In 1957 when *The Hit* was published I hoped that a generation would develop which would have no belief in the American dream, which has always been false as far as blacks are concerned. I think the generation which is about twenty years old today is close to that. The problem is how to move forward on the basis of a new recognition of reality.

INTERVIEWER: One of the themes that you explore in your fiction and which pervades so much of American literature is the search for identity. Perhaps the theme is handled somewhat differently by black writers, though. The black hero's problem doesn't seem to be discovering "who" he is as much as being able to be what he is already.

MAYFIELD: If a black man doesn't know who he is, he need only wait upon the first white person he meets who will indicate it to him. In a war situation such as we find ourselves in, it isn't good to be confused about your identity.

INTERVIEWER: Were you consciously employing myth (in particular, the Ulysses-Telemachus myth) in *The Long Night?* None of your critics seem to have noticed this mythic structure, though a few of them criticized you for contrivance when Steely finds his lost father. His reunion with his father certainly has psychological plausibility.

MAYFIELD: Probably the critics were as ignorant as I am. I went to public school in Washington, D.C., and Telemachus was not in the curriculum.

INTERVIEWER: Would the novel have ended similarly had you written it now?

MAYFIELD: Very difficult question. I think that today I would not have the father return home. Forty-three and cynical? Perhaps.

INTERVIEWER: *The Long Night* raises the question of the hero in black culture. Steely is in search of a cultural hero, perhaps even a cultural past. At times it's Frederick Douglas, Toussaint, and even Jackie Robinson. Is it more difficult for blacks to find heroes? Is there a sense in which the white hero, for better or

worse, was long ago defined in the white culture, while the black
hero is in the process of being defined?

MAYFIELD: Of course. Whites control the communication systems, and quite naturally create white heroes. The black heroes
existed, but they did not allow us to know about them. I heard of
Booker T. Washington and George Washington Carver—hard-
working, conciliatory men—but seldom of DuBois and Nat
Turner and David Walker, Toussaint, and others. Perhaps our
black teachers knew, and, perhaps, unconsciously, they made the
decision not to tell us of them so that we would not become too
bitter at an early age. I think the overall game-plan of our teachers was to inspire us . . . you know, keep a'plugging away . . .
whites won't always be as savage as they are now, and so
on. . . .

INTERVIEWER: What are your writing habits like?

MAYFIELD: I work every day, revise constantly, and read
something completely foreign from what I'm writing—such as
crime fiction.

INTERVIEWER: Has your film career had any effect upon your
writing? Much of your fiction is very visual. It occurred to me
while reading *The Grand Parade* how easily it lent itself to the
cinema.

MAYFIELD: Except for a couple of bit roles, I have only had
one picture in which I played a substantial role, and had something to do with the writing. So I don't consider that I have had a
"film career." I believe it is possible to make good motion pictures
in the United States, but only if you control them, and only a
couple of blacks are in that position today.

INTERVIEWER: *The Grand Parade* was published in 1962.
You have published no fiction since then. Have you permanently
abandoned writing fiction? In favor of what?

MAYFIELD: No. I have written a couple of novels I didn't like, a play which I do like, but nobody else does, and some short fiction pieces which will be published. But while I worked in the office of the President of Ghana between 1961 and 1966 I thought that I could make a better contribution toward achieving the kind of world I want by doing the straight-out political writing I did in the newspapers, magazines, and for radio. I suppose one of the main problems is that I still doubt the fictional pen is mightier than the sword.

Ann Petry

Ann Petry's first novel, *The Street,* has sold well over a million copies since it first appeared in 1946. It concerns the struggles and eventual destruction of a young black woman as she tries to survive with her young son in the ghetto of Harlem. It is a forceful novel that sounds many angry protests against the position of blacks and women in America. Despite the success of the book, her finest work was to come in her later novels, *Country Place* (1947) and *The Narrows* (1953). Her second novel details the devastating effects of World War II on the social and moral structure of a small New England town. Her third novel, *The Narrows* shows Petry at her very best. Once again she is concerned with racial themes, but her focus is more philosophical than political and social. The enemy appears to be the nature of time, rather than the institutions that govern society. She sees the terrifying quality of the past as its arbitrariness, its dependence upon chance. Yet out of these haphazard occurrences comes a culture that is shackled to its past experiences. One character in the novel reflects "on how peculiar, and accidental, a foundation rests all of one's attitudes toward a people. . . . It all depended on what had happened in the past. We carry it around with us. We're never rid of it."

The success of her last novel lies as much in her maturity of style as of theme. She quite skillfully develops brilliant episodes in what is essentially a tragic story. And unlike her first novel, this one is held together by a complex network of images that gives the novel its poetic quality and structure. It does not rely upon the drama of action alone, as I think *The Street* does, but rather employs much more subtle and suggestive literary devices. In *The Narrows* Petry is more interested in creating conflicting points of view which she tries less to resolve than to explore in fine detail. In other words, the novel has a complexity that defies easy or simplistic interpretation.

Her collection of short stories, *Miss Muriel and Other Stories,* was published in 1971. It demonstrates Petry's remarkable versatility. Many of the stories are concerned with her youth in a small town in Connecticut, where she still lives. Her father was the town's druggist and her family a significant minority. But the atmosphere is relatively free of racial problems. There are also stories in this volume that grew out of her experience in Harlem, where she worked as a reporter.

Mrs. Petry is presently working on another novel, after taking several years off to raise a family and write children's stories. We met in early November of 1971. She picked me up at the train station in Old Saybrooke and, on the way to her home, showed me the landmarks that dated back to before the Revolution. She was quick to point out disdainfully the ugly encroachments of commercialism upon her town. She lives in a house that was built in 1800 and has been preserved in its original state. Because she dislikes tape recorders, as well as interviews, she answered my questions by mail a few months after we talked in her home. Almost a year after our initial meeting, we talked briefly once more on the phone in an effort to expand on some of her earlier remarks. The brevity of her answers and her obvious hesitancy to talk about her work belie her warmth. After apologizing for what she considered to be unhelpful answers, she invited me to visit her again when I was not armed with pen and paper.

INTERVIEWER: Do you like talking about your writing?

PETRY: No. I find it painful.

INTERVIEWER: Is it just that it's unpleasant for you, or do you think that a writer shouldn't discuss her own work?

PETRY: I personally don't like talking about it. My feeling is that once I've written something I don't have anything more to say about it. That's it. Talking about it isn't going to change what I did or didn't do. The classic example of the man who tried to explain his work was Shaw. Well, it seems to me that if you have to explain what you write, then you haven't done a very good job. If a critic wants to analyze it, let him. Fine. But I don't want to.

INTERVIEWER: Are you also hesitant to talk about the craft of writing?

PETRY: No, I don't mind. But I'm not an authority. I can only speak in terms of what I try to do or the problems I face.

INTERVIEWER: Do you have any particular difficulty in creating characters?

PETRY: I don't have any particular problem in creating characters. They seem to grow and develop and become alive during the process of writing. Occasionally there's something about a character I don't know. For example I had almost finished writing *The Street* and I still did not know why Mrs. Hedges always wore a turban. One afternoon I was on the Eighth Avenue subway going to the Bronx and it suddenly came to me that Mrs. Hedges was bald. And then I worked out how she came to be bald.

INTERVIEWER: Do you have a set way in which you begin working on a character? Do you know beforehand what he or she will be doing in the story?

PETRY: There are really so many ways. I don't think that a character appears in its entirety. It's part of a process whereby you have probably surprised yourself several times by the time you have finished, because the character changes or grows or does things that you did not expect. It comes to you as you write.

INTERVIEWER: Then you never start out by thinking of a character as having to fulfill some symbolic function in the story?

PETRY: No, because I do not think of characters functioning symbolically. I hope that what starts out as a sketch will become a full-boned portrait, but that portrait is not necessarily very much related to the original sketch.

INTERVIEWER: Then the creation of a character, for you, is instinctive?

PETRY: Yes. I don't think that I can explain the origins of a character, or even why he fits the situation he's in.

INTERVIEWER: There's a complex system of imagery in your short story "In Darkness and Confusion." I wonder whether you were conscious of it as you wrote?

PETRY: I don't think I worked it in consciously. It's something that I became aware of after I finished it. That particular story almost wrote itself. I did it all at one sitting. I don't know about other people, but it seems to me that the subconscious mind is what creates such things in a story.

INTERVIEWER: Do you ever become aware that something is taking on symbolic importance while you are writing a story?

PETRY: I guess that it's always a matter of after the fact, but I always shy away from such things as symbol hunting. If they are there, they are not there because I consciously created them.

INTERVIEWER: How much do you depend upon personal experience for material in your stories? Must you experience, in some way, much of what you write about?

PETRY: I think a writer would be seriously handicapped—well, let's say limited—both as to subject-matter and the creation of characters if these were based solely on personal experience.

INTERVIEWER: I know that you worked as a reporter in Harlem for six years. Did this experience affect your writing in any way, perhaps both your style and subject matter?

PETRY: Doubtful.

INTERVIEWER: When we met at your home last November we talked about critics' frequent arbitrary grouping of black writers which is most apparent in anthologies of black literature. So often critics seem to ignore the differences between black writers in order to establish some mysterious link between them all.

PETRY: That's because we're all black. As I said, we do have a common theme. We write about relationships between whites and blacks because it's in the very air we breathe. We can't escape it. But we write about it in a thousand different ways and from a thousand different points of view.

INTERVIEWER: Does it bother you that, as John A. Williams has complained, regardless of what a black writer does in his work or what subject he may treat, he or she is always designated as "a black writer"?

PETRY: Well, it's just an indication of the fact that black people are in a minority in this country. If I lived in a country where the majority of the people were black people I would be an "author"—and the white folks would be "white authors"—if they were authors.

INTERVIEWER: I wonder whether such identification does not force a black writer always to direct himself only to black audiences? Do you find yourself writing with a particular audience in mind?

PETRY: Not at all. If I permitted myself to think in terms of the reader, I would become so inhibited I wouldn't write—at least for publication.

INTERVIEWER: In addition to the racial problems black writers face in America, they also share the problem that all American writers have—our culture does not greatly value books and reading. What do you identify with the culture you write in?

PETRY: Pro-football, beer, TV serials, and cars.

INTERVIEWER: Have you ever been unable to write a story which you would have liked to write?

PETRY: I've never abandoned a story or a novel once I started working on it. I've abandoned many ideas before I ever put a pen to paper. I once planned or thought about writing a book for young people about Daniel Drayton and Edward Syres, two ships' captains imprisoned for attempting to help slaves escape from the District of Columbia on the schooner *Pearl*. I didn't write that particular book because I became interested in—actually fascinated by—a slave, Tituba, who was one of three women charged with witchcraft at the beginning of the trials for witchcraft in Salem, Massachusetts. Another idea that I once abandoned was to write a book for young people about Jacintha de Siqueira "the celebrated African woman—founding mother of the richest of all Provinces of Brazil" (David Davidson). I gave up this idea because of the research involved—I would have had to spend a considerable amount of time in Brazil, and I would have had to learn to speak Portuguese, or at least learn to read it. These ideas go with the territory and I hope someone else will write about these people. Feel free.

INTERVIEWER: Is there a part of a novel which is more difficult for you to write than any other?

PETRY: Sometimes. I had great difficulty writing the chapter *(The Narrows)* in which Link is murdered.

INTERVIEWER: Is there some point in the novel where you feel that you have everything in hand and the rest will fall into place?

PETRY: I never have a novel "in hand" until it is completed.

INTERVIEWER: Do you ever experience any conflict between meaning and form, or between what you might like to do in a novel and what you think your reader will be able to understand? Or does the form of a novel develop on its own?

PETRY: The form finds itself.

INTERVIEWER: Do you remember how old you were when you first started to write?

PETRY: Fourteen.

INTERVIEWER: Were you anxious to show your work to people?

PETRY: I rarely ever told anyone that I was writing. And I still don't talk about what I write if I can avoid it.

INTERVIEWER: Do you think of your fiction as autobiographical?

PETRY: I could say that none of my work is autobiographical, or that all of it is—everything I write is filtered through my mind, consciously or unconsciously. The end product contains everything I know, have experienced, thought about, dreamed about, talked about, lived for. And so in that sense I am any of the characters that I create, all of them, some of them, or none of them.

INTERVIEWER: Could you say something about your writing habits? When do you work? How much revising do you do? Are you subject to moods during the time you are working on a novel?

PETRY: When I'm writing I work in the morning from 8:00 A.M. to about noon. If I'm going to do any revising I do it in the afternoon. The first draft is in longhand. The planning and the writing go hand in hand for the most part. I revise endlessly. And yet the first chapter of *The Street* was written in one sitting and that first draft was the final one—no changes. And there were no changes in a story entitled "Like a Winding Sheet" or in "Sole on the Drums." I do not work at night if I can avoid it. I am not subject to moods. I doubt if my family or anyone else can tell when I'm thinking about writing.

INTERVIEWER: One reviewer of *The Street* made a comparison between you and Theodore Dreiser. Do you see any similarity? Do you feel that you belong to a naturalistic school of writing?

PETRY: No to both questions. To be absolutely honest about it, it really doesn't interest me. I always want to do something different from what I have done before; I don't want to repeat myself. If I belong to a certain tradition, I don't want to belong, because my writing would be very boring if I always wrote in a particular style.

INTERVIEWER: Could you tell me how the conception for *The Street* came to you? After you have an idea for a novel, how do you go about starting the novel itself?

PETRY: *The Street* was built around a story in a newspaper— a small item occupying perhaps an inch of space. It concerned the superintendent of an apartment house in Harlem who taught an eight-year-old boy to steal letters from mail boxes. As far as procedure is concerned I usually make a rough outline or draft— and I break it down into chapters, and begin to write, and then revise what I've written.

INTERVIEWER: Hoyt Fuller noted in an article that a number of black writers around 1950 abandoned writing novels about blacks. He pointed to *Country Place* as an example. Why do you think this happened with so many black writers? Why did you choose different subjects and themes?

PETRY: I don't know what impelled other black writers to stop writing novels about blacks. I wrote *Country Place* because I happened to have been in a small town in Connecticut during a hurricane—I decided to write about that violent, devastating storm and its effect on the town and the people who lived there.

INTERVIEWER: A few critics have pointed out what they think are your implausible endings, especially those in *The Street* and *Country Place*. I guess what they are referring to are Lutie Johnson's act of murder and Lil's attempted murder. How do you respond to that criticism?

PETRY: I don't think there's anything "implausible" about the endings in *The Street* and *Country Place*—they're perfectly logical given the circumstances and the character of the people.

INTERVIEWER: Why did you use the druggist to narrate *Country Place* rather than having an omniscient point of view as you did in *The Street?*

PETRY: I had never used the first person, and a druggist in a small town seemed to offer great possibilities.

INTERVIEWER: One of your critics has argued that the hope of the town in *Country Place* resides in the minority figures, Neola and Portegee. One also might add the youth, Johnnie Roane. Did you intend something like this? And at the end of the novel there appears to be a restoration of moral order when several minority figures are included in the will. Were you suggesting that social and moral change must occur simultaneously?

PETRY: No to both questions. I think you're reading something into this book that simply is not there.

INTERVIEWER: What are your feelings about Weasel? His name suggests certain unlikable qualities, yet, in some crude way he brings justice to the town, even though he does not always practice it himself.

PETRY: As to The Weasel—very few people are all evil. The Weasel isn't, Mrs. Hedges isn't, nor is Powther in *The Narrows,* or Bill Hod. We're all mixtures of good and evil.

INTERVIEWER: So Mrs. Hedges in *The Street* plays a kind of dual role: she rescues Lutie and Bub on two different occasions, yet she was also part of the vicious system that was entrapping them.

PETRY: Dual role? Well, perhaps. Mrs. Hedges is probably a classic example of the fact that most people are a mixture of good and evil.

INTERVIEWER: *The Narrows* seems a very different novel from the first two. Perhaps your form and content have come together perfectly in that novel. What do you think?

PETRY: I don't know.

INTERVIEWER: Is there any "correct" point of view in *The Narrows?* I think of this in relation to the themes of guilt and time. Abbie thinks that the past determines everything and that she, personally, is responsible for the evil that has occurred. Miss Doris thinks that everyone is responsible. Bill Hod and Weak Knees think of racism as being the cause of the evil. Is any one of these wholly correct?

PETRY: I suppose not, though racism comes closer to being *the* cause.

INTERVIEWER: Is there any implicit condemnation of Link for having undertaken the love affair with a rich white girl?

PETRY: No.

INTERVIEWER: Could you say something about the use of comedy in *The Narrows?* Some of the comic scenes seem to be steeped in "black humor."

PETRY: I have a peculiar sense of humor.

INTERVIEWER: While I was reading *The Narrows* I was struck by certain thematic similarities to Huxley and Faulkner, especially in your treatment of time. Are you conscious of any such resemblance?

PETRY: No.

INTERVIEWER: The racial conflict in *The Narrows* is minimized. Although it plays a large part in determining the outcome of the story, you seem to be treating more universal problems. Do you think that "race" is as important a theme in this novel as it was in *The Street?*

PETRY: Yes.

INTERVIEWER: Your short story, "The Witness," ends with Woodruff slowing his car after he is reminded what the boys had done to him. Will he return and be a witness against them? Or is it just that he doesn't have the strength or desire to go on?

PETRY: He won't be back.

INTERVIEWER: What are your plans for writing?

PETRY: I plan to go on writing novels and short stories and one of these days I plan to write a play—or two—or three.

INTERVIEWER: Did you intend "Mother Africa" to be an allegory? For example, the protagonist is called "Man." Or is it unfair to ask you to explain your own story in this way?

PETRY: I think it is an imposition to ask me to "explain" a story or a novel.

Ishmael Reed

Ishmael Reed is a poet, novelist, editor, college teacher, essayist, and dramatist. Though only thirty-four, he is one of America's most distinguished innovative fictionists and has established himself as the aesthetic spokesman for black experimental fiction. His anthology, *19 Necromancers from Now,* brought together many of the black writers who are rarely permitted into the standard collections of Afro-American literature. In his introductory essay to the book he argues that the mainstream of American literature has historically ignored writers who belong to a uniquely American tradition, who use American slang and idiom, American experience, and original literary forms that cannot be traced to European influences. He exhorts the new black writers and critics to flee "the cultural slave quarters" and develop non-Western literary standards.

Reed's own fiction has led the way in creating those new standards. Unfortunately, though perhaps purposely, his position has been narrowly interpreted to mean that fiction should foster political revolution. In fact, the opposite is true. Revolution is indeed what Reed seeks, but not the political and social upheavals his wary critics have attributed to him. He is instead after a reform of the "imagination," and to this end his fiction satirizes and takes out after the emblems of the cultural establishment and its underlying values. The objects of his "metaphysical" attacks, as he describes them, are Christianity, Western art and morality, the hypocrisy of democratic ideals, American history, and the tyrannical myths that shape the American mind.

His success has largely been achieved by his ability to invent the forms and techniques to carry such themes. His own novels move across an unexplored landscape composed of fantasy, vaudevillian humor, phantasmagoric colors, Voodoo rituals, and surrealistic imagery. His novels generally discard plot and resemble more a dream whose revelations are made through piecing together image and episode. *The Free-Lance Pallbearers* (1967) is Reed's first fantasy and involves a young cultural revolutionary named Bukka Doopeyduk who tries to overthrow the totalitarian state of Harry Sam. Bukka is eventually lynched and hung on meathooks to die. Before "giving up the ghost" his last words are " 'What's the use?' " On the third day after his death the Free-Lance Pallbearers, made up of white liberals and silent blacks who never prevent the martyrdom of their heroes but religiously venerate them after their demise ("Better late den never"), arrive to bury Doopeyduk's body. A new regime arrives to replace Harry Sam, lands on rooftops with its helicopters, and blinks its revolutionary doctrine on and off on neon signs: SAVE GREEN STAMPS. Significantly, the new rulers speak Chinese.

Yellow Back Radio Broke-Down (1969) concerns the myriad adventures of a black cowboy possessed of supernatural powers named Loop Garoo. He is at war with Drag Gibson, the ruthless mythical founder of the West, the government of the United States, prescriptive literary critics, and the Pope. In a confrontation with Bo Shmo, who insists that writers must use their fiction for "liberating the masses" and showing "the oppressor hanging from a tree," Loop argues that a novel can be anything that the inventive mind wants to make it and is not confined to serving propagandistic purposes. At the end of the novel all the figureheads of culture which circumscribe the range and freedom of man's experience are expelled from the land and the world is returned to the domain of man.

The interview was conducted through the mails in the winter of 1972. Over a period of six weeks after the original tape was made, Mr. Reed revised and expanded his initial answers. Some of his tone and humor was modified in the transcription; the full force of his irony and wit often depended upon pauses and verbal expression that the printed word was only partially successful in capturing. At the time of the interview, Mr. Reed was completing his third novel *Mumbo Jumbo* and is now working on a collection of his own critical essays. He continues to read, lecture, and teach at numerous colleges across the country and now resides in Berkeley, California, where he functions as a one-man communications center for writers and artists on the West Coast.

INTERVIEWER: One of the first things one wants to know about fiction such as yours is how you came to do it. Were there other experimental writers who "showed" you what could be done with the novel and, having seen, you put your own hand to it? Or were you working on your own, experimenting in a kind of vacuum?

REED: I think the first fictional influence on me was Nathanael West's work, especially *The Dream Life of Balso Snell*, a piece I've read many times and still can't get over. I'm especially influenced by the style because I feel that West, who went to Paris, was influenced by painters. I think his was an early attempt at the collage, doing what painters have done with the collage. I read that in high school and it never really left me.

INTERVIEWER: Were you trying to write things then yourself?

REED: I had written things in high school and grammar school. I remember one of the first things I attempted was in the second grade. It was based on fairy tales that I had gotten out of the library. It had the fairy tale formula—a young man leaves home and goes out and seeks his fortune. I remember that my mother was working in a Curtis Wright airplane factory for the war effort. She was always a hard worker, always a very self-reliant person. I told her about it and she encouraged me; I think I had very sympathetic parents. But I think I really attempted my first fictional work in college. I wrote a piece during December of 1956. I'll never forget it. It was the Christmas holidays and I was in night school. I wrote a work called "Something Pure." At that time works by Camus and Sartre were pretty much in vogue on the campus and the professors were thrilled about existentialism. So we were indoctrinated to be thrilled about it too. "Something Pure" was a black version of existentialism. It was about a student named Christopher Weeks who has a day off from school. He's a very alienated black Raskolnikov-type individual. Very sensitive. I guess the seeds of Bukka Doopeyduk are in that first short story. Of course, I took Christopher Weeks seriously at the time, but then later on I saw him as really a buffoon, a dupe. But I attempted this existentialist story about the business of despair and alienation and all the clichés that I understood and half-understood at the university. It's very significant that the story had a trick ending. It showed me that I would not be comfortable with the "straight" story. At the end there's a trick ending where the guy goes to a bookstore and Christ lands in a helicopter outside. Christ gives a Madison Avenue pitch and the people laugh at him. He says, "Salvation! Buy it in a jumbo kit and you'll not be cast into the pit." Then Christ and Christopher Weeks leave the scene in the helicopter and go to a Buddhist monastery. The last section of that story was the kind of material I'll be experimenting with for years. I was pretty heavy as a kid. As I grew older I loosened up a bit and I'm thankful for that. But I think I was probably on the way to becoming a monk or something.

INTERVIEWER: Did the story get any attention?

REED: I was in Millard Fillmore night school at the University of Buffalo. My English instructor raved about it and showed it to the people in the English Department. They signed a petition and got me into the day school, and I was quite a celebrity in the English classes. I had a legend going from that one short story. It kind of went to my head. I was working in the library at the time and I found that I was ahead of some of the professors because I would read all the new literary criticism that had arrived. I had discovered the academic game very early. But I became bored with the university and found that I did some of my best work outside of it. I quit in my junior year. I majored in American Studies, and in the middle of my junior year, 1960, I dropped out of college. This was the best thing that could have happened to me at the time because I was able to continue experimenting along the lines I wanted, influenced by West and others. I just didn't want to be a slave to somebody else's reading lists or a slave to what somebody else was going to use as a career and a way of gaining tenure. I kind of regret the decision now because I've gotten some of the most racist and horrible things said to me because of this. It has come from black academicians who kind of hate people who don't have degrees. Even those who say that they are nationalists and blacker than this or that . . . they still put their degrees next to their names as an indication of where they are in this culture. Actually, I never had that with whites. I've been invited to lecture at some of the biggest and best schools in the country. The fact that I didn't have a degree never came up. But with blacks it's a kind of pathology. Maybe I would have avoided a lot of these racist insults had I gotten a degree.

INTERVIEWER: What writing were you doing at this time?

REED: I started working for a newspaper when I dropped out of college. That taught me discipline in writing because I had to turn out so much material each week. The editor was like twenty-eight and I was twenty or twenty-one. We shook the town up. I wrote a play called *Ethan Booker,* but unfortunately I don't have any of this early work. "Something Pure" is in the possession of an actor I knew in high school and college named Richard Monterose. He changed his name. He's in a milk and raisin and cereal commercial that's on television now. He wears a beret. Anyway, the last time I talked to him he said that it was on piles of junk in his mother's house in Buffalo. *Ethan Booker* was a full-length play about a black puritanical college professor who was confronting all these militants in 1960–1961. A friend of mine, an Irish poet named David Sharp, who used to do things like give me Thomas Wolfe's letters on my birthday, read it and thought it was great. I went with him one weekend to New York. We hung out in a place called Chumley's which is run by the Santini brothers. It's a bar and it's got a literary history behind it. Emily Dickenson, Tom Wolfe, and people like that used to go there and they have on the walls covers from the books of those people who used to frequent the place. I was very naive and was impressed by all that. Years later I was thrilled that they put the cover of *Pallbearers* up there on the wall. When I went back to Buffalo I decided that I was going to leave Buffalo and go to New York and become a writer.

INTERVIEWER: What happened in New York?

REED: I went there thinking that I was going to be a W. B. Yeats. It taught me my voice and I developed my style further from contact with such people as Calvin Hernton, David Henderson, Joe Johnson, Steve Cannon, and Tom Dent. They embarrassed me into writing all my own way. Then I went to Newark in 1965, edited a newspaper, and wrote thousands and thousands of prose words. When the paper folded I returned to New York. At the time I had been working on *The Free-Lance Pallbearers.* Living in New York really influenced that book. You wake up in the morning to the blare of truck horns and commotion in the street. You walk outside and right into Halloween in New York.

INTERVIEWER: Were there other influences at work on you while you were writing that novel? Did you know from the beginning what you were trying to do with the novel?

REED: *The Free-Lance Pallbearers* actually started out as a political satire on Newark. It was going to be a naturalistic, journalistic, political novel. But as it went through draft after draft, the style I thought was mine came back and I developed it.

While writing *Pallbearers* I was reading Kenneth Patchen's *The Journal of Albion Moonlight* and Charles Wright's *The Wig*, which is one of the most underrated novels written by a black person in this century. And I was reading a lot of poetry. I learned what poetry is by writing it, and I wanted to bring these techniques to so-called prose. All these things influenced the first book.

INTERVIEWER: I've wondered whether a poet like Gregory Corso or others of that period influenced your writing at this time.

REED: I have an anecdote about Gregory Corso. When I read my first poem publicly in New York, a poem called "Excursions," a long prose poem, Gregory Corso was in the audience and he said, "Ishmael Reed, that sounds like Sigmund Freud."

INTERVIEWER: Did the landscape of *Pallbearers* change from something naturalistic to something surrealistic?

REED: I don't think of it as surrealistic. Surrealism is a painter's movement. The landscape that's created in *Pallbearers* was based on the kind you find in *The Cabinet of Dr. Caligari,* that German Voodoo film in which bokor sends out a zombie to destroy his enemies. The set for that film is almost like a cartoon's and that's the kind of thing I wanted to create. It could almost be rendered in a child's drawing. I wanted to create a tiny world. And I'm glad the novel turned out the way it did because I think that it will be around longer than if it were entitled anything like "Inside Newark" or "San Francisco Confidential." Actually I think the set for the Caligari film was expressionistic. But I don't know what that means. Everytime I think I know I read some other expressionist who's got a different definition.

INTERVIEWER: Do you think of yourself as having done something to or with the novel that has not yet been done? Are your departures from the more traditional novel as much thematic as stylistic? So much of your fiction seems to be taking place in a fantasy or dream or nightmare world. Have you had to develop unique forms to contain your subject matter?

REED: Fantasy or dream world, nightmare world . . . Northrop Frye, in an essay entitled "The Four Forms of Fiction," writes that the word "novel," which up to about 1900 was still the name of a more or less recognizable form, has since expanded into a catch-all term which can be applied to practically any prose book that is not *on* something. That leaves you pretty confused. I think that the Western novel is tied to Western epistemology, the way the people in the West look at the world. So it is usually realistic and has character development and all these things that one associates with the Western novel. When I wrote *The Free-Lance Pallbearers* I wasn't really thinking about writing a novel; I was thinking about telling a story. Story-telling precedes "the novel," which Frye and others say is a very recent and arbitrary form. I consider myself a fetish-maker. I see my books as amulets, and in ancient African cultures words were considered in this way. Words were considered to have magical meanings and were considered to be charms. I think that what's happening in American writing now is that the people who interpret American literature have an old-world orientation, old-world meaning Europe and the eastern United States. You find reviewers still comparing young writers, black and white, with old-world European writers. What you have is people judging American literature who have made no attempt to understand recent American writing. Webster Schott wrote a vicious review of *Yellow Back Radio Broke-Down.* He said the title was really a surrealist joke. Well, having an old world orientation he did not realize that it is a very classic Western (western United States) form. Random House *Dictionary of the English Language:* "An inexpensive, often lurid, novel bound in yellow cloth or paper." Here you have a critic who really was not able to approach the novel because he wasn't acquainted with this. I did research for *Yellow Back Radio* in the Bancroft Library, which is one of the centers of Western Americana. Ánd another critic, L. E. Sissman, who's in love with the old world, said that my book didn't approach what Emily Brontë had done. This is the kind of confusion and ignorance that you have prevailing in the American critical establishment. A man comparing my work—I grew up in Buffalo, New York, an American town—comparing it with a woman writer of nineteenth-century England who was involved with different problems and a different culture. It's going to take a new generation of young black and white critics to assess the thrust of American writing of the last twenty years. I can tell people precisely the aesthetic I'm working with. But you have to have scholars and critics who are just as original as some of the younger black and white writers are.

INTERVIEWER: Was part of the reaction you received from critics their inability to see the innovations that you were making?

REED: Everyone thought that I had made some innovations but the more I get into Afro-American culture, the more I find that I've really not done anything that former writers haven't. Two-thirds of American literature is the part of the iceberg you don't see. I think that there's so much of American literature that we don't know. It's been hidden and suppressed. I was reading a dandy book called *Caleb Catlum's America* (1936) by Vincent McHugh. It's better than Melville but since it's written in vernacular and slang, and since it has something to do with what's going on here instead of the eternal verities of Europe, and since it doesn't have a style reminiscent of Shakespeare or *Moby Dick*, it's been cast aside. It's like a great fantasy, a science fiction book based on American folklore. Its style is absolutely fascinating and innovative. So how could I say that I was an innovator when this sort of book exists? Most Americans aren't educated to American culture; that's why they don't know themselves and are confused.

INTERVIEWER: Is innovative writing by black writers particularly ignored by critics?

REED: Black culture was systematically destroyed by people who came here much later than we did, people who wanted to use us for all kinds of political ends. So they assert that Richard Wright was the beginning of the Afro-American novel because they like the last two chapters of *Native Son,* you know, Max's speech. They like that so they use it, but they have little interest in our culture. In fact, our worst enemies are radical liberals because they have so much influence on how we look in the media and in American culture. They have a vested interest in making us look bad. They are only interested in the social realist, the "experience" of black people. And this treatment limits us and enslaves us. And this is the problem that will concern us from here to the beginning of the next century: that the full diversity and richness and depth of our culture see the light. When I came out with my books I was ignored by the eastern cultural establishment. I was completely ignored on *Pallbearers* because the book didn't fit their mold of what a black writer ought to be doing. When a black writer experiments he gets mugged for it. Then white imitators can come out and claim his innovation. This double standard can be seen, among other places, in the treatment of a book by John Seelye, *The Kid.* This book has been touted by its publishers and reviewers as being unlike any other Western novel, that it's a departure in the Western novel. It was reviewed in the *Sunday Times* which ignored my *Yellow Back* and *Pallbearers.* In *The Kid* there's a character, a black cowboy, who has ESP and supernatural abilities. I was the first in this country to write a Western about a black cowboy with supernatural abilities and ESP, and here is this guy getting all the credit for it, as though it's some kind of innovation. In this country they blame racism on the hard hat or some guy working at a lathe or drilling a hole in the street all day. A lot of people think that because somebody's involved in the arts they're somewhat better as a slave-master than, say, the construction worker. And they always say, "What are you complaining about? What is this? Sour grapes?" The same demands that blacks made in the social area should be made in the cultural areas. One of the problems in this country is that our approach to the solution for our problems has been truncated. The slavemaster not only sets the limits on how you are going to change him but what the target is as well. I think that we have to realize that just because a guy's in New York criticizing books doesn't make him any better than some George Wallace.

INTERVIEWER: Much of the interest in black literature in the last few years has not really been in such things as poetry and fiction. The nonfiction by black writers has received the most attention.

REED: This is very true. When somebody like Peter Prescott comes out and says the most interesting writing from blacks are the autobiographies of Malcolm X and Eldridge Cleaver, it's like saying the most interesting white literature is Richard Nixon's *Six Crises* and Dwight Eisenhower's *Stories I Tell My Friends.* I think it stems from the old ancient Christian notion that heathens don't have souls. If you don't have souls, how can you possibly possess an imagination or be able to write poetry or deal in ambiguity?

INTERVIEWER: In addition to the things you have just talked about, do you think that many readers have had a difficulty with your novels because they are so highly unconventional?

REED: I think that both *Pallbearers* and *Yellow Back* could be reduced to very simple plots. They are very organized and very well structured. If they "get out of hand" for some people it's because they're not really looking at the writing but looking at what the writer is telling them about American society or sociological issues or their own psychology. I made an effort to make *Yellow Back* read like a children's book. I told my editor I wanted it to read so that any child would understand it, and some of the biggest fans of the two books are children. Because of the reception of *Pallbearers* people thought it was esoteric. But there's nothing esoteric about the book when you look at it; it's just a different way of viewing things. I've watched television all my life and I think my way of editing, the speed I bring to my books, the way the plot moves, is based upon some of the television shows and cartoons I've seen, the way they edit. Look at a late movie that was made in 1947—people become bored because there was a slower tempo in those times. But now you can get a nineteenth-century five-hundred-page book in a hundred and fifty pages. You just cut off all the excess, the tedious character descriptions you get in old-fashioned prose and the elaborate scenery. I think that with *Yellow Back* I did make an attempt to "communicate" more than with *Pallbearers* because I do want people to understand and to read the books. As a matter of fact, maybe it's simple to a fault. I've been getting into my third book, *Mumbo Jumbo,* and I think I'm having to prove with it that I could draw, just like when a painter innovates, people criticize him because he can't draw. *Mumbo Jumbo* has all the stuff that you find in a traditional novel. As a matter of fact I call it my "straight" book because I found it necessary to show people that I wasn't one of these 1960s put-on people.

INTERVIEWER: Bo Shmo, in *Yellow Back Radio,* criticizes Loop and says that he's too "abstract," that he's a "crazy dada nigger," that he's given to fantasy, and (the criticism of the social realists) that he can't "create the difference between a German and a redskin." Is this the kind of criticism you received about your own characterization in the books?

REED: I think that the criticism I've received on *Yellow Back* is from people who deny the possibilities of other experience and want everyone to conform to their own experience. . . . There was a period in black folklore when the conjure man was respected. As a matter of fact conjure people wrote their own books. They would list their conjure rites, certain preparations for rites and formulas and charms and advice and proverbs. These were books which didn't deny the possibilities of other dimensions. I was reading an article the other day in which Arthur Koestler said that strict determinism is dead in physics. He went on to say that there are other levels of reality than those we see with the eyes of the common man or the scientist. I think that the traditional hoodoo physics were always amenable to that possibil-

ity. Later what happens is that the conjure man becomes a buffoon and loses his powers. This was a very sorry episode for
blacks in this country when the decline of the conjure man occurred, when blacks went North and were exposed to all the
ideas of Europe. They seemed to lose this kind of wonder and became materialists. What we have now is an attempt to restore the
ancient hoodoo epistemology. Loop Garoo Kid, who does this,
sees "reality" on many levels. Bo Shmo is a guy who has two
minds; Garoo has an infinite number of minds. Bo Shmo is a mun-
dane person and a materialist whom the radicals encourage and
respect.

INTERVIEWER: Could you describe what you try to do in creating a character? Since you are not interested in creating the
"flesh and blood" type of character, what do you aim at?

REED: I look for the essential elements. I look for those qualities which distinguish the character from other people, and everybody has that essence. I attempt to abstract those qualities from
the characters just like someone making a doll in West or East
Africa. This may appear grotesque or distorted but this is the best
way one captures that principle. When I say that I am working
on a "hoodoo" aesthetic I know I'm serious and I know what I'm
talking about and this falls in line with that. They have in Voodoo a thing they call *gros-bon-ange*, and the *gros-bon-ange* is that
which separates from the person after death. It carries all of his
essential elements, the qualities that make him unique from other
individuals. And this is what I try to do. I'm not interested in
rendering a photograph of a person. I'm interested in capturing
his soul and putting it in a cauldron or in a novel.

INTERVIEWER: Do you think of your work as being greatly
influenced by popular culture, for instance, what you read in the
newspapers and see on television?

REED: I read a great deal. I think that I read more than I do
anything else, and I read all kinds of materials. For example,

right now I have a book on electricity as well as a book on the nineteenth-century Congo. I'm also influenced by watching television and listening to the radio. Much of journalism is an American invention, headlines are an American invention. And I was reading a book called *American Vaudeville as Ritual.* It was interesting to me that before vaudevillians would go into a town they would read the local newspaper and derive their skits from that. I think that this explains much of my writing. American vaudeville is a serious mystery drama of civilization. I believe that. It is necessary to change the act from time to time and I think I'm conscious of that when I'm writing. I want a switch, a shift, a shift in syntax, a shift in structure, a change, a surprise! Like instead of Indians invading, you're liable to get Teutonic Germans.

INTERVIEWER: Have vaudevillian techniques influenced your way of telling a story?

REED: My narrative technique involves having a kind of duo that one associates with the vaudeville stage. There's the straight man and the clown, the jokester. Like Laurel and Hardy. And there's a formula for it: one guy is a straight, sophisticated, intelligent, intellectual dude and the other guy keeps breaking into dialect or slang, and slapstick or burlesque. That's what happens in *Free-Lance Pallbearers.* That's what I attempted to do. I was reading a lot of Max Sennet and Bert Williams' scripts about that time, and burlesque, and listening to comedy routines.

INTERVIEWER: In both your novels you keep reminding your reader of the unreality of all that's happening. Two lines that come to mind are "the big not-to-be-believed-in nowhere" and "this incredible nightmare of a NOWHERE." Your characters seem caught in a world where everything is colored by this sense of the unreal. Are there any reprieves from this? Does the world of the imagination then become the only "real" world?

REED: This is a philosophical question and I think that I would have to think about it longer. Ask me that in a couple of years.

INTERVIEWER: When the children take over the town in *Yellow Back* they give as their reason that they want to make "their own fictions." They do not talk about social or political reform. The revolution seems to be taking place in the imagination, not in a political-social environment. Is it a revolution of the imagination that you are working toward in your fiction?

REED: "To create our own fictions" has caused quite a reaction. The book is really artistic guerilla warfare against the Historical Establishment. I think the people we want to aim our questioning toward are those who supply the nation with its mind, tutor its mind, develop and cultivate its mind, and these are the people involved in culture. They are responsible for the national mind and they've done very bad things with their propaganda and racism. Think of all the vehemence and nasty remarks they aimed at the Black Studies programs, somebody like William Buckley, that Christian fanatic, saying that Bach is worth more than all the Black Studies programs in the world. He sees the conflict as being between the barbarians and the Christians. And, you know, I'm glad I'm on the side of the barbarians. So this is what we want: to sabotage history. They won't know whether we're serious or whether we are writing fiction. They made their own fiction, just like we make our own. But they can't tell whether our fictions are the real thing or whether they're merely fictional. Always keep them guessing. That'll bug them, probably drive them up the walls. What it comes down to is that you let the social realists go after the flatfoots out there on the beat and we'll go after the Pope and see which action causes a revolution. We are mystical detectives about to make an arrest. There are some things which we are going to solve and that's the reason the historical establishment is so down on us. They sound like mad monks defending the Church and I think that there's an analogy in that these people really feel they have to save the Western Church. To do this they have to hire thugs who call themselves nationalists and revolutionaries to keep us in line, but as fetish-makers we will get through one way or another.

INTERVIEWER: Is it this kind of revolution which you are envisioning at the end of *Yellow Back Radio?*

REED: The ending of *Yellow Back Radio* was based on an introduction that Carl Jung wrote to *Paradise Lost* in which he traced the origin of Satan. What he claims is that the devil climbed out of art at a certain period along about the time of John Milton and that Milton was using an old gnostic idea of the devil as superman, "a man capable of all things." Jung contends that the devil became eminent in the world. In the ending of *Yellow Back*, which is kind of both a quasi-anarchistic and Tom Mix ending, the symbols of religion, the gods, return to art. They return to where they belong as something one contemplates but that doesn't participate in the world. That's one level of it. It's a trick ending. Some people interpreted it as Loop Garoo going back to Rome. But all the events that Pope Innocent VIII was talking about were taking place in art. And what happens is that people are on their own and Loop Garoo and the Pope return to art.

INTERVIEWER: Do you remember whether the negative criticism you received on both books came from any particular groups? Where did you receive the most enthusiastic responses?

REED: With my first book the hostile reviews were in New York. With my second book, when I was better known, I was able to see that the only hostile reviews were from New York City. I think that's the whole story right there. I got very sympathetic and objective reviews in Saint Louis, in Texas and Wyoming, and Montana, Chicago, Nebraska and Washington, D.C. All these parts of the country that are considered the "corn belt" or where the people are considered square. They gave me a fair reading. But in Manhattan it almost seemed like a conspiracy. It was very weird that Manhattan's thinking could be so much at variance with the rest of the country. I think that might be the problem. Wouldn't it be better if the culture in this country were dispersed? But now you have a cultural "chosen people" in Manhattan. So in order to survive I appealed to the people who read the books. And it looks like my fans are really whites who are interested in the kind of literature that one associates with science fiction writers. I've gotten lots of mail from science fiction fans and science fiction writers. Other fans would be called the silent black majority. These are people, according to a census I read, who belong to a typical black family, the man and wife working very hard; they're self-reliant, sending their children through college, and people who will probably vote for the President in the '72 election. I get my most bitter denunciations from younger students who haven't read much of what they say they believe in: quasi-nationalism, quasi-revolutionary activity, and so on. So I don't think that, although the books may look kind of kooky and wacky to people who read superficially, they appeal to kooks or quacks or lunatics. When it comes to blacks I'm hitting the middle, and when it comes to whites and blacks I'm hitting people who are interested in something other than the run-of-the-mill novel.

INTERVIEWER: Do you see differences between what is being done by black experimental writers and what is being done by people like John Barth, Donald Barthelme, Jerzy Kosinski, and others?

REED: I'm not qualified to talk about the differences. Chester Himes has said that the black people in this country are the only new race in modern times and I think that's probably true. Nothing in history quite happened like it happened here. I think that the young black writer draws from this experience instead of looking over his shoulder to Homer or to the Latins as white writers do, at least many of them. I think that's the difference. And I don't think a white writer is likely to write a poem based on "Curtis Mayfield and the Impressions" like David Henderson did, or write like be-bop musicians play, the way Baraka does so successfully in a book like *Tales*. I just don't see that kind of thing taking place among white writers I read. Of course I find Barth, Kosinski, Brautigan, and Barthelme being at least more interesting than people like John Updike who still uses expressions like "flaxen-haired" and "apple-cheeked" in his novel *Bech: A Book*. A black writer sitting down doesn't have all of Europe looking over his shoulder. I interviewed a famous white woman writer whose most recent book is about a guy who takes a uterus home from a hospital and eats it. Yech! Ugh! How sick! She spoke as if she can't sit down at the typewriter without a bunch of dead people looking over her shoulder, like Henry James and Chekhov. I think that blacks got over that and are trying to set up their own stuff.

INTERVIEWER: Do you think that, aside from stylistic innovations, you are working with themes that have not been greatly used?

REED: I think the themes I deal with in the novels have been dealt with before by black novelists all the way back to 1854, not to mention the poetry that began earlier than that. I can see similarities between what I have done in *Yellow Back* and certain things that William Wells Brown used in his play *The Escape; or, A Leap for Freedom* (1858). I think that it's my style that's unique and it took me a long time to develop that.

INTERVIEWER: Could you tell me something about your work habits?

REED: I write fiction and poetry when I'm inspired, and sometimes those moments are from five minutes to twenty-four hours. All the rest of the time I spend indulging in letters and essays.

INTERVIEWER: Is there any part of a novel that gives you more trouble than another?

REED: The only difficulty I have with novels is beginning them. I think that's the most difficult. And when I say beginning I mean writing in your mind, thinking of plots. I usually keep a notebook next to my bed. Some of the best solutions to problems in my novels come in dreams or in the morning when I'm taking a bath. I get these great insights. And I do a great many— probably too many—revisions. There were thousands of pages that went into *Yellow Back, Pallbearers,* and my new book *Mumbo Jumbo.* So, I do much revising. Of course, a lot of the critics don't think so. Webster Schott in that *Life* magazine review, the infamous *Life* magazine review, said I probably just wrote it off the top of my head. . . . But I think the beginning is the only difficult part. It's very painful to begin the thing, and sometimes you spend a great deal of time thinking about it. I think that writing involves more than just the mechanical act of using a typewriter. A real writer—and only writers know what this is—spends twenty-four hours writing.

Alice Walker

Alice Walker's first collection of poems, *Once,* was published when she was only twenty-four. Her first novel, *The Third Life of Grange Copeland,* appeared two years later. Her second collection of poems, *Revolutionary Petunias,* is due in 1973, and a collection of short stories will be published either in late 1973 or early 1974. All of this suggests how productive Alice Walker has been in so short a time. Along the way she has also managed to publish essays, teach, and raise a family. Yet the most amazing thing is less the ambition she has demonstrated than the maturity she has achieved so early.

The thematic scope of her poetry is the past, both personal and historical. *Once* catalogues her experiences in the civil rights demonstrations of the 1960s and her travels in Africa. The poems are highly personal, recounting first loves and early disappointments. *Revolutionary Petunias* indicates that since her first collection, Walker learned more about both her craft and her subjects. The poems are less marked by abstract observations than by a dependance upon brief anecdotes and precise memories. The language is sharper; the forms, more disciplined. And there is a simplicity of style and imagery which, as Yeats knew, is arrived at only after much labor, but appears spontaneous. More so than the first volume, *Revolutionary Petunias* focuses on specific memories that belong to her family, her small Southern town, and herself.

Walker's most notable accomplishment, however, has been in fiction. *The Third Life of Grange Copeland* traces the life of its hero from his early boyhood through his reckless youth, and finally to his old age. It is a novel of education, in which Walker demonstrates a remarkable ability to show the change and transformation of a character without violating either her characters or human nature. For her subject she chooses a character who is uneducated, oftentimes inarticulate, deprived, abused by his family, and usually trapped by circumstances which he seems unable to control. In other words, she picks an unlikely character in whom to explore the possibility of growth and change. Most impressive about her fiction is Walker's power as a storyteller. She does not indulge in awkward asides in which characters have revelations, or in extended dialogues where they work out the themes of the novel. Walker depends upon her capacity to render theme in terms of action.

The interview was arranged through the help of Miss Walker's editor, Hiram Haydn. Because of a complicated set of circumstances we were forced to conduct the interview through the mail. I sent a long list of questions which she reshaped and worked together, so that—rather than answering specific questions—she most frequently developed brief essays. Her responses are expansive, illuminating, and painstakingly phrased. Miss Walker lives in Jackson, Mississippi, where she is at work on another novel.

INTERVIEWER: Could you describe your early life and what led you to begin writing?

WALKER: I have always been a solitary person, and since I was eight years old (and the recipient of a disfiguring scar, since corrected, somewhat), I have daydreamed—not of fairytales—but of falling on swords, of putting guns to my heart or head, and of slashing my wrists with a razor. For a long time I thought I was very ugly and disfigured. This made me shy and timid, and I often reacted to insults and slights that were not intended. I discovered the cruelty (legendary) of children, and of relatives, and could not recognize it as the curiosity it was.

I believe, though, that it was from this period—from my solitary, lonely position, the position of an outcast—that I began to
really see people and things, to really notice relationships and to
learn to be patient enough to care about how they turned out. I
no longer felt like the little girl I was. I felt old, and because I
felt I was unpleasant to look at, filled with shame. I retreated into
solitude, and read stories and began to write poems.

But it was not until my last year in college that I realized,
nearly, the consequences of my daydreams. That year I made myself acquainted with every philosopher's position on suicide, because by that time it did not seem frightening or even odd—but
only inevitable. Nietzsche and Camus made the most sense, and
were neither maudlin nor pious. God's displeasure didn't seem to
matter much to them, and I had reached the same conclusion.
But in addition to finding such dispassionate commentary from
them—although both hinted at the cowardice involved, and that
bothered me—I had been to Africa during the summer, and returned to school healthy and brown, and loaded down with
sculptures and orange fabric—and pregnant.

I felt at the mercy of everything, including my own body,
which I had learned to accept as a kind of casing, over what I
considered my real self. As long as it functioned properly, I
dressed it, pampered it, led it into acceptable arms, and forgot
about it. But now it refused to function properly. I was so sick I
could not even bear the smell of fresh air. And I had no money,
and I was, essentially—as I had been since grade school—alone. I
felt there was no way out, and I was not romantic enough to believe in maternal instincts alone as a means of survival; in any
case, I did not seem to possess those instincts. But I knew no one
who knew about the secret, scary thing abortion was. And so,
when all my efforts at finding an abortionist failed, I planned to
kill myself, or—as I thought of it then—to "give myself a little
rest." I stopped going down the hill to meals because I vomited
incessantly, even when nothing came up but yellow, bitter, bile. I
lay on my bed in a cold sweat, my head spinning.

While I was lying there, I thought of my mother, to whom
abortion is a sin; her face appeared framed in the window across
from me, her head wreathed in sunflowers and giant elephant-
ears (my mother's flowers love her; they grow as tall as she

wants); I thought of my father, that suspecting, once-fat, slowly shrinking man, who had not helped me at all since I was twelve years old, when he bought me a pair of ugly saddle-oxfords I refused to wear. I thought of my sisters, who had their own problems (when approached with the problem I had; one sister never replied, the other told me—in forty-five minutes of long-distance carefully enunciated language—that I was a slut). I thought of the people at my high-school graduation who had managed to collect seventy-five dollars, to send me to college. I thought of my sister's check for a hundred dollars that she gave me for finishing high school at the head of my class: a check I never cashed, because I knew it would bounce.

I think it was at this point that I allowed myself exactly two self-pitying tears; I had wasted so much, how dared I? But I hated myself for crying, so I stopped, comforted by knowing I would not have to cry—or see anyone else cry—again.

I did not eat or sleep for three days. My mind refused, at times, to think about my problem at all—it jumped ahead to the solution. I prayed to—but I don't know Who or What I prayed to, or even if I did. Perhaps I prayed to God awhile, and then to the Great Void awhile. When I thought of my family, and when —on the third day—I began to see their faces around the walls, I realized they would be shocked and hurt to learn of my death, but I felt they would not care deeply at all, when they discovered I was pregnant. Essentially, they would believe I was evil. They would be ashamed of me.

For three days I lay on the bed with a razorblade under my pillow. My secret was known to three friends only—all inexperienced (except verbally), and helpless. They came often to cheer me up, to bring me up-to-date on things as frivolous as classes. I was touched by their kindness, and loved them. But each time they left, I took out my razorblade and pressed it deep into my arm. I practiced a slicing motion. So that when there was no longer any hope, I would be able to cut my wrists quickly, and (I hoped) painlessly.

In those three days, I said good-bye to the world (this seemed a high-flown sentiment, even then, but everything was beginning to be unreal); I realized how much I loved it, and how hard it would be not to see the sunrise every morning, the snow, the sky, the trees, the rocks, the faces of people, all so different (and it was during this period that all things began to flow together; the face of one of my friends revealed itself to be the friendly, gentle face of a lion, and I asked her one day if I could touch her face and stroke her mane. I felt her face and hair, and she really was a lion; I began to feel the possibility of someone as worthless as myself attaining wisdom). But I found, as I had found on the porch of that building in Liberty County, Georgia—when rocks and bottles bounced off me as I sat looking up at the stars —that I was not afraid of death. In a way, I began looking forward to it. I felt tired. Most of the poems on suicide in *Once* come from my feelings during this period of waiting.

On the last day for miracles, one of my friends telephoned to say someone had given her a telephone number. I called from the school, hoping for nothing, and made an appointment. I went to see the doctor and he put me to sleep. When I woke up, my friend was standing over me holding a red rose. She was a blonde, gray-eyed girl, who loved horses and tennis, and she said nothing as she handed me back my life. That moment is engraved on my mind—her smile, sad and pained and frightfully young— as she tried so hard to stand by me and be my friend. She drove me back to the school and tucked me in. My other friend, brown, a wisp of blue and scarlet, with hair like thunder, brought me food.

That week I wrote without stopping (except to eat and go to the toilet) almost all of the poems in *Once*—with the exception of one or two, perhaps, and these I no longer remember.

I wrote them all in a tiny blue notebook that I can no longer find—the African ones first, because the vitality and color and friendships in Africa rushed over me in dreams the first night I slept. I had not thought about Africa (except to talk about it) since I returned. All the sculptures and weavings I had given away, because they seemed to emit an odor that made me more nauseous than the smell of fresh air. Then I wrote the suicide poems, because I felt I understood the part played in suicide by circumstances and fatigue. I also began to understand how alone woman is, because of her body. Then I wrote the love poems (love real and love imagined), and tried to reconcile myself to all things human. "Johann" is the most extreme example of this need to love even the most unfamiliar, the most fearful. For, actually, when I traveled in Germany I was in a constant state of terror, and no amount of flattery from handsome young German men could shake it. Then I wrote the poems of struggle in the South. The picketing, the marching, all the things that had been buried, because when I thought about them the pain was a paralysis of intellectual and moral confusion. The anger and humiliation I had suffered was always in conflict with the elation, the exaltation, the *joy* I felt when I could leave each vicious encounter or confrontation whole, and not—like the people before me—spewing obscenities, or throwing bricks. For, during those encounters, I had begun to comprehend what it meant to be lost.

Each morning, the poems finished during the night were stuffed under Muriel Rukeyser's door—her classroom was an old gardener's cottage in the middle of the campus. Then I would hurry back to my room to write some more. I didn't care what she did with the poems. I only knew I wanted someone to read them as if they were new leaves sprouting from an old tree. The same energy that impelled me to write them carried them to her door.

This was the winter of 1965, and my last three months in college. I was twenty-one years old, although *Once* was not published till three years later, when I was twenty-four; (Muriel Rukeyser gave the poems to her agent, who gave them to Hiram Haydn—who is still my editor at Harcourt, Brace—who said right away that he wanted them; so I cannot claim to have had a hard time publishing, yet). By the time *Once* was published, it no longer seemed important—I was surprised when it went, almost immediately, into a second printing—that is, the book itself did not seem to me important; only the writing of the poems, which clarified for me how very much I love being alive. It was this feeling of gladness that carried over into my first published short story, "To Hell With Dying," about an old man saved from death countless times by the love of his neighbor's children. I was the children, and the old man.

I have gone into this memory because I think it might be important for other women to share. I don't enjoy contemplating it; I wish it had never happened. But if it had not, I firmly believe I would never have survived to be a writer. I know I would not have survived at all.

Since that time, it seems to me that all of my poems—and I write groups of poems rather than singles—are written when I have successfully pulled myself out of a completely numbing despair, and stand again in the sunlight. Writing poems is my way of celebrating with the world that I have not committed suicide the evening before.

Langston Hughes wrote in his autobiography that when he was sad, he wrote his best poems. When he was happy, he didn't write anything. This is true of me, where poems are concerned. When I am happy (or neither happy nor sad), I write essays, short stories, and novels. Poems—even happy ones—emerge from an accumulation of sadness.

INTERVIEWER: Can you describe the process of writing a poem? How do you know, for instance, when you have captured what you wanted to?

WALKER: The writing of my poetry is never consciously planned; although I become aware that there are certain emotions I would like to explore. Perhaps my unconscious begins working on poems from these emotions long before I am aware of it. I have learned to wait patiently (sometimes refusing good lines, images, when they come to me, for fear they are not lasting), until a poem is ready to present itself—*all* of itself, if possible. I sometimes feel the urge to write poems way in advance of ever sitting down to write. There is a definite restlessness, a kind of feverish excitement that is tinged with dread. The dread is because after writing each batch of poems I am always convinced that I will never write poems again. I become aware that I am controlled by them, not the other way around. I put off writing as long as I can. Then I lock myself in my study, write lines and lines and lines, then put them away, underneath other papers, without looking at them for a long time. I am afraid that if I read them too soon they will turn into trash; or worse, something so topical and transient as to have no meaning—not even to me— after a few weeks. (This is how my later poetry-writing differs from the way I wrote *Once*). I also attempt, in this way, to guard against the human tendency to try to make poetry carry the weight of half-truths, of cleverness. I realize that while I am writing poetry, I am so high as to feel invisible, and in that condition it is possible to write anything.

INTERVIEWER: What determines your interests as a writer? Are there preoccupations you have which you are not conscious of until you begin writing?

WALKER: You ask about "preoccupations." I am preoccupied with the spiritual survival, the survival *whole* of my people. But beyond that, I am committed to exploring the oppressions, the insanities, the loyalties, and the triumphs of black women. In *The Third Life of Grange Copeland*, ostensibly about a man and his son, it is the women and how they are treated that colors everything. In my new book *In Love & Trouble: Stories of Black Women*, thirteen women—mad, raging, loving, resentful, hateful, strong, ugly, weak, pitiful, and magnificent, try to live with the loyalty to black men that characterizes all of their lives. For me, black women are the most fascinating creations in the world.

Next to them, I place the old people—male and female— who persist in their beauty in spite of everything. How do they do this, knowing what they do? Having lived what they have lived? It is a mystery, and so it lures me into their lives. My grandfather, at eighty-five, never been out of Georgia, looks at me with the glad eyes of a three-year-old. The pressures on his life have been unspeakable. How can he look at me in this way? "Your eyes are widely open flowers/ Only their centers are darkly clenched/ To conceal/ Mysteries/ That lure me to a keener blooming/ Than I know/ And promise a secret/ I must have." All of my "love poems" apply to old, young, man, woman, child, and growing things.

INTERVIEWER: Your novel, *The Third Life of Grange Copeland*, reaffirms an observation I have made about many novels:

there is a pervasive optimism in these novels, an indomitable belief in the future, and in man's capacity for survival. I think that this is generally opposed to what one finds in the mainstream of American literature. One can cite Ahab, Gatsby, Jake Barnes, Young Goodman Brown. . . . You seem to be writing out of a vision which conflicts with that of the culture around you. What I may be pointing out, is that you do not seem to see the profound evil present in much of American literature.

WALKER: It is possible that white male writers are more conscious of their own evil (which, after all, has been documented for several centuries—in words and in the ruin of the land, the earth—) than black male writers, who, along with black and white women, have seen themselves as the recipients of that evil, and therefore on the side of Christ, of the oppressed, of the innocent.

The white women writers that I admire: Chopin, the Brontës, Simone De Beauvoir, and Doris Lessing, are well aware of their own oppression and search incessantly for a kind of salvation. Their characters can always envision a solution, an evolution to higher consciousness on the part of society, even when society itself cannot. Even when society is in the process of killing them for their vision. Generally, too, they are more tolerant of mystery than is Ahab, who wishes to dominate, rather than be on equal terms with the whale.

If there is one thing African-Americans have retained of their African heritage, it is probably animism: a belief that makes it possible to view all creation as living, as being inhabited by spirit. This belief encourages knowledge perceived intuitively. It does not surprise me, personally, that scientists now are discovering that trees, plants, flowers, have feelings . . . emotions, that they shrink when yelled at; that they faint when an evil person is about who might hurt them.

One thing I try to have in my life and in my fiction is an awareness of and openness to mystery, which, to me, is deeper than any politics, race, or geographical location. In the poems I read, a sense of mystery, a deepening of it, is what I look for—for that is what I respond to. I have been influenced—especially in the poems in *Once*—by Zen epigrams and by Japanese haiku. I think my respect for short forms comes from this. I was delighted to learn that in three or four lines a poet can express mystery, evoke beauty and pleasure, paint a picture—and not dissect or analyze in any way. The insects, the fish, the birds, and the apple blossoms in haiku are still whole. They have not been turned into something else. They are allowed their own majesty, instead of being used to emphasize the majesty of people; usually the majesty of the poets writing.

INTERVIEWER: A part of your vision—which is explored in your novel—is a belief in change, both personal and political. By showing the change in Grange Copeland you suggest the possibility of change in the political and social systems within which he lives.

WALKER: Yes, I believe in change: change personal, and change in society. I have experienced a revolution (unfinished, without question, but one whose new order is everywhere on view) in the South. And I grew up—until I refused to go—in the Methodist Church, which taught me that Paul *will* sometimes change on the way to Damascus, and that Moses—that beloved old man—went through so many changes he made God mad. So Grange Copeland was *expected* to change. He was fortunate enough to be touched by love of something beyond himself. Brownfield did not change, because he was not prepared to give his life for anything, or *to* anything. He was the kind of man who could never understand Jesus (or Ché or King or Malcolm or Medgar) except as the white man's tool. He could find nothing of value within himself and he did not have the courage to imagine a life without the existence of white people to act as a foil. To become what he hated was his inevitable destiny.

A bit more about the "Southern Revolution." When I left Eatonton, Georgia, to go off to Spelman College in Atlanta (where I stayed, uneasily, for two years), I deliberately sat in the front section of the Greyhound bus. A white woman complained to the driver. He—big and red and ugly—ordered me to move. I moved. But in those seconds of moving, everything changed. I was eager to bring an end to the South that permitted my humiliation. During my sophomore year I stood on the grass in front of Trevor-Arnett Library at Atlanta University and I listened to the young leaders of SNCC. John Lewis was there, and so was Julian Bond—thin, well starched and ironed in light-colored jeans, he looked (with his cropped hair that still tried to curl) like a poet (which he was). Everyone was beautiful, because everyone (and I think now of Ruby Doris Robinson who since died) was conquering fear by holding the hands of the persons next to them. In those days, in Atlanta, springtime turned the air green. I've never known this to happen in any other place I've been—not even in Uganda, where green, on hills, plants, trees, begins to dominate the imagination. It was as if the air turned into a kind of water —and the short walk from Spelman to Morehouse was like walking through a green sea. Then, of course, the cherry trees—cut down, now, I think—that were always blooming away while we —young and bursting with fear and determination to change our world—thought, beyond our fervid singing, of death. It is not surprising, considering the intertwined thoughts of beauty and death, that the majority of the people in and around SNCC at that time were lovers of Camus.

Random memories of that period: myself, moving like someone headed for the guillotine, with (as my marching mate) a beautiful girl who spoke French and came to Spelman from Tuskegee, Alabama ("Chic Freedom's Reflection" in *Once*), whose sense of style was unfaltering, in the worst of circumstances. She was the only really blackskinned girl at Spelman who would turn up dressed in stark white from head to toe—because she knew, instinctively, that white made an already beautiful black girl look like the answer to everybody's prayer: myself, marching about in front of a restaurant, seeing—inside—the tables set up with clean napkins and glasses of water. The owner standing in front of us barring the door. A Jewish man who went mad on the spot, and fell to the floor: myself, dressed in a pink faille dress, with my African roommate, my first real girl friend, walking up the broad white steps of a broad white church. And men (white) in blue suits and bow-ties materializing on the steps above with axe-handles in their hands (see: "The Welcome Table" in *In Love & Trouble*). We turned and left. It was a bright, sunny day. Myself,

sitting on a porch in Liberty County, Georgia, at night, after
picketing the jailhouse (where a local black schoolteacher was
held) and holding in my arms the bleeding head of a little girl—
where is she now?—maybe eight or ten years old, but small, who
had been cut by a broken bottle held by one of the mob in front
of us. In this memory there is a white girl I grew to respect because she never flinched and never closed her eyes, no matter
what the mob—where are they now?—threw. Later, in New
York, she tried to get me to experiment with LSD with her, and
the only reason I never did was because on the night we planned
to try it I had a bad cold. I believe the reason she never closed
her eyes was because she couldn't believe what she was seeing.
We tried to keep in touch—but, because I had never had very
much (not even a house that didn't leak), I was always conscious
of the need to be secure. Because she came from an eleven-room
house in the suburbs of Philadelphia and, I assume, never had
worried about material security, our deepest feelings began to
miss each other. I identified her as someone who could afford to
play poor for awhile (her poverty interrupted occasionally by
trips abroad), and she probably identified me as one of those inflexible black women black men constantly complain about: the
kind who interrupt lighthearted romance by saying, "Yes, well
. . . but what are the children going to eat?"

The point is that less than ten years after all these things I
walk about Georgia (and Mississippi)—eating, sleeping, loving,
singing, burying the dead—the way men and women are supposed to do, in a place that is the only "home" they've ever
known. There is only one "for coloreds" sign left in Eatonton, and
it is on a black man's barber shop. He is merely outdated.
Booster, if you read this, *change* your sign!

INTERVIEWER: I wonder how clear it was to you what you
were going to do in your novel before you started? Did you
know, for instance, that Grange Copeland was capable of
change?

WALKER: I see the work that I have done already as a foundation. That being so, I suppose I knew when I started *The Third*

Life of Grange Copeland that it would have to cover several generations, and nearly a century of growth and upheaval. It begins around 1900 and ends in the sixties. But my first draft (which was never used, not even one line, in the final version) began with Ruth as a civil-rights lawyer in Georgia going to rescue her father, Brownfield Copeland, from a drunken accident, and to have a confrontation with him. In that version she is married—also to a lawyer—and they are both committed to insuring freedom for black people in the South. In Georgia, specifically. There was lots of love-making and courage in that version. But it was too recent, too superficial—everything seemed a product of the immediate present. And I believe nothing ever is.

So, I brought in the grandfather. Because all along I wanted to explore the relationship between parents and children: specifically between daughters and their father (this is most interesting, I've always felt; for example, in "The Child Who Favored Daughter" in *In Love & Trouble,* the father cuts off the breasts of his daughter because she falls in love with a white boy; why this, unless there is sexual jealousy?), and I wanted to learn, myself, how it happens that the hatred a child can have for a parent becomes inflexible. *And* I wanted to explore the relationship between men and women, and why women are always condemned for doing what men do as an expression of their masculinity. Why are women so easily "tramps" and "traitors" when men are heroes for engaging in the same activity? Why do women stand for this?

My new novel will be about several women who came of age during the sixties and were active (or not active) in the Movement in the South. I am exploring their backgrounds, familial and sibling connections, their marriages, affairs, and political persuasions, as they grow toward a fuller realization (and recognition) of themselves.

Since I put together my course on black women writers, which was taught first at Wellesley College and later at the University of Massachusetts, I have felt the need for real critical and biographical work on these writers. As a beginning, I am writing a long personal essay on my own discovery of these writers (designed, primarily, for lectures), and I hope soon to visit the birthplace and home of Zora Neale Hurston, Eatonville, Florida. I am so involved with my own writing that I don't think there will be time for me to attempt the long, scholarly involvement that all these writers require. I am hopeful, however, that as their books are reissued and used in classrooms across the country, someone will do this. If no one does (or if no one does it to my satisfaction), I feel it is my duty (such is the fervor of love) to do it myself.

INTERVIEWER: Have women writers, then, influenced your writing more than male? Which writers do you think have had the most direct influence upon you?

WALKER: I read all of the Russian writers I could find, in my sophomore year in college. I read them as if they were a delicious cake. I couldn't get enough: Tolstoi (especially his short stories, and the novels, *The Kruetzer Sonata* and *Resurrection*—which taught me the importance of diving through politics and social forecasts to dig into the essential spirit of individual persons— because otherwise, characters, no matter what political or current social issue they stand for, will not live), and Dostoevsky, who found his truths where everyone else seemed afraid to look, and Turgenev, Gorky and Gogol—who made me think that Russia must have something floating about in the air that writers breathe from the time they are born. The only thing that began to bother me, many years later, was that I could find almost nothing written by a Russian woman writer.

Unless poetry has mystery, many meanings, and some ambiguities (necessary for mystery) I am not interested in it. Outside of Basho and Shiki and other Japanese haiku poets, I read and was impressed by the poetry of Li Po, the Chinese poet, Emily Dickinson, e.e. cummings (deeply) and Robert Graves—especially his poems in *Man Does, Woman Is;* which is surely a pure male-chauvinist title, but I did not think about that then. I liked Graves because he took it as given that passionate love between man and woman does not last forever. He enjoyed the moment, and didn't bother about the future. My poem, "The Man in the Yellow Terry," is very much influenced by Graves.

I also loved Ovid and Catullus. During the whole period of

discovering haiku and the sensual poems of Ovid, the poems of e.e. cummings and William Carlos Williams, my feet did not touch the ground. I ate, I slept, I studied other things (like European history) without ever doing more than giving it serious thought. It could not change me from one moment to the next, as poetry could.

I wish I had been familiar with the poems of Gwendolyn Brooks when I was in college. I stumbled on them later. If there was ever a *born* poet, I think it is Brooks. Her natural way of looking at anything, of commenting on anything, comes out as a vision, in language that is peculiar to her. It is clear that she is a poet from the way your whole spiritual past begins to float around in your throat when you are reading, just as it is clear from the first line of *Cane* that Jean Toomer is a poet, blessed with a soul that is surprised by nothing. It is not unusual to weep when reading Brooks, just as when reading Toomer's "Song of the Sun" it is not unusual to comprehend—in a flash—what a dozen books on black people's history fail to illuminate. I have embarrassed my classes occasionally by standing in front of them in tears as Toomer's poem about "some genius from the South" flew through my body like a swarm of golden butterflies on their way toward a destructive sun. Like DuBois, Toomer was capable of comprehending the black soul. It is not "soul" that *can* become a cliché, but rather something to be illuminated rather than explained.

The poetry of Arna Bontemps has strange effects on me too. He is a great poet, even if he is not recognized as such until after his death. Or is never acknowledged. The passion and compassion in his poem, "A Black Man Talks of Reaping," shook the room I was sitting in the first time I read it. The ceiling began to revolve and a breeze—all the way from Alabama—blew through the room. A tide of spiritual good health tingled the bottom of my toes. I changed. Became someone the same, but different. I understood, at last, what the transference of energy was.

It is impossible to list all of the influences on one's work. How can you even remember the indelible impression upon you of a certain look on your mother's face? But random influences are these: music; which is the art I most envy.

Then there's travel—which really made me love the world, its vastness, and variety. How moved I was to know that there is no center of the universe. Entebbe, Uganda or Bratislava, Czechoslovakia exist no matter what we are doing here. Some writers —Camara Laye, or the man who wrote *One Hundred Years of Solitude* (Gabriel Garcia Marquez)—have illumined this fact brilliantly in their fiction, which brings me to African writers I *hope* to be influenced by: Okot p'tek has written my favorite modern poem, "Song of Lawino." I am also crazy about *The Concubine* by Elechi Ahmadi (a perfect story, I think), *The Radiance of the King*, by Camara Laye, and *Maru,* by Bessie Head. These writers do not seem afraid of fantasy, of myth and mystery. Their work deepens one's comprehension of life by going beyond the bounds of realism. They are like musicians: at one with their cultures and their historical subconscious.

Flannery O'Connor has also influenced my work. To me, she is the best of the white southern writers, including Faulkner. For one thing, she practiced economy. She also knew that the question of race was really just the first question on a long list. This is hard for just about everybody to accept, we've been trying to answer it for so long.

I did not read *Cane* until 1967, but it has been reverberating in me to an astonishing degree. *I love it passionately;* could not possibly exist without it. *Cane* and *Their Eyes Were Watching God* are probably my favorite books by black American writers. Jean Toomer has a very feminine sensibility (or phrased another way, he is both feminine and masculine in his perceptions), unlike most black male writers. He loved women.

Like Toomer, Zora Neale Hurston was never afraid to let her characters be themselves, funny talk and all. She was incapable of being embarrassed by anything black people did, and so was able to write about everything with freedom and fluency. My feeling is that Zora Neale Hurston is probably one of the most misunderstood, least appreciated writers of this century. Which is a pity. She is great. A writer of courage, and incredible humor, with poetry in every line.

When I started teaching my course in black women writers at Wellesley (the first one, I think, ever), I was worried that

Zora's use of black English of the twenties would throw some of the students off. It didn't. They loved it. They said it was like reading Thomas Hardy, only better. In that same course I taught Nella Larsen, Frances Watkins Harper (poetry and novel), Dorothy West, Ann Petry, Paule Marshall, etc. Also Kate Chopin and Virginia Woolf—not because they were black, obviously, but because they were women and wrote, as the black women did, on the condition of humankind from the perspective of women. It is interesting to read Woolf's *A Room of One's Own* while reading the poetry of Phillis Wheatley, to read Larsen's *Quicksand* along with *The Awakening*. The deep-throated voice of Sojourner Truth tends to drift across the room while you're reading. If you're not a feminist already, you become one.

INTERVIEWER: Why do you think that the black woman writer has been so ignored in America? Does she have even more difficulty than the black male writer, who perhaps has just begun to gain recognition?

WALKER: There are two reasons why the black woman writer is not taken as seriously as the black male writer. One is that she's a woman. Critics seem unusually ill-equipped to intelligently discuss and analyze the works of black women. Generally, they do not even make the attempt; they prefer, rather, to talk about the lives of black women writers, not about what they write. And, since black women writers are not—it would seem— very likable—until recently they were the least willing worshipers of male supremacy—comments about them tend to be cruel.

In Nathan Huggins's very readable book, *Harlem Renaissance*, he hardly refers to Zora Neale Hurston's work, except negatively. He quotes from Wallace Thurman's novel, *Infants of the Spring*, at length, giving us the words of a character, "Sweetie Mae Carr," who is alledgedly based on Zora Neale Hurston. "Sweetie Mae" is a writer noted more "for her ribald wit and personal effervescence than for any actual literary work. She was a great favorite among those whites who went in for Negro prodigies." Mr. Huggins goes on for several pages, never quoting Zora Neale Hurston herself, but rather the opinions of others about her character. He does say that she was "a master of dialect," but adds that "Her greatest weakness was carelessness or indifference to her art."

Having taught Zora Neale Hurston, and of course, having read her work myself, I am stunned. Personally, I do not care if Zora Hurston was fond of her white women friends. When she was a child in Florida, working for nickels and dimes, two white women helped her escape. Perhaps this explains it. But even if it doesn't, so what? Her work, far from being done carelessly, is done (especially in *Their Eyes Were Watching God*) almost too perfectly. She took the trouble to capture the beauty of rural black expression. She saw poetry where other writers merely saw failure to cope with English. She was so at ease with her blackness it never occurred to her that she should act one way among blacks and another among whites (as her more sophisticated black critics apparently did).

It seems to me that black writing has suffered, because even black critics have assumed that a book that deals with the relationships between members of a black family—or between a man and a woman—is less important than one that has white people as a primary antagonist. The consequence of this is that many of our books by "major" writers (always male) tell us little about the culture, history, or future, imagination, fantasies, etc. of black people, and a lot about isolated (often improbable) or limited encounters with a nonspecific white world. Where is the book, by an American black person (aside from *Cane*), that equals Elechi Amadi's *The Concubine*, for example? A book that exposes the *subconscious* of a people, because the people's dreams, imaginings, rituals, legends, etc. are known to be important, are known to contain the accumulated collective reality of the people themselves. Or, in *The Radiance of the King*, the white person is shown to be the outsider he is, because the culture he enters into in Africa *itself* expels him. Without malice, but as nature expels what does not suit. The white man is mysterious, a force to be reckoned with, but he is not glorified to such an extent that the Africans turn their attention away from themselves and their own imagination and culture. Which is what often happens with "protest literature." The superficial becomes—for a time—the deepest reality, and replaces the still waters of the collective subconscious.

When my own novel was published, a leading black monthly admitted (the editor did) that the book itself was never read; but the magazine ran an item stating that a *white* reviewer had praised the book (which was, in itself, an indication that the book was no good—such went the logic) and then hinted that the reviewer had liked my book because of my life-style. When I wrote to the editor to complain, he wrote me a small sermon on the importance of my "image," of what is "good" for others to see. Needless to say, what others "see" of me is the least of my worries, and I assume that "others" are intelligent enough to recover from whatever shocks my presence might cause.

Women writers are supposed to be intimidated by male disapproval. What they write is not important enough to be read. How they live, however, their "image," they owe to the race. Read the reason Zora Neale Hurston gave for giving up her writing. See what "image" the Negro press gave her, innocent as she was. I no longer read articles or reviews unless they are totally about the work. I trust that someday a generation of men and women will arise who will forgive me for such wrong as I do not agree I do, and will read my work because it is a true account of my feelings, my perception, and my imagination, and because it will reveal something to them of their own selves. They will also be free to toss it—and me—out of a high window. They can do what they like.

INTERVIEWER: Have you felt a great deal of coercion to write the kind of fiction and poetry that black writers are "supposed" to write? Does this ever interfere with what you *want* to write?

WALKER: When I take the time to try to figure out what I am doing in my writing, where it is headed, and so on, I almost never can come up with anything. This is because it seems to me that my poetry is quite different from my novels (*The Third Life of Grange Copeland* and the one I am working on now); for example, *Once* is what I think of as a "happy" book, full of the spirit of an optimist who loves the world and all the sensations of caring in it; it doesn't matter that it began in sadness; *The Third Life of Grange Copeland,* though sometimes humorous and cele-brative of life, is a grave book in which the characters see the world as almost entirely menacing. The optimism that closes the book makes it different from most of my short stories, and the po-litical and personal content of my essays makes them different— again—from everything else. So I would not, as some critics have done, categorize my work as "gothic." I would not categorize it at all. Eudora Welty, in explaining why she rebels against being la-beled "gothic," says that to her "gothic" conjures up the supernatural, and that she feels what she writes has "something to do with real life." I agree with her.

I like those of my short stories that show the plastic, shaping, almost painting quality of words. In "Roselily" and "The Child Who Favors Daughter" the prose is poetry, or, prose and poetry run together to add a new dimension to the language. But the most that I would say about where I am trying to go is this: I am trying to arrive at that place where black music already is; to ar-rive at that unselfconscious sense of collective oneness; that natu-ralness, that (even when anguished) grace.

The writer—like the musician or painter—must be free to explore, otherwise she or he will never discover what is needed (by everyone) to be known. This means, very often, finding one-self considered "unacceptable" by masses of people who think that the writer's obligation is not to explore or to challenge, but to second the masses' motions, whatever they are. Yet the gift of loneliness is sometimes a radical vision of society or one's people that has not previously been taken into account. Toomer was, I think, a lonely, wandering man, accustomed to being tolerated and misunderstood—a man who made choices many abhorred— and yet, *Cane* is a great reward; though Toomer himself probably never realized it.

The same is true of Zora Neale Hurston. She is probably more honest in her fieldwork and her fiction, than she is in her autobiography, because she was hesitant to reveal how different she really was. It is interesting to contemplate what would have been the result and impact on black women—since 1937—if they had read and taken to heart *Their Eyes Were Watching God.*

Would they still be as dependent on material things—fine cars, furs, big houses, pots and jars of face creams—as they are today? Or would they, learning from Janie that materialism is the drag-rope of the soul, become a nation of women immune (to the extent that is possible in a blatantly consumerist society like ours) to the accumulation of things, and aware, to their core, that love, fulfillment as women, peace of mind, should logically come before, not after, selling one's soul for a golden stool on which to sit. Sit and be bored.

Hurston's book, though seemingly apolitical, is in fact, one of the most radical novels (without being a tract) we have.

INTERVIEWER: Christianity is implicitly criticized in your work. Is that because it has historically been both racist and anti-feminist?

WALKER: Although I am constantly involved, internally, with religious questions—and I seem to have spent all of my life rebelling against the church and other peoples' interpretations of what religion is—the truth is probably that I don't believe there is a God, although I would like to believe it. Certainly I don't believe there is a God beyond nature. The world is God. Man is God. So is a leaf or a snake. . . . So, when Grange Copeland refuses to pray at the end of the book, he is refusing to be a hypocrite. All his life he has hated the Church and taken every opportunity to ridicule it. He has taught his granddaughter, Ruth, this same humorous contempt. He does, however, appreciate the humanity of man-womankind as a God worth embracing. To him, the greatest value a person can attain is full humanity, which is a state of oneness with all things, and a willingness to die (or to live) so that the best that has been produced can continue to live in someone else. He "rocked himself in his own arms to a final sleep" because he understood that man is alone—in his life as in his death—without any God but himself (and the world).

Like many, I waver in my convictions about God, from time to time. In my poetry I seem to be for; in my fiction, against.

I am intrigued by the religion of the black Muslims. By what conversion means to black women, specifically, and what the religion itself means in terms of the black American past: our history, our "race memories" our absorption of Christianity, our *changing* of Christianity to fit our needs. What will the new rituals mean? How will this new religion imprint itself on the collective consciousness of the converts? Can women be free in such a religion? Is such a religion, in fact, an anachronism? So far I have dealt with this interest in two stories, "Roselily," about a young woman who marries a young Muslim because he offers her respect and security, and "Everyday Use" a story that shows respect for the "militance" and progressive agricultural programs of the Muslims, but at the same time shows skepticism about a young man who claims attachment to the Muslims because he admires the rhetoric. It allows him to acknowledge his contempt for whites, which is all he believes the group is about.

In other stories, I am interested in Christianity as an imperialist tool used against Africa ("Diary of an African Nun") and in Voodoo used as a weapon against oppression ("The Revenge of Hannah Kemhuff"). I see all of these as religious questions.

INTERVIEWER: Could you tell me about the genesis of your title poem "Revolutionary Petunias"? Why was "Sammy Lou" chosen as the heroine of the poem?

WALKER: The poem "Revolutionary Petunias" did not have a name when I sat down to write it. I wanted to create a person who engaged in a final struggle with her oppressor, and won, but who, in every other way, was "incorrect." Sammy Lou in the poem is everything she should not be: her name is Sammy Lou, for example; she is a farmer's wife; she works in the fields. She goes to church. The walls of her house contain no signs of her blackness—though that in itself reveals it; anyone walking into that empty house would know Sammy Lou is black. She is so incredibly "incorrect" that she is only amused when the various poets and folksingers rush to immortalize her heroism in verse and song. She did not think of her killing of her oppressor in that way. She thought—and I picture her as tall, lean, black, with short, badly straightened hair and crooked teeth—that killing is never heroic. Her reaction, after killing this cracker-person, would be to look up at the sky and not pray or ask forgiveness but to say—as if talking to an old friend—"Lord, you know my heart. I never wanted to have to kill nobody. But I couldn't hold out to the last, like Job. I had done took more than I could stand."

Sammy Lou is so "incorrect" she names her children after Presidents and their wives: she names one of them after the founder of the Methodist church. To her, this does not mean a limitation of her blackness, it means she feels she is so black she can absorb—and change—all things, since everybody knows that a black-skinned Jackie Kennedy still bears resemblance only to her own great aunt, Sadie Mae Johnson.

But the most "incorrect" thing about Sammy Lou is that she loves flowers. Even on her way to the electric chair she reminds her children to water them. This is crucial, for I have heard it said by one of our cultural visionaries that whenever you hear a black person talking about the beauties of nature, that person is not a black person at all, but a Negro. This is meant as a put-down, and it is. It puts down all of the black folks in Georgia, Alabama, Mississippi, Texas, Louisianna—in fact, it covers just about everybody's Mama. Sammy Lou, of course, is so "incorrect" she does not even know how ridiculous she is for loving to see flowers blooming around her unbearably ugly gray house. To be "correct" she should consider it her duty to let ugliness reign. Which is what "incorrect" people like Sammy Lou refuse to do.

Actually, the poem was to claim (as Toomer claimed the people he wrote about in *Cane* who, as you know, were all as "incorrect" as possible) the most incorrect black person I could, and to honor her as my own—on a level with, if not above the most venerated saints of the black revolution. It seems our fate to be incorrect (look where we live, for example), and in our incorrectness, stand.

Although Sammy Lou is more a rebel than a revolutionary (since you need more than one for a revolution) I named the poem "Revolutionary Petunias" because she is not—when you view her kind of person historically—isolated. She is part of an ongoing revolution. Any black revolution, instead of calling her "incorrect" will have to honor her single act of rebellion.

Another reason I named it "Revolutionary Petunias" is that I like petunias and like to raise them because you just put them in any kind of soil and they bloom their heads off—exactly, it seemed to me, like black people tend to do. (Look at the blues and jazz musicians, the blind singers from places like Turnip, Mississippi, the poets and writers and all-around blooming people you know, who—from all visible evidence—achieved their blooming by eating the air for bread and drinking muddy water for hope.) Then I thought too, of the petunias my mother gave me when my daughter was born, and of the story (almost a parable) she told me about them. Thirty-seven years ago, my mother and father were coming home from somewhere in their wagon—my mother was pregnant with one of my older brothers at the time —and they passed a deserted house where one lavender petunia was left, just blooming away in the yard (probably to keep itself company)—and my mother said Stop! let me go and get that petunia bush. And my father, grumbling, stopped, and she got it, and they went home, and she set it out in a big stump in the yard. It never wilted, just bloomed and bloomed. Every time the family moved (say twelve times) she took her petunia—and thirty-seven years later she brought me a piece of that same petunia bush. It had never died. Each winter it lay dormant and dead-looking, but each spring it came back, more lively than before.

What underscored the importance of this story for me is this: modern petunias do not live forever. They die each winter and the next spring you have to buy new ones.

In a way, the whole book is a celebration of people who will not cram themselves into any ideological or racial mold. They are all shouting Stop! I want to go get that petunia!

Because of this they are made to suffer. They are told that they do not belong, that they are not wanted, that their art is not needed, that nobody, who is "correct," could love what they love. Their answer is resistance, without much commentary; just a steady knowing that they stand at a point where—with one slip of the character—they might be lost, and the bloom they are after wither in the winter of self-contempt. They do not measure themselves against black people or white people; if anything, they learn to walk and talk in the presence of DuBois, Hurston,

Hughes, Toomer, Attaway, Wright, and others—and when they bite into their pillows at night these spirits comfort them. They are aware that the visions that created them were all toward a future where all people—and flowers too—can bloom. They require that in the midst of the bloodiest battles or revolution this thought not be forgotten.

When I married my husband there was a law that said I could not. When we moved to Mississippi three years after the lynching of Cheney, Schwerner and Goodman, it was a punishable crime for a black person and a white person of opposite sex to inhabit the same house. But I felt then—as I do now—that in order to be able to live at all in America I must be unafraid to live anywhere in it, and I must be able to live in the fashion and with whom I choose. Otherwise, I'd just as soon leave. If society (black or white) says, Then you must be isolated, an outcast—then I will be a hermit. Friends and relatives may desert me, but the dead—Douglass, DuBois, Hansberry, Toomer, and the rest—are a captive audience. . . . These feelings went into two poems, "Be Nobody's Darling," and "While Love is Unfashionable."

INTERVIEWER: There is one poem in *Revolutionary Petunias* which particularly interests me—"For My Sister Molly Who in the Fifties." Can you tell me about what went into the structuring of this rather long poem, and perhaps something about the background of it?

WALKER: "For My Sister Molly Who in the Fifties" is a pretty real poem. It really is about one of my sisters, a brilliant, studious girl who became one of those Negro Wonders—who collected scholarships like trading stamps and wandered all over the world. (Our home town didn't even have a high school, when she came along). When she came to visit us in Georgia it was—at first—like having Christmas with us all during her vacation. She loved to read and tell stories; she taught me African songs and dances; she cooked fanciful dishes that looked like anything but plain old sharecropper food. I loved her so much it came as a great shock —and a shock I don't expect to recover from—to learn she was ashamed of us. We were so poor, so dusty and sunburnt. We

talked wrong. We didn't know how to dress, or use the right eating utensils. And so, she drifted away, and I did not understand
it. Only later, I realized that sometimes (perhaps), it becomes too
painful to bear: seeing your home and family—shabby and seemingly without hope—through the eyes of your new friends and
strangers. She had felt—for her own mental health—that the gap
that separated us from the rest of the world was too wide for her
to keep trying to bridge. She understood how delicate she was.

I started out writing this poem in great anger; hurt, really. I
thought I could write a magnificiently vicious poem. Yet, even
from the first draft, it did not turn out that way. Which is one of
the great things about poetry. What you really feel, underneath
everything else, will present itself. Your job is not to twist that
feeling. So that although being with her now is too painful with
memories for either of us to be comfortable, I still retain (as I
hope she does) in memories beyond the bad ones, my picture of a
sister I loved, "Who walked among the flowers and brought them
inside the house, who smelled as good as they, and looked as
bright."

This poem (and my sister received the first draft, which is
hers alone, and the way I wish her to relate to the poem) went
through fifty drafts (at least) and I worked on it, off and on, for
five years. This has never happened before or since. I do not
know what to say about the way it is constructed other than to
say that as I wrote it the lines and words went, on the paper, to a
place comparable to where they lived in my head.

I suppose, actually, that my tremendous response to the
poems of W. C. Williams, cummings and Basho convinced me
that poetry is more like music—in my case, improvisational jazz,
where each person blows the note that she hears—than like a ca-
thedral, with every stone in a specific, predetermined place.
Whether lines are long or short depends on what the poem itself
requires. Like people, some poems are fat and some are thin. Personally, I prefer the short thin ones, which are always like painting the eye in a tiger (as Muriel Rukeyser once explained it). You
wait until the energy and vision are just right, then you write the
poem. If you try to write it before it is ready to be written you
find yourself adding stripes instead of eyes. Too many stripes and

the tiger herself disappears. You will paint a photograph (which is what is wrong with "Burial") instead of creating a new way of seeing.

The poems that fail will always haunt you. I am haunted by "Ballad of the Brown Girl" and "Johann" in *Once,* and I expect to be haunted by "Nothing is Right" in *Revolutionary Petunias.* The first two are dishonest, and the third is trite.

The poem "The Girl Who Died #2" was written after I learned of the suicide of a student at the college I attended. I learned, from the dead girl's rather guilty sounding "brothers and sisters" that she had been hounded constantly because she was so "incorrect," she thought she could be a black hippie. To top that, they tried to make her feel like a traitor because she refused to limit her interest to black men. Anyway, she was a beautiful girl. I was shown a photograph of her by one of her few black friends. She was a little brownskinned girl from Texas, away from home for the first time, trying to live a life she could live with. She tried to kill herself two or three times before, but I guess the brothers and sisters didn't think it "correct" to respond with love or attention, since everybody knows it is "incorrect" to even think of suicide if you are a black person. And, of course, black people do not commit suicide. Only colored people and Negroes commit suicide. (See "The Old Warrior Terror": Warriors, you know, always die on the battlefield). I said, when I saw the photograph, that I wished I had been there for her to talk to. When the school invited me to join their Board of Trustees, it was her face that convinced me. I know nothing about Boards and never really trusted them; but I can listen to problems pretty well. . . . I believe in listening—to a person, the sea, the wind, the trees, but especially to young black women whose rocky road I am still traveling.

John Wideman

After studying literature at Oxford as a Rhodes scholar, John Wideman published his first novel, *A Glance Away*, in 1967. His second novel, *Hurry Home*, came out three years later, and his third novel, *The Lynchers*, was published in 1973. His academic training shows up in allusions to and imitations of the literary figures he admires, especially T. S. Eliot. *A Glance Away* echoes the early poetry of Eliot both in mood and style and has a central character who—Wideman admits—resembles Prufrock. His second novel uses an Hieronymous Bosch painting as a controlling metaphor and structural device, as well as employing surrealistic techniques in its narrative method.

The Lynchers continues his thematic concern with race, identity, and the workings of the imagination, and reflects his earlier formal interest in myth, ritual, and symbol; yet this novel is very different in many ways. Whereas the first two novels mirrored Wideman's European influences, *The Lynchers* turns to wholly American themes, myths, diction, and locale. The novel revolves around the aborted effort of a group of young blacks to lynch a policeman in the South, an action which the author describes as the most ritualistic and symbolic in portraying racial relations in America. Though the lynching fails, its planning alters the lives of all those involved. It causes less a political upheaval than an imaginative one. And exploration of the imagination is the recurring and pervasive concern in all three novels. Out of necessity his characters are forced to push the imagination to its limits in an effort to order their lives and free themselves from the threatening experiences of the past. At the same time we are made aware that Wideman is as interested in solving the problems of life as he is in solving the problems of the novel, especially the experimental novel. His imagination, like his characters, is being tested to see whether it can reshape the inherited form of the novel or invent a new one.

At the time of the interview, which was conducted in a series of phone conversations in October of 1972, Wideman was at work on a series of interrelated short stories and a novel about the most native of American rituals—athletics. Currently, he teaches black literature and creative writing at the University of Pennsylvania.

INTERVIEWER: Your first two novels, *A Glance Away* and *Hurry Home,* are very differently conceived one from the other. The second experiments rather radically with the form of the novel.

WIDEMAN: Well, each book presented different kinds of problems. I would say in the first book, with a close reading, that you would see pretty quickly that I am interested in the formal aspects of the novel. I am doing apprenticeship work, I am going to school to various other writers, using other's techniques, but also trying out some things that I hope are original. I had a real interest in experimenting, in expanding the form of the novel even in the first book. I think then that the second book continues that. The first book was much less self-consciously organized; in the second book I thought a lot about what precisely I wanted to do from page one to the very last page. There was a progression in technique and craft in *Hurry Home,* so that I had a little more certainty about what I could do. I could set up goals or objectives far more consciously in it and I think this is even more true in *The Lynchers* because there I began the book with a completed plot. I could write a section and know that it was something that would be near the end of the novel.

INTERVIEWER: Is it more difficult when you are just beginning a novel to know how the parts will relate to the whole?

WIDEMAN: When you're beginning, even though you may be
telling yourself otherwise, the process is very much in bits and
pieces. You think there might be connections, but you're not
really sure. You never really can be sure until the last word is
written and you see what you have. For instance, *A Glance Away*
didn't begin as a novel. I wanted to write something long but it
didn't come. I kept writing shorter pieces. I had maybe fifteen or
twenty shorter pieces just lying around. Then I began to re-read
them and I suddenly found that two or three main characters
emerged if I cut out about ten of the stories. So it became very
natural to think of ways of putting these bits and pieces together.
But I tried with all three books to set up a regular work-schedule.
In that way, whether or not you have an idea, you're producing
something. There is a lot of brute work involved in getting several thousand words down on paper. It takes time, but you have
to do that at some stage, whether the words are very polished or
not. You have to get the raw material down.

INTERVIEWER: Do you think of *A Glance Away* as being a
realistic novel?

WIDEMAN: It starts off with a warning that it is not going to
be totally realistic. The Prologue uses many poetic rather than
traditional prose devices for organization. It warns any reader
that he is not going to be able to effect a traditional kind of relationship to the material following the Prologue. So it moves
pretty quickly away from realistic convention. By the end it attempts to orchestrate on the page the inner thoughts of people
and treat those in the same way a conventional novel would treat
dialogue; and there are levels of interaction between the characters' minds that permit them to roll over time and place. All of
that makes it not at all a realistic novel.

INTERVIEWER: There seems to me to be a tension in both
novels, perhaps most pronounced in *Hurry Home*, between traditionally realistic content and your interest in innovative forms.

WIDEMAN: There were contradictions in my own experience that meant that on the one hand I had a great concern for and a great store of realistic material from which I could draw in a very concrete way. On the other hand, I had quite a bit of formal training in literature so that I just couldn't sit down and write a book that didn't show some consciousness of my literary as well as my actual experience.

INTERVIEWER: One of those literary voices that keeps echoing in *A Glance Away* is that of T. S. Eliot. What has been Eliot's influence on you?

WIDEMAN: As with most complex relationships there are various stages. The first stage was when I was a sophomore or junior in high school. I read *The Waste Land* and there was no way in the world that I could get through the ramifications of the poem. Ten or fifteen years later I read in an interview with Ellison that he had had a similar reaction to Eliot. As I grew older I came to understand the whole texture of the poem, its tonal qualities, the effects of the movement from vernacular to high literary speech, the echoes of foreign languages. But I think that I share some of Eliot's vision as well, particularly in *Hurry Home* and now in *The Lynchers*, because one of the themes that Eliot is dealing with is cultural collapse.

INTERVIEWER: Have there been more recent influences upon your writing?

WIDEMAN: About five years ago I began to read other black writers and I began teaching a course in black literature. This whole exposure has been crucial in my development as a writer. It awakened in me a different sense of self-image and the whole notion of a third world. The slave narratives, folklore, and the novels of Richard Wright and Ralph Ellison have been most important to me. And these things are just beginning to become embodied in the things that I write. Toomer's *Cane* as an individual work was very important to me because of its experimentation and open form and also because of Toomer's vision. But actually

I go back to the eighteenth century and the beginning of the novel when I talk about influences of experimentalists—to Defoe, Fielding, and particularly Laurence Sterne. If there is any single book I learned a hell of a lot from, it's *Tristram Shandy*. My scholarly work at Oxford was on the development of the novel in this period. It's interesting that the novel began by imitating facts or what passed itself off as fact, and now we have novels imitating novels.

INTERVIEWER: Do you think that this preoccupation of the contemporary writer with form is changing?

WIDEMAN: There are indications that the pendulum is swinging back again. Someone like John Fowles gives you story, plot, and a lot of the old nineteenth-century trimmings. *The Lynchers* is also in a very realistic tradition. I hope that I have learned from the nonrepresentational school about fantasy and playing around with different forms. The novel started out with these two tendencies—realism and fantasy. *The Lynchers* is in part plot-oriented; I wanted to create drama and get the reader involved with it. On the other hand, the subject of the book is imagination. The novel absorbs some of the philosophical assumptions that caused experiments in form over the last several years, and attempts to merge them with a more traditional plot-line.

INTERVIEWER: Is it a safe generalization to say that the processes of the imagination is the underlying thematic consideration that pervades all three of your novels?

WIDEMAN: (laughing) That's a valid enough generalization. In various conversations you recreate the books you've written and at different times you understand different things about them; it is tied up with your perceptions at the moment. In my last two books I had imagination on my mind, I had notes in my journals and wrote about how to capture some of the ambiguities about imagination. It's a unifying theme in the novels and is something that is very much on my mind at the moment. It's a natural preoccupation because the imagination plays such a powerful role in the relationship between blacks and whites in America, which is also a predominant theme in my work. It's not what we are, it's what we think we are. From the very beginning Western civilization has an idea of what black men are, and that idea has come down to us generation after generation, has distorted and made impossible some kinds of very human and basic interaction. The mechanics of that are both very frightening and very fascinating. I'm sure that it comes out in my work all the time. In *The Lynchers* it doesn't make any difference whether the conspirators pull their plot off or not, it doesn't make any difference whether we have an Armageddon in America or not; what does matter is what certain social realities have pushed these characters to, what attitudes are taken by both blacks and whites. In fact, a subterranean apocalypse does come to pass because people are changed more by their imagination than they are by actual external events.

INTERVIEWER: The first several pages of *The Lynchers* are made up of quotations from various sources about slavery and racism. Was your purpose for using these to break down the distinction between the "real" and the "fictional"?

WIDEMAN: All the quotations are actually taken from newspapers and documents. I wanted to immerse the reader in a reality that for one reason or another he wasn't ready to accept, one which under normal circumstances would seem fantastic to him. I thought this might be a traumatic way of introducing him into a different kind of world. Somehow documents have a different kind of resonance from fiction. I do not have to try to convince anybody that those things happened. They happened; that's all. So when the reader gets involved in the other imaginative world that the novel comprises, perhaps some of his defenses are down.

INTERVIEWER: Can you remember what the genesis was for *Hurry Home?*

WIDEMAN: My best friend in Pittsburgh lived with an aunt and uncle and I noticed that the uncle had a lot of framed documents on the wall. I never payed much attention to the uncle. Then one day I was waiting for my friend and I looked at these things and they were really quite prestigious credentials. One of them was a law degree. Who he was and what he was stuck in my mind. Why would a black man who went through law school and made all the sacrifices one must make to do that, then just disappear, just decide to go down a different path altogether? I attempted to answer that question in the book.

INTERVIEWER: The last line of *Hurry Home* is "So Cecil dreamed." There are suggestions throughout the second and third sections of the novel that all that transpires may be taking place in Cecil's mind or fantasy. Does this line invite us to wonder whether any of this has really happened except in a kind of dream? In what sense might it be a dream?

WIDEMAN: I don't want the ending to be a trick. I don't want it to negate what's come before. Rather than that, I hope that the reader sees that what was specifically Cecil's experience becomes conflated with the whole collective history of his race, that there is a thin line between individual and collective experience which permits one to flow into the other. It has to do with imagination. Cecil can suffer because somebody centuries ago suffered on a slave ship. In the novel this happens through an imaginary voyage, but I feel very strongly that people have this capacity to move over time and space in just such an empathetic way. It's almost silly to talk about whether it's a fantasy or whether it's happening because all of our experience has that same collapsible quality. It's a question of trying to blur that line between dream and reality.

INTERVIEWER: Then, as with Stephen Dedalus, history is a dream?

WIDEMAN: History is a spiraling process. "So he dreamed" follows a metaphor about the garbage cans and how in the moonlight there seemed to be circles going around the cans and they seemed to be endless. The question of "So he dreamed" and this metaphor go together. They recapitulate the way the book has been moving and they pose again the question that Cecil asks throughout the book, "Why did you do that?" To go back into one's past is in fact dreaming. What is history except people's imaginary recreation? In one generation you have Charlemagne the hero, and in the next he's the villain. You have Christians writing history, you have Muslims writing history, you have blacks writing history. Each will create a myth. And so too if you're asking about somebody's life. You will find various versions, you will get various dreamers. It's appropriate to look at Cecil's attempt to go back into his past and to create an identity as also an attempt to create a dream. There is an arbitrariness in meaning that is somehow close to the logic of dreams. The line between Cecil's actual past and his dream past—what is it? Where is it?

INTERVIEWER: The only way that he can find an answer to who he is and what he has done is by returning to the past?

WIDEMAN: In attempting to answer the question that is formulated at the beginning of the novel, "Why did you do that?" Cecil realizes he must go back very far and he also realizes that in an essential way he didn't have a past, that he was surrounded by certain versions of himself, that he had no history, or at least he was presumed to have no history. So he sets out to find whether that's true. That's one of the imperatives—"Why did you do that?"—"Why did you throw that can down the steps early in the morning and wake people up?" Well, he doesn't know the answer. He just picked up the kind of ethic that says, "Go to law school, pull yourself up by your bootstraps, hustle, get ahead." So, he had made tremendous personal sacrifices and cut himself off from so many things. He had gotten his law degree but he didn't understand why he had done any of the things he had done. In that sense his past was invisible to him as well as it was invisible to the culture. He just decided that, after having made so many decisions in the dark, he had to lime out some of his background, he had to delineate it, he had to understand why he was doing what he was doing, he had to make sense of the present.

INTERVIEWER: Does that question change in its meaning each time it occurs?

WIDEMAN: I hope that "Why did you do that?" has a symphonic effect, that it accrues meaning with each instance. At first it might be the very specific question of why he threw the can down the steps; but it is also "Why did you go to law school?" "Why did you go to Europe?" "Why did you go to Africa?" "Why have you chosen the kind of life you've chosen?" I hope that this question spirals. As you go deeper and deeper into it you find out that it has ever-widening circles of significance. You will remember that when Cecil throws the can down the stairwell, it unfolds in a spiral movement.

INTERVIEWER: Is part of Cecil's journey into the past made possible through racial memory?

WIDEMAN: Racial memories exist in the imagination. I believe that there are certain collective experiences that get passed on. I don't know whether through the genes, but there may be other processes that science doesn't have the slightest idea about. Certain things have been repeated generation after generation so that there are archtypes. A man like Cecil is not simply a product of a family; his family reaches out toward larger and larger circles. One can read what an African said about slavery and if he's a sensitive reader then that may strike something in his memory. Once that happens you have a synthesis so that the individual memory becomes larger. The individual identity becomes merged with someone else's from a past generation.

INTERVIEWER: Were you consciously working with certain myths in the novel? Did they—as much as the plot—help to structure Cecil's experiences?

WIDEMAN: I'm sure that to some degree these things are conflated in my own mind, but I can list for you any number of informing myths that relate to various episodes. Cecil's passage through the black section of town on his way to get a haircut, after he has returned home, more or less parallels the Passion, and he is in fact crucified by his own people just as Christ was crucified by the Jews. That archtype is there. The shoeshine boy corresponds to a specific character in the Biblical story; there is a crowd there and the whole episode is structured around Saint John's version of the Passion. And I had in mind the tone and music of both Bach and Heinrich Schütz. In fact part of the narrative is a direct statement from the Schütz *Saint John Passion*. When Cecil goes back to Africa his Uncle Otis tells him the story about Roderic and the Visigoths and the Moors. All that is based upon an actual story. Otis also repeats the story of Tarik, the Moorish warrior who led the invasion of Spain. There are innumerable other legends and myths that act as an underpinning, that give plot to the specific plot that the novel has. Of course, on another level there are much larger kinds of informing myths—Cecil is questing for his own identity, the return to the womb, the return to his birthplace, man's cyclical journey.

INTERVIEWER: Cecil sees a relationship between his experience and what he sees in Bosch's paintings. Did Bosch have an influence upon you as you were writing *Hurry Home?* Were the last two sections of the novel in any way a novelistic imitation of a Bosch painting?

WIDEMAN: I used Bosch for tone, exaggeration, and the surrealistic manner that I sometimes employed. But also for specific details. Under a picture of Bosch is where two of the characters meet, and the pretext for going to Europe is to see the real thing. The picture is used again outside The Proto where Cecil meets a friend and they talk about Bosch. So, it's a narrative thread as well as being a tonal influence. I don't think that it's necessary for anyone to have a great familiarity with the painter to understand the book, but I think that if you are acquainted with his work, then you share some of the visual excitement.

INTERVIEWER: The last question I want to ask is how the title of *A Glance Away* is related to the novel as a whole?

WIDEMAN: I wanted to take a character who was in pretty bad shape and lift him out of his environment and place him back in again and see if in fact he could start fresh. That means that one of the things the book is concerned with is time. At one point a character becomes conscious in looking at his mother's face that she has aged. The way time passes sometimes makes time seem like no more than a "glance" and a "glance away." When you look away from somebody you open up this immensity of time, this gap that is almost impossible to talk about in terms of years or days or seconds. That's a rather terrifying idea. If you look away from somebody you really don't know what is going to be there when you look back. This has to do with history, it has to do with the relationship of the two people, and some strange thing about time. In your own life you see this arbitrariness of time; ten years can seem much less important than ten seconds.

John Williams

Although John A. Williams was already thirty-five when he published his first novel in 1960, in the next twelve years he produced five more novels, a biography of Richard Wright, a journal of his travels through the United States in 1963, a controversial appraisal of the Martin Luther King movement, and edited several other books. Along with Ralph Ellison and James Baldwin, Williams has enjoyed more critical attention than any other contemporary black novelist. But the interest has been an unbalanced one. As his critics point out, Williams is indeed concerned with racial, social, and political themes in his fiction. However, such material enables Williams to focus on the philosophical and psychological issues that are the core of his work. The situation of blacks in America provides him with the perfect metaphor for studying the nature and influence of history, for testing whether man, either as an individual or a race, can transcend the role that history seems to have determined for him. As Williams always reminds us, the individual black must not only struggle with his own past but with his race's. In his most recent novel, *Captain Blackman*, Williams actually has his character, a soldier in Vietnam, move back in time to re-experience all the American wars in which blacks have fought, because he must understand the past in order to make sense of the present.

To one degree or another all of Williams' characters are

trying to break free from the limitations that history has placed upon them. In *The Angry Ones* (1960) Steve Hill insists upon and claims the social and economic rights that have been denied the black man in America. His triumph is that he marries and finds a good job. Ralph Joplin of *Sissie* (1963) discovers that he must not only be free from the external forms of racism but also from the deep psychic scars that prejudice has inflicted. His success lies in his ability to understand and accept the peculiar psychological conflicts which he finds only blacks are heir to. Williams' later novels, *The Man Who Cried I Am* (1967) and *Sons of Darkness, Sons of Light* (1969), are directed outward toward institutional racism and entertain the possibility of changing the course of history through political involvement. The hero of *The Man Who Cried I Am* is a writer who learns that direct political action alone can create the necessary changes. Eugene Browning in *Sons of Darkness, Sons of Light* (1969) carries that realization one step further and begins a revolution.

While Williams' characters struggle with the political realities around them, they must also contend with guilt. Stated simply, Williams conceives of a moral universe in which man survives only by violating that moral system. For instance, Ralph and Iris Joplin in *Sissie* find it necessary to reject their mother but they cannot escape the moral and psychological consequences of their act. Such guilt is relieved through the passage of time and through the discovery of love which makes the guilt worth bearing. Love rescues them both from a hostile society and from their own divided selves. Yet, by the later novels Williams suggests that personal love can exist only when the individual has already committed himself to improving the conditions of all men. Whereas the characters of the first three novels could find love regardless of the threatening social and political atmosphere about them, the characters of the last three novels, if they are to keep their private love intact, must turn it outward to include all men. In effect, the private and the public, the personal and the political, must be fused if either is to endure.

The interview was conducted on a bright chilly day in early November of 1971. We talked continuously for about two hours. Williams was cordial but reserved. As his remarks in the interview make clear, he approaches critics with caution. He speaks in a low, subdued voice, letting the words carry the weight of his meaning. The following February he expanded a few of his original answers and responded to several new questions. I began the interview by asking Mr. Williams about his article "The Literary Ghetto," in which he attacked critics and publishers for their continued but more subtle forms of racist treatment of black writers.

INTERVIEWER: You said in an article that appeared in *The Saturday Review* that you wished for once that you could read a review of a novel by a black writer in which it wasn't compared only to novels by other black writers. Does such treatment of black writers have its roots in racism?

WILLIAMS: I think it's racism and I think it's something that black writers dealt with, with accommodating behavior, for several years, and we still do. The fact is that when you can point out the elements of racism in the business as I did in that article, it doesn't make a goddamn bit of difference. They still do it. On the soft cover of *The Man Who Cried I Am*, it says, "The best novel about blacks since Ralph Ellison." That is defining the territory where black writers are allowed to roam. But you know, I'm a contemporary of Styron, Mailer, and Bruce J. Friedman. Chester Himes and Richard Wright were contemporaries of Hemingway, toward his later years. And Ellison. But we never somehow get into the area where we're compared with white contemporaries. It's always with black contemporaries. What else can you say, except that it is racism?

INTERVIEWER: The point of the article then was that comparisons should be made along literary rather than racial lines?

WILLIAMS: Well, yes, sure . . . I'd like for somebody to begin stacking up *Native Son* with some of Frank Norris' stuff, and I'd like to see Chester Himes stacked up to some of these detective story writers and some of the fiction writers who are still writing fiction from his generation. I'd like to see how I'd stack up against Styron and others who are my contemporaries. Now this doesn't mean that I'm seeking to divest myself of my identity. But I think that one of the reasons why these comparisons are not made in many cases is that black writers would come out better. It's sort of like with Jack Johnson, the heavyweight champion. You can't have those black guys winning at everything, or even looking as though they could possibly win. That's bad business. Things begin to happen to the economic structure of the literary world.

INTERVIEWER: Do you think that black writers are doing things to the form of the American novel which simply are not understood by readers and critics?

WILLIAMS: In terms of form itself, the novel is changing. I think that black writers are initiating—if not forcing—a kind of change from the "straight ahead" American novel, vis-à-vis, Hemingway and Fitzgerald. There's an inclination to do to the novel what Charlie Parker did to jazz. I don't know whether you remember this period in jazz music that is called "Bop," where the method was to take . . . well, you could take any tune that was standard, say "Stardust," for example. They would go through it once and then would come through again with all their improvisations, so that it was only recognizable in part. You knew where the players were at certain points in the music, and only by virtue of touching on those old standard parts in the second passage through did you realize that it was really "Stardust." That's the way it works. And I think that's what's happening to the novel. You see it in William Melvin Kelley's last book, *Dunford's Travels Everywheres*, which is not only an exercise in form but also an exercise in language. Ishmael Reed's books. George Lamming has a book which just came out called *Natives of My Person* which is an allegory about seventeenth-century English slave trade. I read novels like these and it's incredible. You're reading English but it comes through in such a way that it doesn't seem like English; it comes through like Spanish, French . . . anything else than what you're familiar with.

INTERVIEWER: Is the difference between what these writers are doing and what white writers are doing mainly a literary one, or is there something else too?

WILLIAMS: I think that there is a difference in approach to "consciousness" between black and white writers. I don't think white writers have ever had to consciously or subconsciously concern themselves about real problems of life and survival. You can take Salinger's Holden Caulfield. The mentality that issues forth from books like that is that the evil is not within us. It's an outside thing, which perhaps has to be combated. But it's going to be combated on white horses by white knights in white suits of armor. There's no question about it. There's no concern expressed for the world that's not white. The difference with black writers is that their concern has been made extremely conscious, not only by their position in the literary world—the editors and critics— but also by virtue of their awareness of what the situation is.

INTERVIEWER: Then the black writer has been forced to be more concerned with social and political issues just because of his position in society?

WILLIAMS: I think "forced" is the right word. There are many, many black writers today, and in the Renaissance, and even prior to that, who would have been happy to have had acceptance on the terms of being a writer. I think it's the critics who have made the decision for us. By boxing us into an area where our books have been labeled "protest." A very narrow pigeonhole. And I think it sort of deprived us of the ability to mirror through our work all of humanity. So "forced" is a good word, forced in terms of our area being well defined, well drawn for us.

INTERVIEWER: Do you think of yourself as belonging to a realistic tradition in fiction? Have you purposely avoided experimentation?

WILLIAMS: I suppose I am a realistic writer. I've been called a melodramatic writer, but I think that's only because I think the ending of a novel should be at the ending of the book. Not on page sixty-two or page twenty-five. In terms of experimenting, I think that I've done some very radical things with form in *The Man Who Cried I Am* and in *Captain Blackman,* which had to be an experimental novel in order to hold the theme of the novel. What I try to do with novels is to deal in forms that are not standard, to improvise as jazz musicians do with their music, so that a standard theme comes out looking brand new. This is all I try to do with a novel and, like those musicians, I am trying to do things with form that are not always immediately perceptible to most people.

INTERVIEWER: Do you recall your first attempts at serious writing? How old were you? What kind of things were you writing?

WILLIAMS: I started writing when I was overseas in the Navy during the War, and it wasn't very good. It was mostly what one would call "free verse" poetry. I always had a feeling that I was capable of being a writer. I never felt that I was deluding myself by trying to be a writer. The problem with writing, for me personally, lay outside writing itself. It was considered an illness to be involved in the arts since in the black community there were no artists to speak of. One did not earn one's keep by writing poetry or novels. That was out there in never never never land. What I really wanted to do was get a good job, work from nine to five, or ten to four, and live in that fashion. But it became clear to me after several years that even so simple a thing as that was subject to stresses because of discrimination. It was only then that I turned to writing fulltime. Pretty much for the same reason James Baldwin did, to remain sane, to feel that one was really in touch with oneself, that you were not a ghost, but a functioning person capable of thinking and perceiving and feeling.

INTERVIEWER: Have you gone through periods where you felt that you had said everything there was to say, or periods where you felt that your writing was not accomplishing what you wanted it to?

WILLIAMS: I don't go through periods now when I think that I won't be able to write again because of some mental block. But I do feel occasionally that I've said just about all I wanted to say. But after a few days that passes. I've also had the feeling that writing has not moved things as much as I wanted things to be moved and perhaps there might be something else I could do that would get things done. To this extent I've considered quitting writing simply because it hasn't, for myself, produced the things I want to see produced, the things I feel must be produced within my lifetime. But you get past that feeling with the passage of time.

INTERVIEWER: Have you observed any pattern in how ideas for novels come to you? Must you experience most of the things you write about?

WILLIAMS: No, I haven't observed any pattern. I've had some ideas for novels for several years without putting down a line, and every time I think of these ideas I add something more. I don't believe in outlines, at least they've never worked for me. When I finally sit down to write, I'm off and running because I've had the material stored up for so long. I would prefer to experience certain things myself, but I know that's not absolutely necessary. I can project on the basis of my own experiences, the experiences of others, and the testimony of still other people.

INTERVIEWER: Is any one part of a novel more difficult to write than another? Do you hit any lags, perhaps after you get the basic action down? Is there a kind of crisis point after which —if you get past—you know that everything else will fall into place?

WILLIAMS: For me the first fifty pages of a novel are the hardest. This may be a psychological thing. After I hit fifty pages

I know that I've got a novel. It's not that the conception of the novel is difficult for me. But by the end of the first fifty pages I've smoothed out the form and I've got the structure licked. Then I'm off from that point.

INTERVIEWER: Could you describe your work habits? Where do you write? How much each day?

WILLIAMS: I work every day. The time can vary from three to five hours, with many, many breaks in between. If it's going well I'll work at night as well, up to maybe nine o'clock or so. I no longer feel that I have to have a certain kind of atmosphere. In fact I never felt that way. I've always prided myself on being able to write anywhere, and I guess I still can. I have no ritual to go through in order to prepare myself for writing. I sit down and I write, although I have had periods when I have the urge to sharpen about two dozen pencils or polish shoes. It's not a ritual as much as it is giving myself time to think about being consciously aware of thinking of what I am going to deal with that morning, where I have to go back over the work I had done the day before, what it is I am going to repair or change or heighten.

INTERVIEWER: Can you recall the circumstances in which you began working on *The Angry Ones*? Did you have any difficulty in finding a publisher for your first novel?

WILLIAMS: It was in some ways a very autobiographical novel. I felt very intensely about that book and about things that were happening to me at the time. I once rewrote the whole damn book in a day and a half at one sitting because there seemed to be the possibility of it being published by New American Library. The preliminary reports had been good but after that day and a half of rewriting that book, it was turned down. It had been turned down by a number of publishers. What made me sit down and write the book in the first place was that I didn't have anything else to do. It was a question of holding on to my sanity, a question of writing down some of the things that had happened to me. Seeing those situations in print made me rather determined never to forget them. That gave me a new grip on life, feeling that there was a lot out there that I had to do.

INTERVIEWER: Are you conscious of having been influenced by other writers?

WILLIAMS: Nobody has really influenced me. This is because I read without discrimination when I was a great deal younger. In terms of form, my single influence has been Malcolm Lowry in *Under the Volcano*. I tried to emulate him in *Sissie* and improve on what he did with the telescoping of time. But I think I did it much better in *The Man Who Cried I Am*.

INTERVIEWER: What nonliterary influences have there been on your work?

WILLIAMS: I don't really know. I've read an awful lot of history. A great deal of it pre-ancient history. I sometimes get very depressed because I know that all of this business is quite temporary. We become too self-important about our society, our crafts and skills, our families, and so on. I believe, with some other people, that human life on this planet goes in cycles. We're here for maybe ten, twenty, thirty thousand years. And then something happens, a cataclysm, and the poles start sliding around, and it's all gone. Then you start evolving again. I suppose I'm one of the rare guys you'll talke to who believes this. Nonetheless, I'm here, and I'm sort of constrained to act in patterns that are normal for the time I live in. And I suppose that happens so that you'll have some assurance of life existing even after a cataclysm. I don't know what you would call all this. I'm pessimistic about the progress that humans are going to make with each other within the timespan that we have, how many hundreds or thousands of years that may be.

INTERVIEWER: Do you think that music has influenced you?

WILLIAMS: I've always liked jazz and some classical music. If I had been from a well-to-do family when I was a child I would have been a trumpeter. But when the time came to move on to a trumpet we simply could not afford it. I haven't been too much for music lately. I don't know why, whether or not it has to do with work. . . . You're too busy playing the baby's records. But I like music, and I always say, "we ought to play a stack of records on Saturday or Sunday." But we never do. Somehow I wind up watching football games, just like any other piece of stone on Sunday afternoon.

INTERVIEWER: Have you felt the influence of Albert Camus?

WILLIAMS: Maybe, I don't really know. I just don't know. These are things I think about. I can't say I consciously move about as a devotee of any particular philosophy.

INTERVIEWER: Which of your novels are you most pleased with?

WILLIAMS: Well, I guess that I keep changing novels because I do different things with each one. Out of two previously published novels my preference was for *Sissie*. That was before I wrote *The Man Who Cried I Am*. I felt that in that novel I said things better and with a vehicle that had infinitely more horsepower. In the novel coming out in May, I think something different is taking place and I think that I brought that off well. So, I liked that too. Maybe when I am sixty or seventy years old I can look back and really see the differences and see which one I like. But now, things keep changing. I liked *Sons of Light, Sons of Darkness* least of all.

INTERVIEWER: Why is that?

WILLIAMS: It's a potboiler. I just feel that it came too easily.
It was one of those novels that I don't like very much, that I call
a "straight ahead" novel. You start at A and wind up at Z and
then you get off the train.

INTERVIEWER: Has *The Man Who Cried I Am* had the most
critical acclaim?

WILLIAMS: That is what I keep hearing. But I think I hear it
for the wrong reasons. People keep talking about "King Alfred."
There were many other things in that novel besides "King Alfred"
but all they talk about is "King Alfred." I can't say that that
pleases me too much, although I believe there exists such a plan
as this. The acclaim has been political. I wouldn't mind so much
if it was both political and literary. But the literary acclaim has
been missing.

INTERVIEWER: It's been suggested that some of the characters
in *The Man Who Cried I Am* are paralleled by real life figures,
that Richard Wright is represented by one of the characters and
yourself by another.

WILLIAMS: I think that there are elements that could be
taken as the character of Richard Wright. Actually the character
that everyone thinks is me, is only me partially. I had Chester
Himes in mind.

INTERVIEWER: Max and Harry in that novel are two authors
who are forced into becoming politically conscious and active.

WILLIAMS: I think "political" is a big word, but I think I
know what you mean. And you're right. They have been forced
into this kind of political role. And when I say political role,
what I'm talking about is a larger humanistic role. It's outside the
scope of just putting books together. The thrust may be political,

per se, involving what your government is doing, but it is also an involvement in what other people are doing. It's being concerned about people, somehow relating to them, even with all their personal problems. I like to think that important writers are without flaws in terms of how they deal with other people. I feel this and sometimes say to myself that this is very childish. I think that a man who is a writer, who is good with words, should have an obligation to be a good man in his day-to-day life. It would be nice if the writer did have the responsibility to be more humane with people. Unfortunately we know that this isn't true. You can talk of Faulkner, or you can talk about Dostoevsky, bigots both.

INTERVIEWER: Do you see certain similarities between the heroes in all your novels? Is it essentially the same hero?

WILLIAMS: Some people say that it's the same character in each book, that he goes through all the books. I think to a large extent they're different characters. If you wanted to be strict about it, you could say that literally they're the same character. If you wanted to be most strict about it, you could say that they are the same two characters. Steve's confidant is Obie. In *Night Song* the characters would be Keel and Eagle. In *Sissie*, it's Ralph and his sister. In *The Man Who Cried I Am* it's Max and Harry. In *Sons of Darkness* the two actually are Hod and his girl. In my new novel, *Captain Blackman,* the protagonist runs throughout the story. He's one man. He is the person around whom the whole story revolves, but there are other people who are pulled into the story as the story progresses. And they flush it out from a point of view that Captain Blackman could not possibly see it from. With two characters you can more fully develop a situation than you could with only one who would have to be babbling off at the mouth all of the time, or thinking all of the time for the reader to get the complete story. I've always felt that I need two people to handle the dialogue, to move it, two people who know each other well. I find that too much narrative becomes a pain in the ass. You get on a roller coaster and start breaking out the flags. Dialogue is always better.

INTERVIEWER: Do you see a progression in your heroes? In your first novel the hero is in search of a good job; in your most recent novel the hero starts a revolution.

WILLIAMS: Wait till you read the next one (laughing).

INTERVIEWER: Is there a difference between what Steve thinks is necessary to be human and what Eugene does?

WILLIAMS: I think so. Browning thinks in revolutionary terms out of the boredom and frustration of middle-class existence. And Steve, who hasn't had that, is thinking of getting where Browning is. He's not thinking about a revolution: he's thinking about three squares and a nine-to-five routine.

INTERVIEWER: Most of your characters have a need for and are in search of love. If they find it, they are saved.

WILLIAMS: I believe in love. Which means that I live in a society. I also believe that all things, revolutions included, begin with individuals and individual choices.

INTERVIEWER: Then love is looked to as a kind of ultimate solution?

WILLIAMS: I don't see that anything else has worked. Not even money. And I think that love grows out of some kind of respect. Most people just don't understand it or the processes of it. It's the only thing that can work.

INTERVIEWER: There seems to be a progression from the first novel, where money is thought to be a final solution, to the second novel, where love seems to take that place.

WILLIAMS: Well, yes, but that's in the realm of books. I think economically things were better in the second novel. Not much, but better. When you get to *Sissie,* of course, ostensibly, things are even better. You've got Ralph running around Europe . . . and—it's not necessarily true—but it seems that anybody running around Europe must have the money to get back. He has some kind of economic status, however small. And as my own economic condition has improved, I think this has been matched by the conditions of the characters in my books. One of the books I'm working on now deals with a guy who has worked in a foundry for twenty-five years, but even so he owns a house in a fairly exclusive neighborhood. He's probably the only guy on the block who works with his hands. I spend a great deal of time in the opening chapter describing his kitchen, and the car which he loves (a big four-hundred-horsepower job). You've got a black man who appears to be economically solvent and perhaps he is. But he's still black and what that really means is that he's never really secure.

INTERVIEWER: The theme of racial assimilation was important in your first novel and perhaps not as important in some of the later ones. Did your views change?

WILLIAMS: I tell everybody that regardless of whatever "revolutionary movement" is now current, I think we've got assimilation and there is probably more of it, in spite of a necessary period of separatism. There's got to be integration. People are deluding themselves by saying that we won't have it. This particular neighborhood is sort of a post-Village neighborhood and interracial couples are fairly frequent. If you had time to walk around on a nicer day you'd see it. It's pretty incredible. And there's more of it now than there was ten or fifteen years ago. I think that there is a lot of talk going on about how little there is and how many people are opposed to it. And I'm sure that certain so-called militants really mean it when they say they're opposed to it. But I've seen changes in the philosophy of Nicki Giovanni who lives two blocks away from here. I've been over to her place a few times, and you know she was vigorously opposed to any kind of interracial marriage. I don't know what brought about the change, certainly not us [Williams and his wife] because we're not that close. But I see changes taking place. I had a run-in with Don Lee over this situation. In his review of *The Man Who Cried I Am,* he brought in my marriage on the tail end of it . . . I told him I thought it was out of order. We almost came to pretty good blows there. We've since made peace.

INTERVIEWER: Are you conscious of your usual treatment of white liberals in your novels? Without exception, I think, they wind up exploiting blacks.

WILLIAMS: I guess I'm pretty conscious of it. And I think that's pretty much the way things are. I can say this with some assurance since I do a lot of work in the white world, my editors are all very white, my agents have all been white. There are only a couple of black agents around, but I've never felt that I could go to an agent just because he was black. I'm not that crazy. An agent is an agent, just like a publisher is a publisher. It's a money-making proposition. But I've been, over a period of years, depressed about some of my white friends. I know white liberals very well. I've known white liberals, friends, who showed me the guns they brought in from Colorado or New Mexico. And I say, "What do you want that for?" "Well, just in case." "In case of what?" "Well, you know . . ." Everybody's worried about black people getting guns but if they ever had a shakedown in some of the middle-class apartments around this city, it would be incredible. Absolutely. I don't want to be misleading here. I have many white friends whom I don't categorize as being liberal, conservative, or anything else. I try to deal with them as people and I feel that they deal with me as a person. I don't think there is more that can be asked of a relationship across the races except mutual respect.

INTERVIEWER: Racial guilt, which you discuss in your introduction to *Sissie,* is a recurring theme in your novels. Do you consider this one of your major themes?

WILLIAMS: It could very well be, and I have personally felt
some of this, though to a lesser degree now. When you are the
first one in your family in seven or eight generations to go to college at a great sacrifice to yourself and your family, there has to
be some degree of guilt. But my older kid is now in graduate
school and he's teaching, and he's married. And number two is a
junior at Cornell. So the pattern is started. Nobody is going to
have to feel guilty about going to college, as silly as that was.

INTERVIEWER: How can your characters escape from the
enormous guilt they feel?

WILLIAMS: Well, I suppose if they are going to be my characters in my books, they relate to the idea that with time one feels
less and less. I would imagine that . . . well, for example, the
book I'm working on now. The foundry worker has a son who is
at Columbia. And there's no sense of guilt there. All the guys his
age have kids away at school. That's the thing to do now. I would
suppose that the longer I live and the more I write, the less I feel
personally. And this will be reflected in my characters.

INTERVIEWER: Must your characters—I think here especially
of the characters in *Sissie*—come to some understanding of themselves and their situation before they can be relieved of the guilt?

WILLIAMS: Yes, I think coming to an understanding of what
happened gives the release. And understanding often comes with
time. If you're dealing with a novel, you're restricted by time and
space. So, you've got to set up certain things to make this happen.

INTERVIEWER: You suggest in the preface to *Sissie* that the
matriarchal system in America is a myth. Who invented the
myth?

WILLIAMS: I think I would say that the white man did.

INTERVIEWER: As a way of releasing himself from responsibility?

WILLIAMS: Well, I don't know whether it would be that or that it would be something more simple. That is, it put the black male outside the activity in the scheme of things.

INTERVIEWER: In *Sons of Darkness* Dr. Jessup represented a certain kind of radicalism in the novel. Is the thrust of the novel away from Jessup's ideas for social change and toward Eugene Browning's?

WILLIAMS: Yes, because he's the kind of guy who's around today. It's sort of like Marcus Garvey whose "back-to-Africa movement" was very much applauded by Southerners, the KKK guys. He could send his scouts to the South in cities where a strange black guy usually disappeared overnight. But Garvey didn't lose anybody. That's because he was working hand-in-hand with the KKK, not hand-in-hand but at least they knew what he was doing and approved of it. Now Jessup is one of these guys who believes that he can make deals with the devil and come away unscorched. And Browning just never had that spirit. Browning is the kind of activist-nonactivist that all of us would like to be; so that we can press a button and set things in motion without paying the consequences. And in this sense, his thing is really a big daydream.

INTERVIEWER: Browning thinks he can do this without incurring any guilt?

WILLIAMS: He would like to.

INTERVIEWER: Is he becoming aware at the end of the novel of those consequences?

WILLIAMS: Of course. Yes.

INTERVIEWER: Have your thinking or ideas changed since
you first began writing fifteen years ago? Are you surprised when
you look back to see that you were thinking one thing or another?

WILLIAMS: No, I'm not. I didn't know how things would
change, but I always expect things to change. What I was writing
about then was what I wanted to write about. What I write about
now is what I want to write about now. I think that there have
been moments when I have, perhaps with *Sons of Darkness, Sons
of Light,* given under to the pressures around me and done a
book on revolution. But I'm not sorry I did it. In the process of
working it out I came to see pretty much the kind of things that
would have to happen for any revolution to become a success and
also the things that couldn't happen. In that book I was dealing
with nine tunnels and bridges leading into Manhattan. Well, hell,
since last spring when the bridge-and-tunnel workers had a
strike, I discovered that there were something like thirty-four
bridge-tunnel approaches to Manhattan. A hell of a revolutionary
I'd make! . . . if I thought I could seal off Manhattan at nine
points, leaving twenty-five more wide open.

INTERVIEWER: What have been some of the reactions to your
book on Martin Luther King? Do you think that the book was
misunderstood?

WILLIAMS: I don't read reviews of a book until they're out for
a year. Once in a while my wife will insist that I read a particularly good or bad one. With the King book I was glad that I had
made that rule. I read some of the reviews just this September.
They were pretty bad. I think that the misunderstanding was wil-
full. A lot of people wanted to misunderstand, wanted to accuse
me of being a traitor, a panderer for the FBI. A lot of people
jumped on me, a lot of people in the black community. I got beat

pretty badly. I think that over the past fourteen months or so there's been a better reaction to the book than when it first came out. Again, time, you know. But I really took a beating on that. It wasn't that I didn't expect to. I just didn't anticipate the degree of ferocity. . . . There were a lot of people running around saying, "Well, he's finished as a writer. He'll never write again." You start asking yourself, "Is that really true? Am I finished as a writer?"

INTERVIEWER: Why did you write the book?

WILLIAMS: I thought that it would be a good thing for the black community to understand how much we're at the mercy of the system. And, of course, nobody wanted to believe that we were that badly off. Or that we could be that easily used. That's really the answer to it. Not in 1971.

Charles Wright

The fictional world of Charles Wright is best described as a surrealistic painting come to life in the streets of New York City:
gratuitous violence, sexual aberrations of every kind, wave after
wave of piecemeal experiences whose "parts won't come together." Or viewed in another way, it is the streets of New York
contained but threatening to break out of the novels in which he
puts them. In Wright's fiction, not only are the lines between the
real and the fantastical made thin, they are destroyed. The imagination continually tries to break loose from the strictures of realistic fiction as well as the realities of American life. But the real
world keeps outstripping the imagination. So, in a novel like *The
Wig* Wright pushes the imagination to its limits in order to envision grotesqueries that even America, so he thought, could not invent. But the black militant groups, the see-through plastic
dresses, the wigs, and the Chicken Man all came to pass and
were absorbed into American culture. The imagination is a weak-
ling when confronted with America's brutish capacity to thrive on
the grotesque. In his latest book *Absolutely Nothing to Get
Alarmed About* (1973), Wright forgoes the guise of fictionist and
writes a journal based upon pieces he published in *The Village
Voice*. But as with the novels, he discovers that the greatest

source for fantasy is the real world. The nightmares and black comedy in these pieces are indistinguishable in form and content from what was left to the imagination to create in the novels.

Unlike many American fictional heroes who actually seek out the unusual and bizarre as a way of escaping the stultifying effects of what they feel is a stagnating society, Charles Stevenson of *The Messenger* (1963) and Lester Jefferson of *The Wig* (1966) want nothing more than to fit into the Great Society (Lester even buys a wig because the salesman guarantees him that it will help), to have the quiet lives that Thoreau said were filled with desperation. Instead of finding such simple pleasures, they reel headlong toward chaos and death where the only sin is "believing, hoping" and where even "ice cream bars" evoke paranoia. In the closing scene of *The Wig* Lester submits to castration because "Having children is the greatest sin in this country."

The method of Wright's novels is phenomenological. The inability to piece together the fragments of experience is matched by the style and structure of the books. Depending upon brief episodes rather than plot, both the novels avoid a linear development that would give the veneer of realism. In other words, stitching together the experiences of the novels is as difficult or as impossible for the reader as it is for the characters themselves. Like the characters, we are left with elusive images—as likely to be from classical literature as pop culture—which should illuminate the experience from which they come; but they don't. We discover that the novels are really held together by literary device rather than meaning; our interest is less in resolutions or conclusions than in the specific quality of feeling in each separate episode.

The interview was done in two parts. I met with Mr. Wright in New York City in October of 1971. He appeared for the interview in matching and faded blue denim pants, jacket, and fisherman's hat, and was ill at ease for most of the session. He talked very quickly and rarely directed his remarks to the questions asked. In the summer of 1972 we talked long distance while he was staying in Veracruz, Mexico. The change of locale seems to have rescued him from terror of New York. His answers on the second occasion were lucid and detailed. Frequently he would return to previous answers to clarify or expand on them. He is presently working on short fiction and plans to begin a third novel.

INTERVIEWER: This question may call forth too obvious an answer, because when we met last year in New York you talked about wanting to leave the City and both of your novels concern characters who are trying to escape there, but why did you go to Veracruz?

WRIGHT: Years ago Katherine Anne Porter was here in Veracruz. When I was younger I was sort of hung up on Katherine Anne's work and I decided to come here. But, of course, things have changed for me after nine years. It's no longer a Graham Greene setting as it was then. I don't know whether you have read too much of Katherine Anne's work, but one gets the impression that she was not totally happy in this particular city. The same can be said for me also.

INTERVIEWER: Now that you are in Veracruz are you going to keep writing about New York City?

WRIGHT: It seems at present that I am writing about things that happen down here, but I plan to continue writing the things I do for *The Village Voice*. The short stories I've done here . . . although the setting is Mexico, the characters are mostly American. If I do the novel I want to, I will call it *The Gulf of Oz*.

INTERVIEWER: Do you find it easier to write about American things down in Mexico because you have a certain distance?

WRIGHT: It doesn't seem so. There may be superficial changes in America, but I think if you have the country clear in your mind then everything is fine. All I have to do is to look through the August issue of *Harpers*. There's a photograph in black-and-white on page seventy-eight of an Italian woman and her daughter standing on their porch in Newark, and there's a statue of what appears to be a Madonna covered in plastic. Now below that are flowers, and I will bet my life that those flowers are plastic. When I was delivering circulars in the Bronx I knew neighborhoods like that. So, if nothing else, I have good old *Time* magazine to get a realistic picture of what's going on in America by just looking at the photographs. But I don't even think that I would really need the photographs because everything seems to be very, very clear in my mind.

INTERVIEWER: Did you feel that you had to get away from New York?

WRIGHT: Either that or crack-up or else commit some violence. There were several disappointments for me there from which I still haven't recovered. *The Wig* was one of them. That's my retarded child. I had to get away.

INTERVIEWER: It's not clear at the end of *The Messenger* whether Charles will be able to escape New York. Do you think he will?

WRIGHT: Well, I certainly hope he does.

INTERVIEWER: Do you have any plans for returning to New York?

WRIGHT: Yes, I'll probably go back in a couple of months. If I get set up on the novel I might stay here until December or January. Who knows? I'm very impulsive. Like when I returned to Mexico this time I decided on a Thursday night that I was leaving the following day. And I left. But even here I sometimes think, "Oh, God, let me get out of this place." I know this place so well; it's a small city and no one stays here. Even the natives don't stay here. If they are shrewd enough they make a connection so that they can leave. The tourists never stay longer than three or four days. There's really nothing here.

INTERVIEWER: But it is an alternative to New York. I remember in *The Messenger* that Charles looks out at the city one morning and describes it as "surrealistic." Does that term characterize his whole experience there?

WRIGHT: Yes, yes, indeed.

INTERVIEWER: The surrealism in your stories is so prevalent that it becomes almost ordinary, it seems to have worked its way into everyone's life.

WRIGHT: (Laughing) I agree with you one hundred percent. But there are a great many people out there, who live in New York City, who don't believe this. For example, I received a letter from a young man, a Puerto Rican who lives in New York. It said, "Dear Mr. Wright, I read you in *The Village Voice* but ninety percent of the things you write about I don't believe really happen."

INTERVIEWER: When Eli Bolton in Clarence Major's novel *All-Night Visitors* encounters the same kind of experiences he finally feels that "nothing seemed real." Did your experiences in New York seem unreal, and did you then attempt to create something in the imagination that did appear real?

WRIGHT: They seemed quite real. But I suppose Clarence Major creates a fictional world in order to make something real. I think perhaps that is what I do because I know that the world out there is very real, or at least a part of me knows that it is very real. But it's also terrible and so frightening. And although sometimes the things I write about are frightening, it seems so much more comfortable in this fictional world where I would like to remain. Say, "No, no, no," and not go out there. I have to go downtown today and mail a story to my editor because I want her to get it soon. I don't want to get on the bus here at the corner. I would much prefer to remain in my room, but I can't.

INTERVIEWER: What I am wondering about is that both of the novels, *The Messenger* and *The Wig*, seem to be trying to find some meaning, to put all the parts together. But the parts don't want to seem to come together so you go to fantasy instead. Do you see art—writing a novel—as a superior way of puttings things together because people try to put things together in their lives and sometimes they're successful and sometimes they're not. What advantages do you see in going to fantasy?

WRIGHT: You take these things and put them together and, of course, you somehow have a plan.

INTERVIEWER: Is fantasy better than realistic fiction?

WRIGHT: I don't think it is. I don't think that one is better than the other. It's whatever suits your purpose. I could have written *The Wig* as a realistic novel . . . but, oh God! Before the Black Panthers appeared on the scene, I started a short action-type of novel in the Hemingway style about a group of blacks like the Panthers, except that they didn't have black berets and black leather jackets. But who knows, if I would have continued the novel perhaps they would have even had those. I sent a few sample chapters to my agent and she said, "Oh, God, Charles. We can't publish this!" And a few years later the Panthers were there. That frightened me. So I decided to write it as a fantasy because I wanted to see if I could do it in both ways.

INTERVIEWER: Does the fantasy come easier now that you are removed from New York?

WRIGHT: I don't know. I haven't even thought about that and I don't want to think about it because I'm living a fantasy (laughing). Here it is and it's unbelievable.

INTERVIEWER: Do you see *The Messenger* and *The Wig* as being very different novels?

WRIGHT: Yes.

INTERVIEWER: What are the differences as far as you're concerned? I see basic differences, especially in style, but there are also several similarities.

WRIGHT: Different and at the same time they're the same? Is that what you said? I think that Graham Greene a few weeks ago said that there's only one novel you have to tell, and that you (laughing) write it over and over again. As you know *The Messenger* was a first novel with almost nothing going for it and almost no advertising campaign. Yet, it took off on its own, found its own audience, and was well received by the critics. I realized that they were waiting for me to write a sequel to *The Messenger* or another novel like that. I said that I'll be damned if I'll do what is expected of me. Of course, I didn't have any idea that I was going to write anything like *The Wig*. However, in spite of the fantasy in *The Wig* and the realism in *The Messenger*, the novels are similar. At least, physically the heroes are the same.

INTERVIEWER: Do you like comparisons to be made between the two?

WRIGHT: The strange thing that I don't understand—or understand only in a sense—is that the readers and critics felt very sympathetically toward Charles of *The Messenger*. He may be going through a bad time but eventually he will be all right. It's what the ordinary person goes through . . . well, maybe not the *ordinary* person (laughing). At the same time, I think that Lester of *The Wig* is tragic. My God, if anyone needs understanding and sympathy, it's him. He will eventually go mad, kill himself, or kill a dozen other people.

INTERVIEWER: What's the real difference between the two?

WRIGHT: I think that the "slice-of-life" things that happen to Charles are quite typical. He goes through life, sensitive and aware, but really quite ordinary. The things that happen around him do not have a cancer. Hemingway said something like, "Nothing can hurt you or affect you if you don't want it to . . . if you don't let it get next to you." That's what kept Charles going. At times it does get next to him and it takes a terrible toll, both mentally and physically. But he doesn't let it get him down. It's a survival technique. Lester, who could easily be his brother, is really different because he takes a long-range view of things. What happens to him is that he sees it as a part of a larger design. This could be a sickness, but he feels this. The things that happen to him cut into him, not like a razor blade, but like a dagger. Because of that these emotions build up in his mind.

INTERVIEWER: Are you conscious of any stylistic influences upon *The Wig?*

WRIGHT: No. I suppose somewhere in the back of my mind I was thinking about James Joyce. Someone has said that it reminded him of Nathanael West because *The Wig* is not a plotted novel; it's in episodes and you might think of it in relation to vaudeville. I avoided reading other contemporary writers because I didn't want to be influenced. They might come along and say somebody else did a thing like that. I was totally at work on my own and I didn't know what the hell I thought I was doing. . . . I take it back—I knew exactly what I was doing. The first draft was in the third person and then I changed it into the first person. I rewrote *The Wig* in twenty-nine days in New York City. Twenty-nine days, that was the happiest period of my life (laughing). I never felt so happy in my whole life. One of the interesting things about the novel is that all of it was pure imagination, yet they came to pass—the slang, the see-through plastic dresses, abortions, vibrators.

INTERVIEWER: Have you felt the influence of writers who are not your contemporaries?

WRIGHT: The only one I would say is Hemingway. There's nobody else. I've learned many things, including from Uncle Norman [Mailer], who I think is as sweet as sugar. But I'd say no one else.

INTERVIEWER: What interested you about Katherine Anne Porter's fiction?

WRIGHT: I suppose it was her style, something offbeat that I could identify with. In the *Paris Review* interview Katherine Anne said that when she was ten years old, someone asked her what she wanted to be when she grew up. She said that she didn't know, but she shouted, "I want glory." And that's what I am trying for.

INTERVIEWER: When did you first start writing?

WRIGHT: That was in high school, little pieces called "So Long, Buddy." When I read it in class everyone would start, and one of the students said that I had copied it out of *Reader's Digest*. I was furious because even back then *Reader's Digest* was not a magazine I would have read (laughing). At the same time, I was flattered. The story was about a soldier with a limp. I was reading Hemingway at the time and I remember being very impressed with "Indian Camp."

INTERVIEWER: What did you do when you finished high school? You didn't go to college, did you?

WRIGHT: No, no. What did I do when I got out of high school? Well, in those days they didn't have draft dodgers (laughing), so I went into the army. That wasn't out of high school directly, though. I just sort of hung around, as they say.

INTERVIEWER: What kind of experiences did you have in the army?

WRIGHT: I would say that mine were really good. After I learned to survive I had a marvelous time.

INTERVIEWER: How long were you in the army?

WRIGHT: Two years. One year in the United States and one year in Korea. The first two days were really something else. On the third day a soldier told me that if you stay in the army you learn what you have to do and what you can get away with. You have to be a politician. I always remembered that. The army was a fantastic experience and I don't regret it at all. I didn't see any fighting because when I got there all the fighting was over. All the fighting that occurred took place in the company that I was in. I was always that strange one, the one that was different; that created problems for me, but I always won. It was a game of wits. I was not only a loner but I looked much younger than I was, and I was black and little and skinny. There was no one to protect me but myself—no black buddies, no white buddies. No one. Just me.

INTERVIEWER: Will you ever try writing about your army experiences?

WRIGHT: I've thought of it, yes. Doing a comic novel (laughing). One of my friends suggested that's what I should do. Maybe one of these days I will.

INTERVIEWER: Did you ever try writing straight realistic fiction?

WRIGHT: (Laughing) I think perhaps once upon a time. That was only natural, and it was very bad. That was when I was at a writer's colony with James Jones. It was a Korean War novel that Putnam's was interested in. But they were also interested in getting Jim. If they could have latched on to Jim, they would have published my novel. Mine was a James-Jones-type novel, except for certain set pieces of poetic stuff that I do. It was just a straight, hard-hitting war novel.

INTERVIEWER: I wonder whether you ever worry that your innovations might cause some people to get lost?

WRIGHT: Most of them were lost. Most of them, the few readers who read *The Wig*, are still lost. But I thought it was perfect and I thought that I was communicating. The most shocking thing was when I was out at the University of California–Irvine branch, I thought that the young black ones would be aware, that they would understand it. Oh, no. When Lester gets castrated at the end? They said, "How dare you end it that way." But since then I occasionally receive a letter from someone who understood it. The best review of it was by the late Conrad Knickerbocker in the *New York Times*. He was a man I admired for many years. When I was a messenger I used to think, if I ever publish a novel, I would like him to review it. And it so happened that he understood it so well that . . . (laughing) it was uncomfortable.

INTERVIEWER: What has been the reaction of other black writers to your work?

WRIGHT: Among the younger black writers like Ishmael Reed and Cecil Brown—that's one thing that makes me very happy—they like it. That makes me feel good.

INTERVIEWER: Have you received any criticism from critics who say that such fiction will not aid in a revolution?

WRIGHT: No, not from critics. But quite often, from young blacks in colleges where I might be lecturing. How juvenile they are. A young man once told me that he wanted to be a playwright and start a theater in the streets. He wasn't even going to use professional actors. Beautiful. But he regretted that he couldn't continue with the classes in playwrighting with William Inge, of all people. Can you imagine? How tragic that is. To tell me about your revolutionary theater in the streets and then to regret this!

INTERVIEWER: Do you see any black writers emerging as true cultural figureheads; such as, perhaps, LeRoi Jones?

WRIGHT: Well . . . oh, oh, LeRoi, what is there to say? I think he's a good man. And I think he's a very good playwright, and he's very concerned. He's doing marvelous things up in Newark. But he's the only one: look at the thing with Eldridge Cleaver and George Jackson who just died. There's so much infighting. But it's all only for the moment. Next year it may be Cold Dog Eskimo.

INTERVIEWER: What kind of writing habits do you have?

WRIGHT: (Laughing) I have the worst . . . well, not the worst, but I place among the top ten. It depends upon how I feel, number one. I may screw around all night long until about midnight. Then when I start to work, I work. I'll build and design houses for maybe two days. And then for ten days I'll do nothing but write.

INTERVIEWER: Your next book will be a collection of pieces from *The Village Voice?*

WRIGHT: *The Village Voice* is the only thing that has kept me going. Without it I don't know what would happen to me. *Absolutely Nothing to Get Alarmed About* is a collection of old *Village Voice* pieces. Some of them I've changed. It reads exactly like *The Messenger.* It was originally called *Black Studies* but the salesmen thought that it would get put on the wrong bookshelves.

INTERVIEWER: What exactly is the difference between your journalism and your fiction?

WRIGHT: It's a very thin line. I intend to break every cocksucking heart in America with *Absolutely Nothing to Get Alarmed About*. And I think I'm slowly but surely succeeding.

INTERVIEWER: My last question: what is a "paranoid ice cream bar"? It appears in *The Wig* if you remember.

WRIGHT: What *is* a "paranoid ice cream bar"? I don't know (laughing). Well, ah. . . . What's a paranoid ice cream bar? There's no paranoid ice cream bars. But maybe there are. If Good Humor doesn't have them, maybe they will. Especially if they've read *The Wig*. I don't know; it's like when everybody is getting *on* a train, I'm going the opposite way.

Al Young

The poetry and fiction of Al Young are remarkable reminders to us that joy and love are still fit subjects for literature. His poetry attains a pastoral quality while at the same time employing sharp images from pop culture (he compares his heart to "a region vaster and deeper than/Marlboro Country") and contemporary diction ("Just because you wear a natural baby/don't mean you aint got a processed mind"). The controlling image throughout his poetry is that of the "dance," which both helps to structure his poems and to describe his conception of a universe that is in constant movement. As he suggests in the interview, his poetry concerns the journey of the self as it seeks unity with other men and nature, a journey in which man finds nothing new, but rather rediscovers and is reminded of the unchanging self that has always existed. All experience is a trip back into the self where man delights in recovering the underlying unity of himself with the rest of nature. And that revelation can be gained as easily by seeing squirrels "shittering/outside thru the trees of my bedroom window" as by taking "thoughtful journeys to supermarkets," because, despite the apparent disparity between the graceful beauty of the squirrel and the banal ugliness of the supermarket, "There's meaning to all this itemization." Man's effort must be to locate the dance, the song, the rhythm of life even in the mortar and steel of urban living in modern America. Love becomes the ulti-

mate expression of this unity, and its many forms and moods constitute the material for several of Young's most successful poems.
Indeed, God can only be found in an encounter with one's lover,
who is a "paradise/I would gladly invade."

The purposeful vision that pervades Young's poetry is likewise present in his short novel *Snakes*. Without sacrificing his
sense of the realistic, he depicts the successful initiation into manhood of a high-school boy who ends the novel—unlike the archi-
typal American adolescent in fiction—feeling "For the first time
in my life I don't feel trapped." As in his poetry, the path to identity lies more in discovering one's past and less in realizing what
one is to become, than in what one already is. Significantly, the
vehicle for MC's self-discovery is music. Recalling Young's use of
the dance image in his poetry, music enables MC to conceive of a
world that is held together by the imagination and the spirit.
Confessing that the novel is in part autobiographical, Young insists that it is simply the story of a boy's high-school experiences
rather than a document of black protest.

The interview was conducted through the mails and a series
of phone conversations. Mr. Young presently lives near San Francisco with his wife and child, and teaches writing at Stanford
University. Recently he completed the screenplay for the movie
version of Dick Gregory's autobiography and is at work on his
second novel, *Who Is Angelina?*

INTERVIEWER: You are both a fiction writer and a poet. I
wonder whether one ever gets in the way of the other? Does poetry demand a different approach to language and subject-matter
than does fiction? Do you ever start writing something in one
form and decide later it would be better in the other?

YOUNG: I find that I must operate in a different way for each
genre. For example, there are times when I conceive of a theme,
or something happens to me that I want to capture immediately,
and I'll try to capture it as a poem. Later on I might look back
and see where it has story possibilities. Of course, the reverse has
also happened. I've written stories that would have been better

off as poems. I find that poetry satisfies my more immediate needs for expression and communication; whereas, if I really need to build something up, if I have to treat a subject in depth or if I want to express myself in depth, then I'll use a longer form and hope that the emotional impact will build up in segments in the reader's consciousness over a gradual period of time. But both my poetry and prose come from the same place. There always seems to be some essence I'm trying to communicate and I have become aware of this process in my later years especially.

INTERVIEWER: What started you writing?

YOUNG: Chester Himes said in his autobiography that boys who aren't properly disciplined by their fathers become either writers or criminals. I've thought a lot about that statement. I don't know what made me a writer. I certainly didn't come from a family that was big on reading. As a child—and so much of my childhood was spent living with my grandparents—I remember there being books around the house. They were usually popular novels or big medical books, and, of course, the Bible. I didn't take too much interest in these books because they didn't have pictures. But I did start to read just for the pleasure of reading. I must have been around nine or ten years old and I would read just about anything. This continued through my early twenties. I rarely left the house without a book. I felt that reading provided me with an outlet that wasn't accessible elsewhere. So that if you like to read it is very often coupled with a love for trying to express yourself in writing.

INTERVIEWER: How old were you when you first began writing?

YOUNG: I started writing around the age of six or seven. I had a jump on some of the other kids because I was able to read before I went to school from looking at words and being read to. My parents used to read the comic strips or they'd read stories to me. They would always ask about them until eventually I figured them out. By the time I got to school I knew how to read and it made first grade a little boring. But as soon as I learned how to read I started to write. I started writing seriously around the age of fifteen, but I knew long before then that I would be a writer. I knew it around the age of nine or ten because I used to write science fiction and adventure stories. Sometimes they were just the re-tellings of things I had already read or things I had seen in the movies. I started this in the fifth grade.

INTERVIEWER: I know that you lived in many parts of the country for different periods of time, but wasn't most of your life spent in the South?

YOUNG: I lived in the South for the first third of my life, moved to Detroit, and then to California, with brief intervals in New Orleans, Pennsylvania, and Chicago. I've moved around quite a bit. Before I was twelve years old I'm sure that I had gone to at least a dozen grade schools.

INTERVIEWER: Did that make you feel rootless?

YOUNG: It didn't make me feel rootless but I'm sure that it's had a strange effect on me. Even after I moved to Detroit I went back and forth between Michigan and Mississippi. I think that having had to make so many different friends at schools has made me mobile in being able to live in a wide variety of different-styled communities. It does something to you inside too. It gave me the feeling that there is no stability in external circumstances, that the only thing you have to hold onto is within yourself.

INTERVIEWER: Do poems always come to you in the same way?

YOUNG: A poem begins with images which are intimately related to feelings. I don't like to separate the two. That's one of the things that you're forced to do when you teach. You start dissecting poems for the purpose of analysis and after a while you start to think that way. You say, "Well, I'm going to write a poem. First I'll wait for the feeling and then I'll imbue it with the

proper images." What happens with me is that I generally perceive things in terms of memory through imagery. I will have a
feeling about something, perhaps something from my childhood.
Before the words come, the pictures and the feelings will well-up
inside of me. These images will be charged with emotion. The
problem is to get them down in language that will carry or evoke
some essence of that feeling. The third section of the long poem
"The Song Turning Back Into Itself" perhaps illustrates what I'm
saying. It is simply one of my earliest memories in Ocean Springs,
Mississippi, on the Gulf Coast near Biloxi. It's an attempt to use
the imagery of my memories to recreate some of the earliest memorable feelings I had. I remember my father out in the backyard
sawing wood. "Consider the little house/of sunken wood/in the
dusty street/where my father would/cut his fingers/up to his
ankles/in fragrant coils/of lumber shavings/the backyard of nowhere." This was the kind of life we were living there. Extremely
poor. But in a strange kind of way they're very happy memories.

INTERVIEWER: What determines the physical shape of a
poem for you? Is it a particular problem for you since you experiment with so many different forms?

YOUNG: Lately I find myself working in forms that are more
traditional than I have previously. The most difficult thing about
writing "free verse" (I never really liked that term but everyone
understands it, so I'll use it) is that you have to create your own
form each time you write a poem. This can be very exasperating
if you have a sensitivity for shaping things. Now I know a lot of
poets who really don't worry about that at all. It's all a "language
trip," it's all "do your own thing," which I tend not to like. I don't
like that approach because—as with music—I find that the more
interesting a poem is the more curious its shape. I think that form
is not something you should impose artificially from without; it
more resembles something that grows naturally out of what
you're trying to say. When I'm writing a poem I get a very rough
first draft down. Then I begin to see possibilities: how it can fall
into place, how I can make a design out of it.

INTERVIEWER: Do you go through periods when you feel that you have exhausted yourself and won't be able to write again? How do you get past such times?

YOUNG: I've never had such periods. I always have more than enough to say. It's more a matter of finding the time. Right after completing a certain sequence of poems or when the sequence is about to end, I find that I have been carried along on some emotional or psychological current, usually stimulated by what's happening in my life at a particular time. I often will find that I've written myself out in that direction and I'll have to go down into myself or my life to make contact with unexplored areas for new things and not write poetry for a while. I just let things build up in me again.

INTERVIEWER: In your poem, "The Song Turning Back Into Itself 4," you write, "I violinize peace/in the Nazi era" and "Let us change the design/of their celluloid architecture/into a shape where love could live." Are you here speaking as "the Poet"? Is this really about the function of poetry in the modern world?

YOUNG: Yes, I'm talking about "the Poet." Whatever else a poet might be involved with, I think that in a sense he is something of a magician or shaman. In our particular era the poet who is just concerned with himself as poet seems very impotent. Society doesn't really seem to have much use for him. So you get a lot of poets whining about how they're ignored. The true poets of our age are often to be found working in other areas. I see people like Duke Ellington or Chuck Berry as poets; of course, I am using that term very loosely. But I think that even the poet that's just involved with words should feel that his language can change things, if only by changing the way one other person looks at "reality." Poets should alert people to the fact that they have imaginations. There's something else down beneath that flesh and blood and gray matter. And that's the only thing that's going to change the direction we're moving in. It doesn't matter whether you look to the West or to the East; we're all getting squashed and becoming more and more dehumanized by the forms our governments are assuming.

INTERVIEWER: In your poem "A Dance for Militant Dilettantes" you satirize the image of the black writer, created, in part, by publishers. Have you felt pressure from publishers to write books which conform to that image? Did you, for instance, have any difficulty finding a publisher for *Snakes* because it wasn't militant enough?

YOUNG: Things are changing and I am very happy to see the changes come. Perhaps the "black rage," the supermilitant, the blacker-than-black era was a necessary phase. *Snakes* went to a number of publishers before it was accepted. I don't know whether it was turned down because it wasn't militant enough but many editors were all too eager to tell me that I wasn't "telling it like it is." One editor said, "A little too sweet for a ghetto novel." I was infuriated with this narrow vision of most editors but I wasn't crushed by it because I see it as just another form of our native racism. We're used to talking about the sociopolitical-economic aspects of racism but cultural racism crystallizes so much else.

INTERVIEWER: The editor just seemed to have another stereotype of what the black is or should be.

YOUNG: Yes. The image of the black keeps changing. You have different kinds of stereotypes but they're stereotypes just the same. You don't have Kingfish Stevens or Rochester anymore, or the "fifties" black man in the button-down collar and the ivy league suit, but you have fist-waving blacks now. It's just another way of avoiding dealing with people as people.

INTERVIEWER: But you think that black writers are reacting against this?

YOUNG: I think it's changing because black writers are becoming aware of the fact we've been put into a bag and as long as we let ourselves be put there, we're still enslaved.

INTERVIEWER: I would like to ask you a few particular questions about your novel, *Snakes*. Do you think it was influenced by any other novels?

YOUNG: I wasn't conscious of it resembling any other novels. I think it was more influenced by music. I wanted to produce a book that had all the good feeling and depth and strangeness of the fifties and early sixties. And I wanted to evoke what rhythm and blues do. I wanted to capture that particular unspeakable quality in the book. *Snakes* is curious in that it started off as one short story but it grew into two or three stories. I thought it might become a story cycle even though I've never been taken by the idea of a story cycle. Suddenly it started to turn itself into a book of some kind. At that point I could just ride with it. I think that it owes more to a living than a literary tradition. Almost all of my writing proceeds from a tradition of the spoken word rather than the written. In my writing I strive for oral appeal. As a kid I used to enjoy staying up late. I'd be in bed in another room. My brother and I were put to bed when there was a special guest in the house or some relative who had come from a distance. Southern people would sit up all night and talk. I'd pretend to be asleep but I'd be catching all of it. You can't imagine the kind of storytelling that went on! I think this oral influence has been greater on my narrative style than anything literary.

INTERVIEWER: You said that *Snakes* was more influenced by music than by other novels. Generally speaking black fiction has the same debt to music. Could you say something about your ideas on music, especially as they influenced this novel? Were you using music the way other black writers like McKay, Toomer, and Jones used it, as both a thematic and structural device?

YOUNG: I don't know whether I was using it the way they used it. I think that most black people in America are very musically conscious. Music tends to be of single importance in every aspect of Afro-American life, particularly blues, pop music, jazz, and Gospel music. The black writer who is writing about Afro-American life will naturally have to deal with music in some way or other. It's just there. I got a lot of inspiration from music, as well as from painting and the dance. One of my principle interests is this whole process of music and its effects on Afro-American life. So, in writing *Snakes* I wanted to have the kind of appeal that much of the early rhythm and blues had before they became plasticized. That's what I wanted the prose to be like.

INTERVIEWER: The story involves a group of four kids who start a band, but it seems from the beginning that it is doomed not to last.

YOUNG: It was inevitable that the band MC formed must fall apart. But I think central to understanding the whole novel is the fact that these are four teenage kids. This is their first touch of success and what the book is really about is what happens to these four youths under the influence of this localized success. MC goes one way, Shakes goes in another direction. Jimmy Monday quits and joins the navy because he wants security. Billy Sanchez goes into professional music as a jazz musician. We see just how ephemeral these ties are at this particular time and place. That's what the book is really about. Critics like to say it's about black ghetto life closely scrutinized. But its effect is just the opposite of something like "black rage." It's a story about four kids.

INTERVIEWER: Why do the photographs of his parents seem so important to MC? Do they awaken in him some yearning for the past?

YOUNG: Well, the photographs are one of his few connections with the past. Besides his grandmother, MC is sort of out there on an island by himself. This is one of the points of the book. So many Americans are without pasts, real pasts! MC looks at the photographs for some clue as to where he came from. He looks at these photographs of his mother and father and they become almost religious objects to him. It seems very unreal to him that his parents died when he was an infant.

INTERVIEWER: Could you say something about how your long poem "Dancing" was put together? What is the progression in the poem?

YOUNG: "Dancing" was written at the end of the 1960s. It was an attempt on my part to explain where America was at, at that particular time, and where I stood with respect to my country. You'll remember that the assassinations were all going on. I was trying to explain to myself what was happening in America. I started to see my life starting from 1939 as being inescapably interwoven with the life of the country from that year on. I tried to find parallels between what was happening in the country and what was happening in my own life, which in recent years has loosely been involved with spiritual struggle. "Dancing" was, then, for me the summation of my life to the end of the sixties.

INTERVIEWER: How does the image of the "dance" work in your collection of poems *Dancing*? It is perhaps the most recurrent image in your poetry.

YOUNG: For me the "dance" is the most dramatic and satisfying image for what's really going on in creation. Everything is a dance—the rise and fall of the tides, the change of seasons, the movement of the stars. This to me is incredible and so I use the metaphor of the dance to describe the natural movement of my own life. Though I haven't looked at it in this way, it does appear to be the central metaphor in my poetry.

INTERVIEWER: Could you explain the title of your book and series of poems *The Song Turning Back Into Itself*? Does it thematically describe what is going on in the poems as well as suggest something about your techniques?

YOUNG: I see everything as proceeding in a circular fashion. I really believe in the cyclical theory of history and evolution. Several years ago that title came to me. In fact, it was originally the title of a poem that doesn't appear in that book. I'm not one for analyzing the sources of poems and imaginative materials, but I think this grew out of listening with another ear to different kinds of Afro-American music. Mainstream popular music of the 1960s in America drew heavily upon Afro-American ethnic and folk sources. I saw this process of return as a song turning back into itself. Cast thy song into the air and after many an air it will return to you—that sort of thing. There's also a mystical consideration here. In essence you're never anyone but yourself. You go through all these changes but in a sense you're always turning back into what you really are. I wanted the poems to sum up a certain aspect of a period of my life. I think they do.

Bibliography

This bibliography is intended to serve as a useful guide to the works of the authors interviewed in this volume. I have avoided listing books which they have edited, works which have not yet been collected, and unpublished material—unless a publication date had already been established.

BONTEMPS, ARNA

God Sends Sunday. New York: Harcourt, Brace and Co., 1931.

Black Thunder. New York: Macmillan, 1936.

Drums at Dusk. New York: Macmillan, 1939.

Personals. London: Paul Breman, Ltd., 1963.

COLTER, CYRUS

The Beach Umbrella. Iowa City: University of Iowa Press, 1970.

The Rivers of Eros. Chicago: Swallow Press, 1972.

The Hippodrome. Chicago: Swallow Press, 1973.

DEMBY, WILLIAM

Beetlecreek. New York: Rinehart, 1950.

The Catacombs. New York: Pantheon, 1965.

DODSON, OWEN

Powerful Long Ladder. New York: Farrar, Straus, 1946.

Boy at the Window. New York: Farrar, Straus & Young, 1951.

The Confession Stone: Song Cycles. London: Paul Bremen, Ltd., 1970.

ELLISON, RALPH

Invisible Man. New York: Random House, 1952.
Shadow and Act. New York: Random House, 1964.

GAINES, ERNEST J.

Catherine Carmier. New York: Atheneum, 1964.
Of Love and Dust. New York: Dial Press, 1967.
Bloodline. New York: Dial Press, 1968.
The Autobiography of Miss Jane Pittman. New York: Dial Press, 1971.

HARPER, MICHAEL S.

Dear John, Dear Coltrane. Pittsburgh: University of Pittsburgh Press, 1970.
History Is Your Own Heartbeat. Urbana: University of Illinois Press, 1971.
Photographs, Negatives, History as Apple Tree. San Francisco: Scarab Press, 1972.
Song: I Want A Witness. Pittsburgh: University of Pittsburgh Press, 1972.
Debridement. New York: Doubleday, 1973.
Nightmare Begins Responsibility. Urbana: University of Illinois, Press, 1973.

HAYDEN, ROBERT

Heart-Shape in the Dust. Detroit: Falcon, 1940 and Myron O'Higgins, *The Lion and the Archer,* Published privately, limited ed., 1948.
A Ballad of Remembrance. London: Paul Breman, Ltd., 1962.
Selected Poems. New York: October House, 1966.
Words in the Mourning Time. New York: October House, 1970.
Night-blooming Cereus. London: Paul Breman Ltd., 1972.

MAJOR, CLARENCE

Love Poems of a Black Man. Omaha: Coercion Press, 1964.
Human Juices. Omaha: Coercion Press, 1965.
All-Night Visitors. New York: Olympia Press, 1969.
Swallow the Lake. Middletown, Conn.: Wesleyan University Press, 1970.

Dictionary of Afro-American Slang. New York: International Publishers, 1970.

Symptoms and Madness. New York: Corinth Books, 1971.

Private Line. London: Paul Breman, Ltd., 1971.

The Cotton Club. Detroit: Broadside Press, 1972.

The Syncopated Cakewalk. New York: Barlenmir, 1972.

No. New York: Emerson Hall, 1972.

Slaveship and Relationship. New York: Emerson Hall, 1973.

MAYFIELD, JULIAN

The Hit. New York: Vanguard Press, 1957.

The Long Night. New York: Vanguard Press, 1958.

The Grand Parade. New York: Vanguard Press, 1961.

PETRY, ANN

The Street. Boston: Houghton Mifflin, 1946.

Country Place. Boston: Houghton Mifflin, 1947.

The Narrows. Boston: Houghton Mifflin, 1953.

Miss Muriel and Other Stories. Boston: Houghton Mifflin, 1971.

REED, ISHMAEL

The Free-Lance Pallbearers. Garden City: Doubleday, 1967.

Yellow Back Radio Broke-Down. Garden City: Doubleday, 1969.

Mumbo Jumbo. Garden City: Doubleday, 1972.

Conjure. Amherst: University of Massachusetts Press, 1972.

WALKER, ALICE

Once. New York: Harcourt, Brace, Jovanovich, 1968.

The Third Life of Grange Copeland. New York: Harcourt, Brace, Jovanovich, 1970.

Revolutionary Petunias. New York: Harcourt, Brace, Jovanovich, 1973.

In Love & Trouble: Stories of Black Women. New York: Harcourt, Brace, Jovanovich, 1974.

WIDEMAN, JOHN

A Glance Away. New York: Harcourt, Brace, Jovanovich, 1967.

Hurry Home. New York: Harcourt, Brace, Jovanovich, 1970.

The Lynchers. New York: Harcourt, Brace, Jovanovich, 1973.

WILLIAMS, JOHN A.

The Angry Ones. New York: Ace Books, 1960.

Night Song. New York: Farrar, Straus and Cudahy, 1961.

Sissie. New York: Farrar, Straus and Cudahy, 1963.

This Is My Country Too. New York: Signet, 1965.

The Man Who Cried I Am. Boston: Little, Brown, 1968.

Sons of Darkness, Sons of Light. Boston: Little, Brown, 1969.

The King God Didn't Save. Boston: Little, Brown, 1970.

Captain Blackman. Garden City: Doubleday, 1972.

WRIGHT, CHARLES

The Messenger. New York: Farrar, Straus, 1963.

The Wig. New York: Farrar, Straus & Giroux, 1966.

Absolutely Nothing to Get Alarmed About. New York: Farrar, Straus & Giroux, 1973.

YOUNG, AL

Dancing. New York: Corinth Books, 1969.

Snakes. New York: Holt, Rinehart, Winston, 1970.

The Song Turning Back into Itself. New York: Holt, Rinehart, Winston, 1971.

810.9 O'Brien, John, ed
OBR

Interviews with
black writers

DATE			

12801